AF791169

Insider's Guide

Doing Business in SHANGHAI 2003

China Knowledge Press

Railway
Expressway
EXPRESSWAY UNDER CONSTRUCTION
Viaducts
Highway
Nanjing
Changzhou
Nantong
JIANGSU
Wuxi
Suzhou
Tai Lake
SHANGHAI
Jiaxing
Hangzhou
Shaoxing
ZHEJIANG
Ningbo
Baoshan
Zhabei
Yangpu
Hongkou
Huangpu River
Jiading
Putuo
Jing'an
Huangpu
Changning
Luwan
HONGQIAO AIRPORT
ZHE-JIANG
Pudong New Area
Minghang
Xuhui

MAP OF SHANGHAI
YANGTZE RIVER
JIANGSU
Chongming
CHONGMING ISLAND
Taicang
Kunshan
Jiading
Baoshan
CHANGXING ISLAND
Nanxiang
Pudong
City
PUDONG AIRPORT
Qingpu
Minhang
Songjiang
Nanhui
HUANGPU RIVER
SHANGHAI
Fengjing
Fengxian
Jinshanwei
Pinghu
HANGZHOU BAY

CITY MAP
Jiading District
Outer Ring Rd
Shanghai-Nanjing Expressway
Putuo District
Caoyang Rd
Rd
Wuning Rd
Daduhe
Jinshajiang Rd
Zhongshan North Rd viaduct
Caoyang
Rd
Wuning Rd
Changshou
Rd
Jing Dis
Wuning Rd
Normal University of East China
Suzhou Creek
Beizhai Rd
West
Rd
Changning Rd
Yuyan
Jiangsu
Dingxi
Wuyi
Rd
Changning District
Gubei
Pingtang
Rd
Rd
Shuicheng Rd
Zunyi Rd
Kaixuan Rd
Rd
Xianxia Rd
Gubei
Jianhe
Rd
Hongqiao
Yan'an West Rd
Xinhua Rd
Rd
Rd
Huashan
Rd
Hongqiao Rd
Hongqiao Rd
Zhongshan West Rd. viaduct
Huaihai West Rd
Wanping
Hongqiao Airport
Highway
Panyu
Jiaotong University
Jianguo
Hongqiao Rd
Rd
Huqingping
Minhang District
Hongzhong Rd
Hongmei Rd
Hongxu Rd
Wuzhong Rd
Yishan
Laoxi North Rd
Xujiahu
Wuzhong Rd

LEGEND
Municipal Government
Metro
Metro under construction
Railway station
Light Railway
Ferry
Tunnel
Shanghai Int'l Studies University
Hongkou District
Zhongshan North Rd viaduct
Zhabei District
Linping Rd
Railway Station
North-South Viaduct
Tianmu West Rd
Haining Rd
Jiangxi Nth Rd
Sichuan Middle Rd
Wusong Rd
Henan Middle Rd
Fujian Middle Rd
Xizang North Rd
Qufu Rd
Suzhou Creek
Jiangning Rd
Shimen Rd
Chengdu North Rd
Xikang Rd
Shaanxi North Rd
Xinzha Rd
Beijing West Rd
Beijing East Rd
Nanjing East Rd
Jiangxin M. Rd
Zhongshan
Bund Park
Lujiazui
Ave
Binjiang
Tunnel
Pudong New Distric
Jing'an Temple
Nanjing West Rd
People's Park
Fuzhou Rd
Yan'an East Rd
Yan'an Middle Rd
Jinling East Rd
No.1
Huangpu River
Dongchang Rd
Changle Rd
Huaihai Middle Rd
Luwan District
Laoximen
Huang District
Henan South Rd
Xizang South Rd
Huangpi South Rd
East Rd
Zhangyang Rd
Wulumuqi Rd
Xiang yang Rd
Shaanxi South Rd
Ruijin Rd
Fuxing Middle Rd
Fuxing East Rd
Hengshan Rd
Zhongshan South Rd
Zhong hua Rd
Jianguo Middle Rd
Chongqing South Rd
Lujiabang Road
West Rd
Xuhui District
haojiabang Rd
Xietu Rd
Ruijin South Rd
Nanpu Bridge
Pudong Airport
Zhongshan South Rd viaduct

Published by China Knowledge Press Pte Ltd.

China Knowledge Press Pte Ltd.
2 Tan Quee Lan Street
Singapore 188091
Fax: (65) 6310 8738
Email: info@chinaknowledge.com
www.chinaknowledge-press.com

ISBN 981-04-6818-0
Printed in Singapore

FOREWORD

On the eve of 2002, as I was to pen this foreword, a news flashed : 'The fastest train in the world that 'flies without wings' at a speed of more than 400 kph to be officiated by China Premier Zhu Rongji and German Chancellor Gerhard Schroeder. For the month of December alone, I was juggernauting piles of such meaty news about Shanghai where journalists around the world would front it as headlines. This municipality of 17 million people of which 13.2 millions are Shanghainese and the rest made up of 3.8 millions of 'floating population', non-residents and foreigners is now poised to create dazzling stories.

This confidence that Shanghai residents have in their city's destiny derives partly from history – a history that did much to shape their personality through the 20th century. Looking back at Old Shanghai, we witnessed its birthplace of world renowned companies like AIG, HSBC and lists of China's corporate giants, and breeding ground of colorful tycoons and successful entrepreneurs where we find their remarkable achievements in Hong Kong, Taiwan, Singapore and North America. Today, its rebirth as an international financial, commercial, and trading hub is once again putting Shanghai at the center-stage to world's audience. The new financial district of Pudong, studded with skyscrapers, showcases its mega cylinders of growth where a substantial amount of world's largest Foreign Direct Investment (FDI) in China had sponged onto the city.

This Guide contains three parts and a useful business directory. Part One begins with an introduction of the past and present development of Shanghai, its history and geography, administration and infrastructure. Part Two covers numerous aspects necessary for doing business in Shanghai, from tax, accounting, legal, human resource, importing and exporting, commercial and industrial properties to incentive schemes offered by various industrial parks. Part Three presents business opportunities on various industries as follows: Agriculture, Banking and Finance, Construction, IT, Logistics, Manufacturing, Professional Services, Real Estates, and Wholesale and Retail. At the back of the Guide, we have compiled comprehensive and useful listings of local and foreign businesses.

With our Motto of "providing independent insight" and founding principle of "investor's right to know", we hope our team of China specialists and professionals, made up of several industry analysts, researchers, economists, legal experts, auditors, real estates consultants and other contributors, would benefit readers with the most up-to-date, accurate and reliable research and information.

Let's board this escalator to the land of opportunities.

Charles Chaw Chong Loong
Research Director
Singapore
1st January 2003

Contents

DIRECTORY

Today's Shanghai

"Paris of the Orient", "Ten Miles of Foreign Territory", "the Paradise of Adventurers" are just a few old names that used to describe the materialistic metropolis before the Communist revolutions.

Since 1949, Shanghainese started a different life experience as Marxist-Leninism and Maoist Thoughts swept over the previous filthy capitalist hotbeds and pushed workers to the frontiers. Factories erected, reservoirs dug, slums cleaned, houses redistributed, production and consumption were under meticulous planning and tight control. Shanghai's dynamism diminished, so did its prominence in China – especially when urban youths were dispersed into the country's vast rural area and major projects laid in more "secure" hinterland to prevent any "imperialist invasions".

Emerging from these years of oblivion, the Chinese reformists finally and firmly opened the door for the most populous city in China. In early 1990s, Pudong, formerly a forsaken area to the east of the Huangpu River, was handpicked to be the test field to re-ignite this economic locomotive for the whole of East China. After a decade of busy installing and relocating cranes, wooing businesses and residents, Shanghai is now home to many brand-new skyscrapers in the world and, to a certain degree, also manifests the huge disparities of contemporary China.

Shanghai is now attracting world audiences with every move it makes. Having successfully hosted the Fortune Global Forum 1999 and APEC 2001, Shanghai stood out to be the winner to host the World Expo 2010 – just days before China's first anniversary of its WTO entrance. The city is almost synonymous with the "prime location", whenever an overseas investment proposal prompts CEOs from multinationals. Shanghai is hyping numerous grand urban projects with extranvaganza – deepwater port, bridges, tunnels, subway, light rail, magnetic levitated train and so on. History is eventually returning to favor Shanghai again.

CITY LIFE IN SHANGHAI

Public Health

Regaining economic momentum, Shanghai has spared no effort to push the reform of the local medical and healthcare system. A new social network of disease prevention, control and monitoring has been established. By the end of 2001, the city had 3,813 medical and public health institutions, including 432 hospitals, 3,210 clinics, and 26 anti-epidemic outlets. More than 105,100 professionals are working with these organizations, including 48,500 doctors and 37,700 nurses.

With continuous improvements in living quality and medical system, the average life expectancy of Shanghainese reached 79.66, with 77.47 for male and 81.83 for female. As a result of tight birth control in Shanghai which is also a phenomenon in other economically developed societies, the natural population growth recorded -2.7‰ in 2001, which makes Shanghai the first city in China with a negative rate in population growth.

Cultural Facilities

By the end of 2001, the city had 36 public establishments to promote mass culture and art, 32 public libraries, and 20 museums. The city also owns 29 performing troupes. Since 1990, a number of large, contemporary, multi-

Shanghai Library

functional cultural and recreational facilities have been added into the list. These include the new Shanghai Museum, Shanghai Library, Shanghai Grand Theater, Shanghai Book City, Shanghai Circus City, Shanghai Urban Planning Exhibition Hall and Shanghai Science and Technology Museum.

Shanghai Library is a modern public library that has a combined floor area of 83,000 square meters. It boasts a collection of 13.2 million volumes of books and 3,036 seats in 38 reading rooms, 24 research reference rooms and 8 multimedia rooms. An 842-seat conference hall, a 500-sq m exhibition hall, and a seminar room with facilities for simultaneous interpretation are also available.

Shanghai Museum

Located at the People's Square – the heartland of Shanghai City – Shanghai Museum, an RMB576 million project, was opened to the public in 1996. With a round top and a square base, it reflects the ancient Chinese belief in the "hemispherical dome cosmology". The museum contains ten galleries displaying Chinese ancient artworks like bronze, pottery, ceramics, jadeware, sculptures, coins, Chinese paintings and calligraphy. Hosting a rich collection of more than 123,000 pieces of precious cultural relics, Shanghai Museum enjoys prestige both at home and abroad.

Diagonally opposite Shanghai Museum and across the Central Avenue lies the newly built Shanghai Grand Theater. The main theatre has a capacity of 1,800 seats and a front stage of 728 sq m, and the other two theatres are

able to accommodate 600 and 200 audience. With a total floor area of 70,000 sq m and infusing state-of-the-art technology, the crystal palace-like theater is a world-class arena for performing Chinese and western ballet, opera and symphony.

Shanghai Grand Theatre

If the Shanghai Grand Theatre is the emblem of performance arts, the adjacent 19,000 sq m Urban Planning Exhibition Hall is a testament to Shanghai's colorful history of urbanization. Opened in 1999, it traces the developmental history of the city since the Song Dynasty and showcases the current urban area in an 800 sq m model.

Urban Planning Exhibition Hall

Without
China knowledge

With total investment of RMB1.755 billion and an architectural area of 98,000 sq m, the magnificent Science and Technology Museum was built on an area of 6.8 ha and opened to the public at the end of 2001. The museum owns 6 major exhibition zones and three special theatres with panoramic or spherical screens.

Shanghai Book City is located at Fuzhou Road, a famous Cultural Street where books, stationeries, antiques and all kinds of collectibles can be found. As the first book superstore in town, the book city sells more than 120,000 titles and accommodate tens of thousands readers and customers everyday.

Mass Media

Currently, there are two main stations, namely, Shanghai People's Radio Station with six channels, and the Oriental Radio Station with four channels. Three television stations are in operation, which includes Shanghai TV with seven channels, Shanghai Oriental TV with four channels and Shanghai Educational TV.

By the end of 2001, Shanghai had 101 newspapers in circulation, including 11 dailies. In 2001 alone, 1.7 billion copies of newspaper, 185 million copies of magazines and 268 million copies of books were published in Shanghai. As the city attracts world spotlights, 46 media with 12 nationalities had already established their subsidiaries in Shanghai.

Events

In 2001, Shanghai hosted 278 international exhibitions and conferences which attracted 4.8 million audience and reached deals worth RMB55 billion. Those trade fairs cover a wide range of industries, such as IT and electronics, packaging, automobile, food and beverage, furniture, agriculture etc.

In the same year, Shanghai had also hosted the 3rd Shanghai International Arts Festival, Shanghai International Fashion Culture Festival, Shanghai Spring International Music Festival and the 5th Shanghai Film Festival.

Noticeably, APEC Summit 2001, participated by 6,000 high profile leaders and officials from 19 economies and over 3,000 reporters and journalists, was successfully held in Shanghai in October. The city had hosted the 1999

Fortune Global Forum too. On 3rd December 2002, Shanghai beat other four candidates and won the bid for World Expo 2010 successfully.

A contrast of modern highrises and old houses in the city

Living

Whatever products and services existing elsewhere can be literally found in Shanghai. Services like banking, engineering, telecommunication, accountancy, consultancy and entertainment are either well rendered or in a quick catching-up process. As the city possesses attractive social and cultural environment and developed infrastructure, it entices an increasing

number of overseas professionals and businessmen with their families every year. Housing options for expatriates vary from high-standard villas, serviced apartments to ordinary flats in Shanghai. The monthly rentals may range from USD250-500 for an ordinary flat to USD3,000-5,000 for a villa. At the same time, living conditions have also improved greatly for the locals. By the end of 2001, district residents' living area averaged at 12.1 sq m per person, a considerable advancement from the old days when it was common for a family to share a single room or the attics without proper sanitary equipment.

Shopping centres are never short of electronic products

In 2001, GDP per capita of Shanghai had exceeded USD3,500. The average disposable income of urban residents was RMB12,883, an increase of almost 10% over the previous year. And that of rural residents was RMB5,850, up 5.1% over the previous year. The annual expenditures of urban and rural residents were at RMB9,336 and RMB4,753, respectively. However, residents' personal savings totaled RMB300 billion, or averaged at RMB22,600, a great potential purchasing power.

Statistics show that per hundred urban dwellers now possess 154 color TVs, 100 air-conditioners, 56 VCD players, 50 mobile phones, 38 personal computers and even 7 sets of fitness equipment.

ATTRACTIONS IN SHANGHAI

The Bund

The Bund originates from an Anglo-Indian term for the embankment of a muddy waterfront. Called "wai tan" in Chinese, it refers to a stretch of the west bank of the Huangpu River. It was Shanghai's Wall Street, a place of feverish trading and an unabashed playground for Western business sophisticates.

The refurbished Bund is now a tourist spot in Shanghai

Still a grand strip of hotels, banks and shopping streets, the Bund remains an intrinsic part of Shanghai's character. Everyday, Chinese and foreign tourists pad along the Bund's grand edifices reminiscent of neoclassical 1930s downtown New York or renaissance in any European cities. The 52 buildings are a great collection of different architectural styles such as Gothic, Baroque, Roman, Renaissance, British, French and East Indian. Among them are the old homes to Hong Kong and Shanghai Bank, the Banque de l'Indochine, and AIA. Today, the Bund is a spectacular demonstration of the financial and economic development of Shanghai.

A grand display of different architectural styles along the Bund

Zhongshan East No. 1 Road along the Bund

Nanjing Walking Street

Often cited as China's No.1 Commercial Street, Nanjing East Road was formerly a small path in the British Settlement in Shanghai. It was until the 1930s that four big Chinese department stores pushed it onto the throne of the business center of the Far East. The 5.5 km road is now composed of the Nanjing Walking Street and a shorter extension linking to the Bund. Along the street are Shanghai No.1 Department Store, New World, Isetan, Shanghai Landmark Tower, the Century Park and many other elegant commercial centers and hotels.

Nanjing Walking Street

Huaihai Middle Road and Xintiandi

Huaihai Middle Road is all about shopping, with newly erected spacious department stores shining under the sun along a road colorfully lined with flowerboxes. Called Xiafei Road in the past French Settlement, Huaihai Road has always been equivalent to sophisticated shopping and stylish

hospitalities. Shopping malls like Times Square, Hong Kong Plaza and Shanghai Square line up along the east side of the road.

Xintiandi, or known as New Heaven and Earth in Chinese, is a newly constructed area near Huaihang Middle Road. It now hosts a wide range of boutiques selling fashionable goods, creative home furniture and arts and crafts, and many trendy restaurants with exotic and fusion cuisines. Supermarkets and department stores can be found here too, such as Metro, Carrefour and Isetan.

Xintiandi

Yu Garden

The nearby Yu Garden, or "yu yuan" in Chinese, offers huge varieties of delicious snacks, souvenirs, arts and crafts in a traditional Chinese ambience. Its original owners, the Pan family in China's Ming Dynasty during the 15th century, spent 18 years to develop the area. It was the headquarters during the Shanghai Little Dagger Society Uprising of 1853. Today, it has been restored and attracts throngs of Chinese and international tourists amazed by its perfect combination of halls, pavilions, terraces, rockeries, ponds and bridges – typical components of a traditional Chinese garden.

The People's Square

Located at the heartland of Shanghai, between the bustling Nanjing Road and the levitated Yan'an Viaduct, the garden-style square undertakes multiple functions to promote the city's culture, transportation and commerce. An extensive renovation was carried out from the end of 1993 to 1 October, the National Day of 1994. Once a racecourse in pre-1949, the People's Square is now the home to Shanghai Municipal Government, the Grand Theater, Shanghai Museum and the Urban Planning Exhibition Hall. It is a must-visit place where one can feel the crowdedness, modernization and diversity of the city of Shanghai. Century Park is on the north, with an underground Metro Line 2 station.

The Oriental Pearl TV Tower and the Jinmao Tower

With a height of 468 meters, the Oriental Pearl TV Tower is the highest TV Tower in Asia and the 3rd highest in the world. Eleven spheres with various sizes are inlaid "from the blue sky down to the green lawn", resembling a string of pearls. The sphere at a height of 263 meters is an observation hall from where a breathtaking panorama of the metropolis is clearly presented. Within walking distance of the Oriental Pearl Tower there is the 88-storey Jinmao Tower. With a height of 420.5 metres, it is the tallest in China and the 3rd tallest skyscraper in the world. Completed in August 1998, the skyscraper has cost USD 560 million. Grand Hyatt Shanghai occupies 53 to 87 floors, which makes it the tallest five-star hotel in the world.

The Oriental Pear TV Tower is the landmark of Pudong and Shanghai

The tallest building in China - Jinmao Tower, is the third tallest in the world.

Brief History

THE ORIGIN OF HU AND SHEN

Shanghai is called "Hu" for short, and "Shen" as a nickname in Chinese. About 6,000 years ago, the western part of today's Shanghai dried up into land, and its eastern part rose above sea level about 2,000 years ago. During the Spring-Autumn and Warring States Periods (770-221 BC), this area was once the fiefdom of Huang Xie, the Chun Shen Jun (Governor) of Chu Kingdom. It is believed that the name of "Shen" comes from the title of the governor. During the Jin Dynasty (4th-5th centuries), fishermen living along the Songjiang River and the coast of East China Sea created a fishing tool called "Hu". By combining the name of the fishing tool and waters, they coined a Chinese character "Hu" to name the place – as it sits at the estuary of the Yangtze River, the longest river in China.

ANCIENT SHANGHAI

Shanghai began as Huating County, an administrative district established in the year of 751 AD. The county, located in an area known as Songjiang District today, had its boundary reaching today's Hongkou District in the north, Xiasha in the east and the coast in the south. In 991 AD, the town of Shanghai was set up. During the period of 1260 1274, the town evolved into an important trading port, and in 1292, the then central government of Yuan Dynasty approved the formal establishment of Shanghai County in this area. This is widely deemed as the official beginning of the city of Shanghai.

Shanghai continued to grow through the Ming dynasty (1368-1644). At the beginning of the 15th century, the county had an estimated number of 64,000 households. A new tunnel was cut north to the Yangtze in order to permit better drainage and to prevent the outlet to Yangtze River and East China Sea from being filled with silt. Shanghai became the gateway to the mighty Yangtze River.

In the 16th century (mid of the Ming Dynasty), Shanghai became the center of national textile handicraft industry. It grew rapidly during the Qing Dynasty (1644-1911), when the development and use of cotton became widespread. In 1685, Shanghai set up its first customs office. By that time, Shanghai was already a city with population of 200,000. In the 18th century, the city became a prosperous production center of cotton, fabric and garment.

SHANGHAI IN THE PAST

After the Opium Wars in the mid-19th century, with the invasion of foreign powers, Shanghai was forced to open its port to foreign trading and serve as a gateway to inland China. It became a semi-feudal and semi-colonial city. The British, the French and the Americans took up autonomous concession zones in the city, each of which was independent of Chinese law. All three brought in their own colonial influences, which can still be seen today in the European architecture of the buildings along the Bund and in the Old French Concession area. The used-to-be French Concession area is now home of the famous shopping street, Huaihai Road. Containing a high concentration of shops, restaurants, cafes and boutiques, many of the old buildings are today being torn down in favor of glossy department stores and high-rises.

In 1895, Japan defeated China in the First Sino-Japanese War; China was forced to allow westerners and Japanese to invest directly in China. As a result, the population of foreigners in Shanghai grew substantially. A period of commercialization and industrialization, though dominated by foreign forces, followed. In the next half century, Shanghai developed a distinctly western character and experienced a period of economic prosperity. It gained the reputation as one of the world's most exciting and sophisticated cities.

However, the rich got richer and the poor poorer, and many local Chinese lived desperately in poverty. With weak and corrupted Chinese officials and rampant exploitation by foreigners, rebellion and revolt became inevitable. This began when a group of revolutionists overthrew the Qing Dynasty and established a new Republic of China with Sun Yat-sen as president. Marxism soon became a popular ideology among Chinese intellectuals; and in 1921, the Communist Party of China (CPC) was founded in Shanghai, and in 1925 communists staged an uprising in Shanghai to help the republicans take over the city. Although they supported the then powerful Kuomintang (Nationalist Party) led by Chiang Kai-shek, Chiang abruptly ended his alliance with the communists and violently suppressed the communists in Shanghai in 1927. Today, people can trace this history by visiting a number of sites commemorating the birth of CPC and its original members, including the Memorial Hall of the Site of the First CPC National Congress and Dr. Sun Yat-sen's Former Residence.

The world's greatest houses of finance and commerce descended on Shanghai in the 1930s. The place had the tallest buildings in Asia, and more motor vehicles on its streets than the rest of China put together. Shanghai became a byword for exploitation and vice, with countless opium dens, casinos and brothels. The Japanese invaded China and seized Shanghai in 1937. They occupied the city till the end of World War II in 1945. Following the war, Shanghai soon reemerged as China's major domestic and international trading, banking and shipping center, but the Chinese civil war interrupted Shanghai's growth.

Shanghai underwent a historic transformation in May 1949 when the People's Liberation Army of CPC liberated it from Kuomintang rule and took on the job of eradicating slums, rehabilitating hundreds of thousands of opium addicts, and stamping out child and slave labor. China's leaders moved quickly to de-emphasize Shanghai's importance to the country's overall economy and drained capital away from the city to support other areas of China. Difficult years followed, marked by the Great Leap Forward, famines and the Cultural Revolution (1966-1976).

A MODERN SHANGHAI

After Mr. Deng Xiaoping rose to power, he initiated a program of market liberalization and reforms to promote China's economic development in late 1978. In 1984, Shanghai was designated among the 14 coastal open cities for foreign investment. To rebuild its glory in the past and to lead the economic development of the whole Yangtze River Delta, the state government inaugurated Pudong New District, previously a piece of sleeping farmland, in 1990.

In the 1990s, the city grew rigorously as new subways, highways, expressways crisscrossed its territory, and the stock exchange, numerous skyscrapers and luxurious hotels appeared overnight. Foreign influence has once again made Shanghai a Chinese consumer heaven. Domestic stores rub shoulders with the boutiques of Louis Vuitton, Christian Dior, Ralph Lauren and other top international brands. Female Shanghainese are among the most fashionable women in China.

Although Beijing remains China's capital city, Shanghai is known as the de facto economic, financial, international trade and transportation center of the mainland. It may soon regain its mantle as Asia's most dynamic cosmopolitan city.

Geography

LOCATION

Shanghai is located at 120°29′E and 31°14′N on the Yangtze River estuary in eastern China. To its east lies the East China Sea and Hangzhou Bay lies to its south. Chongming Island, north of Shanghai, sits in the middle of Yangtze River where its runs to the sea. Shanghai borders Jiangsu Province and Zhejiang Province in the northwest and southwest, respectively.

Shanghai is 1,460 km away from the capital city of China, Beijing, and only one-hour ride from Suzhou, an emerging economic center of Jiangsu, and two hours' drive from Hangzhou, Zhejiang's provincial capital, via train or expressway.

TOPOGRAPHY

Situated in lower reaches of Yangtze River – part of the Yangtze River Delta alluvial plain, Shanghai is predominantly made up of flatlands with only a few lowlands and small hills in its southwest. The average altitude of the municipality is about 4 m. Qingpu, Songjiang and Jinshan were under sea level until 6,000 years ago; land area east to Jiading-Fengxian line was not formed until the ocean regressed from the mainland 4,000 years ago.

Dianshan Lake, 63 sq km in size, lies in Shanghai's west where altitude is below the city's average level. There is a dense waterway network in Shanghai. Two rivers form its trunk – Huangpu River (114 km) and Wusong River, or Suzhou Creek (125 km), with the latter a tributary of the former. Huangpu River runs northwestward through the city's entire territory and pours into Yangtze River at Wusong. It is the busiest river way for Shanghai Port. However, due to gradual river channel sedimentation and frequent shipment of large tonnage vehicles, Shanghai is determined to set up a deepwater seaport off its southeast coast.

Chongming Island of Shanghai, with a total land area of 1,083 sq km, is the third largest in China, albeit by far smaller than Taiwan and Hainan. It

Administrative Regions of Shanghai

was during the beginning of Tang Dynasty (618-907AD) that it revealed its land surface. There are still a few islands set in the north and the south of Shanghai's sea area, such as Changxing and Dajinshan. Dajinshan, with a height of 103 m above sea level, is actually the peak in Shanghai.

LAND AREA

In 1949, the total area of Shanghai was only 636 sq km. In 1958, 10 counties of Jiangsu joined the city and expanded its territory by almost 10 times. In 2001, Shanghai Municipality measures 6,340.5 sq km, a mere 0.06% of the country's total. The territory spans over 120 km from north to south and spread a latitudinal 100 km wide. The total land area is 6,219 sq km and water surface 122 sq km. As two more counties were approved to be the districts of the municipality in early 2001, Chongming is now the only county left in Shanghai.

Administrative Regions	
Urban Area (9 districts)	Huangpu, Jing'an, Luwan, Hongkou, Changning, Zhabei, Putuo, Xuhui, Yangpu
New Area (1 district)	Pudong
Suburban Area (8 districts, 1 county)	Minhang, Baoshan, Jiading, Nanhui, Songjiang, Fengxian, Jinshan, Qingpu, Chongming county

Shanghai Land Area & Population

	1995	1996	1997	1998	1999	2000	2001
Rural Land Area	4,283	4,283	3,697	3,092	2,416	2,416	2,417
Urban Land Area	2,057	2,057	2,643	3,249	3,924	3,924	3,924
Total Land Area (sq km)	6,341	6,341	6,341	6,341	6,341	6,341	6,341
Rural Population	3.44	3.43	2.86	2.36	1.86	1.85	1.42
Urban Population	9.57	9.61	10.19	10.71	11.27	11.37	11.85
Total Population (million)	13.01	13.04	13.05	13.07	13.13	13.22	13.27

POPULATION

When the People's Republic of China was founded in 1949, Shanghai had a population of 5.2 million, which already made it the largest city in the country. During the period of 1954-1984, Shanghai had migrated 1.39 million people out of the city for economic construction elsewhere in China. Due to its well-managed birth control, Shanghai became the first city with a negative natural population growth rate in 1993. In 2001, the city's birth rate dropped to 4.3‰ and the mortality rate stood at 7‰ which made its natural population growth at –2.7‰.

Nevertheless, by the end of 2001 the number of the city's residents reached 13.27 million, or 2.6 times that in 1949. As Shanghai's economy is taking off, it attracts human influx as well as investment. Statistics show that transient population in Shanghai is estimated at 3.87 million, or one in four people you meet in Shanghai may probably come from elsewhere.

Given a total population size of more than 17 million, the metropolis's population density exceeds 2,680 per sq km. Urban population accounts for 76.2% of the total, the highest among all administrative regions in China.

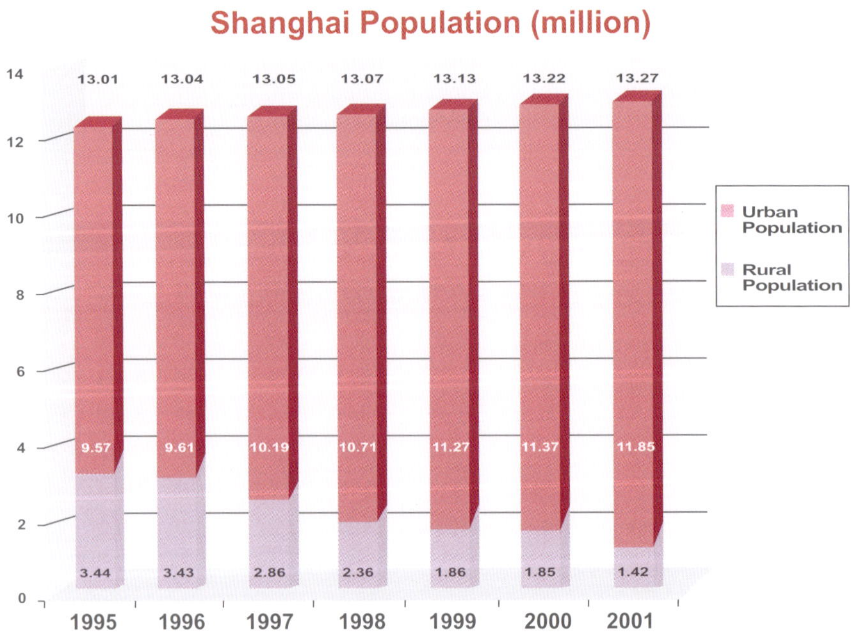

CLIMATE

Located in northern subtropical oceanic monsoon climate zone, Shanghai has four distinctive seasons and abundant sunshine and rainfalls. Spring and autumn are short, summer and winter relatively long, and annual average temperature stands at 15.7°C. July and August are normally the hottest season in a year, with average temperature at 28°C; the lowest average temperature is usually posted in January, about 4°C. Extreme temperature sometimes reaches 36-37°C in summer and –5~–7°C in winter.

Shanghai Climate

Month	Mar	Apr	May	J un	Jul	Aug	Sep	Oct	Nov	Dec	Jan	Feb
Season	Spring			Summer			Autumn			Winter		
Average Temp. (°C)	8.3	14	18.8	22.3	27.8	27.7	23.6	18	12.3	6.2	3.5	4.6
Average highest temp (°C)	12.6	18.5	23.2	27.3	31.8	31.6	27.4	22.4	16.8	10.7	7.6	8.7
Average lowest temp. (°C)	4.9	10.4	15.3	20.1	24.7	24.7	20	14.3	8.6	2.7	0.3	1.4
Rainfalls (mm)	78.1	106	122.9	158.9	134.2	126	150.5	50.1	48.8	40.9	44	62.6
Dress Recommended	Woolen sweater, coat			Shirt			Long sleeve shirt, woolen sweater, coat			Woolen sweater, overcoat		

Frost-free period lasts 230 days in Shanghai, approximately, and annual precipitation is around 1,200 mm. However, 60% of the total rainfalls appear in the high-water season from May to September. There is a so-called "plum rains" period from mid-June to early July when rains are almost incessant. Typhoon often occurs during July-September period.

Authorities

COMMUNIST PARTY OF CHINA

According to the Constitution of the People's Republic of China, the state's fundamental law, China is a socialist state led by the Communist Party of China (CPC).

The Third Plenary Session of the 11th CPC Central Committee, held in December 1978, formally decided to shift the party's work focus to economic development and set a policy of reform and opening up to the outside world.

In Shanghai, the CPC Municipal Committee is the paramount authority. It exercises great influence and power in the city's political and economic developmental progress, and oversees social stability and security. The Municipal Congress of the Party is held once every five years, and is convened by the Standing Committee. Accordingly, every district or county and state-owned enterprises have their own committees or branches.

Mr. Huang Ju, formerly secretary-general of CPC Shanghai Committee, was newly placed in the party's almighty 9-member Politburo Standing Committee in the 16th CPC National Congress in November 2002. Born in 1938, he is among the four Tsinghua University alumni in the Standing Committee. The successor to Huang is Mr. Chen Liangyu, co-currently the governor of Shanghai.

www.sh.gov.cn

Mr Chen Liang Yu

CHINESE PEOPLE'S POLITICAL CONSULTATIVE CONFERENCE

Besides CPC, there are also eight non-Communist democratic parties, or "participating political parties", each with an established committee in Shanghai:

- China Association for the Promotion of Democracy
- China Democratic National Construction Association

- China Democratic League
- Chinese Peasants and Workers' Democratic Party
- China Zhigong Party
- Jiusan Society
- China Kuomintang Revolutionary Committee
- Taiwan Democratic Self-governance League

Political Structure of Shanghai Municipality

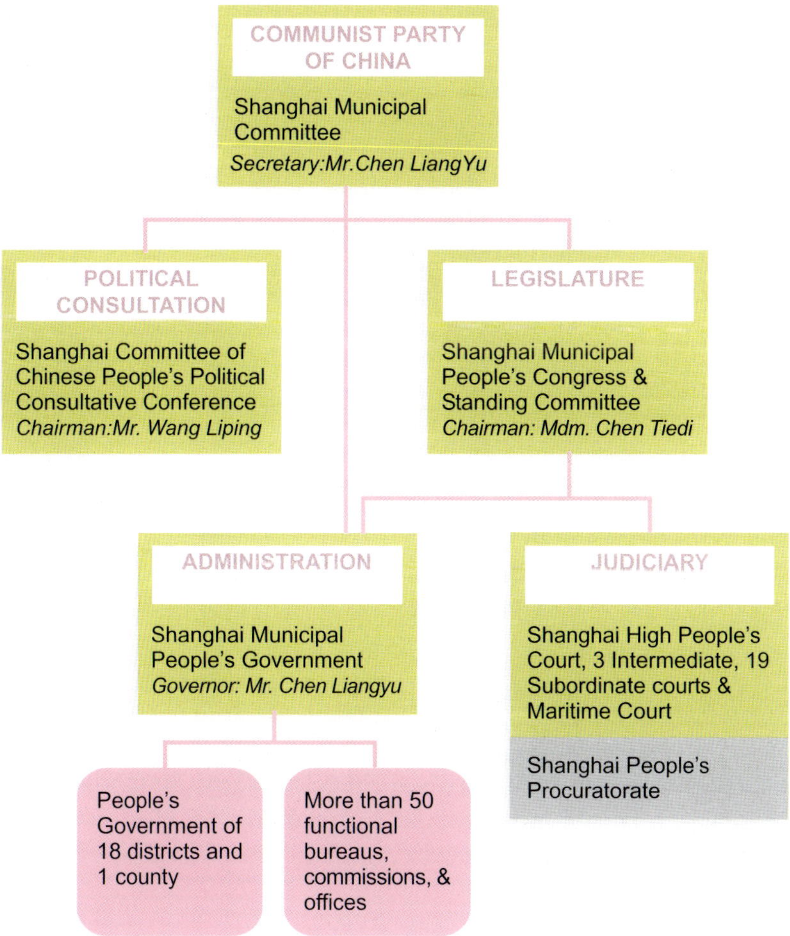

The Chinese People's Political Consultative Conference (CPPCC) is the main political platform for these parties to communicate with CPC, express their political views, exercise democratic supervision, and participate in some policy-making activities related to the economic and political reforms.

Shanghai Committee of CPPCC has 762 existing members, of which 63.08% are non-CPC members. Seventy percent of the members hold university degrees and strong professional backgrounds. Within the committee, there are eight specific subcommittees and one administrative department. The current chairman of CPPCC Shanghai is Mr. Wang Liping.

Website: shszx.eastday.com

PEOPLE'S CONGRESS

The People's Congress is the nation's legislative body and forms the political system of China. Shanghai Municipal People's Congress (SMPC) exercises local legislative power; revises and supervises the implementation of the local regulations; examines and approves Shanghai's economic and social development plans and the municipal government's reports, budget and their implementation; and elects and decides on the choice of leading members of the SMPC Standing Committee, the municipal governor, vice-governors, the chief of Shanghai High Court and the chief procurator of Shanghai Procuratorate.

The members of People's Congress are elected for a term of five years. The current SMPC has 865 representatives who were elected in 1998. It usually meets once a year, and when not in session, a Standing Committee exercises power. SMPC comprises nine working committees with specific functions, an administrative department, and a research office.

The current chairman of SMPC is Mdm. Chen Tiedi, formerly the president of Tongji University and the deputy secretary of CPC Shanghai Committee.

Website: www.spcsc.sh.cn

GOVERNMENT INSTITUTIONS

Shanghai Municipal People's Government is the administrative organ of the metropolis. It exercises administrative functions through its various bureaus and commissions. It also leads subordinate governments at district or county level.

The Shanghai governor, Mr. Chen Liangyu, was elected with his eight deputies in the 5th session of the 11th SMPC in February 2002. In October, Chen was picked as the secretary-general of CPC Shanghai Committee to fill the post as left by Huang Ju. In the 16th CPC National Congress held in

Shanghai Municipal Government at the People's Square

Beijing in November, Chen was further promoted to a member of the CPC Central Committee and the Politburo. Born in 1946, he graduated from the Military Logistics Engineering Institute in 1968. Prior to his current standing, Chen formerly served as the chief secretary of Huangpu District CPC committee and a deputy governor of Shanghai.

Economic Development

Shanghai Development Planning Commission

The main duties include:

- to make the medium and long-term strategies for urban, economic, and social development
- to set annual economic and social development targets, forecasts and supervises economic growths, and suggests solutions
- to formulate industrial policy, coordinate sector balance, and encourages high-tech industries
- to plan and finance key public projects and total volume of fixed assets investment, approve and report to the State Council on the development of large projects
- to direct FDI inflows
- to set, adjust and supervise prices and administrative fees
- to analyze demand supply conditions, implement the State's plans on key exports and imports

Website: www.jhw.sh.gov.cn

Shanghai Economic Commission

The main duties include:

- to implement industrial development laws, rules, regulations and policies
- to supervise and analyze the development tendency of local industries
- to set development plans for local high-tech, pillar and urban industry
- to guide state-owned enterprises in restructuring

Website: www.shec.gov.cn

Shanghai Industrial and Commercial Administration

The main duties of the administration are:

- to implement relevant laws, rules, regulations and policies
- to register industrial and commercial enterprises, checks and ratifies registered company names, and issues certificates upon approval
- to monitor misdemeanors in local market, such as monopoly, illegal competition and fraud
- to deal with customers' complaints and protect customers' rights
- to monitor and administrates advertisement distribution and the companies' operations
- to protect copyright of registered brands, supervises the use and printing of brands

Website: www.sgs.gov.cn

Shanghai Commerce Commission

The main duties of the commission are

- to implement relevant laws, rules, regulations and policies on commerce
- to study and prepare development plans for commerce in Shanghai, and to adjust and control reserves of strategic commodities
- to promote innovations in marketing, encourage developments in chain stores, distribution and logistics, brokerage, and direct sales
- to push forward technological advancement and development of E-commerce
- to guide and monitor organizations including restaurants, hotels and advertising firms, and to supervise alcohol, salt, butchery, auction, and leasing businesses

Website: syw.sh.gov.cn

Shanghai Foreign Economic Relations and Trade Commission

The main duties of the commission are:

- to implement laws, regulations and policies related to foreign trade, foreign investment and other foreign economic cooperation matters

- to formulate strategies in promoting foreign investment and foreign trade
- to deal with applications for foreign-funded project and approve the establishment of foreign-invested enterprises
- to examine, guide and monitor the development of export processing industries and entrepot trade
- to invite foreign organizations to visit Shanghai and arrange Shanghai officials to participate in international events

Website: www.smert.gov.cn

Shanghai Foreign Investment Board

The board's major duties are

- to examine and approve the establishment of FIEs
- to appraise and redirect foreign-funded projects with investment amount of more than what the municipal authorities can approve
- to issue certificates of registered FIEs and Taiwan, Hong Kong, Macau-invested enterprises
- to lead subordinate organizations in districts and counties in relevant matters

Shanghai Foreign Investment Board
15/16F, New Hongqiao Plaza
83 Loushanguan Road
Shanghai 200336
Tel: (86) (21) 62368800
Fax: (86) (21) 62368024

Website: www.investment.gov.cn

The board also has representative offices in Los Angeles, Osaka, London and Frankfurt.

Los Angeles Representative Office
#425 World Trade Center
350 South Figueroa Street
Los Angeles, CA 90071
Tel: (1)(213) 6251890
Fax: (1)(213) 6251935

Osaka Representative Office
Tel: (81)(6) 66155523
Fax: (81)(6) 66155531

London Representative Office
G/F Bank of China Building
90 Cannon Street
London EC4N 6HA, UK
Tel: (44)(20) 76268088
Fax: (44)(20) 76268089

Frankfurt Representative Office
Tel: (49) 16091149540

Urban Planning and Construction

Shanghai Construction and Administration Committee

- oversees urban and rural construction
- administers and regulates construction (including renovation and decoration) industry and construction material industry
- organizes the examination and preliminary designs of approved projects

Website: www.shucm.sh.cn

Shanghai Urban Planning Administration Bureau

- implement laws, regulations and policies regarding urban planning
- organizes Shanghai urban master planning and detailed planning; examines and approves planning and urban design projects
- administers and follows up on the issue of permits for construction land and project plans
- participates in outdoor advertisement examination and approval
- showcases urban planning, organizes and manages urban planning

information system

Website: www.shghj.gov.cn

Shanghai Housing Development Board

Led by Shanghai Construction and Administration Committee, it undertakes the tasks of urban housing development and construction administration in Shanghai.

Website: www.housing.sh.cn

Shanghai Municipal Engineering Administration Bureau

The bureau is responsible for civil engineering projects in Shanghai, which include the construction and maintenance of city streets, roads, bridges, tunnels and piping works.

Website: www.shsz.gov.cn

Shanghai Urban Transportation Administration Bureau

The bureau is in charge of the planning, construction and maintenance of urban transportation facilities, including public transport interchanges, river ports and routes, stops or stations for passenger and cargo.

Website: www.jt.sh.cn

Shanghai Port Authority

The Authority manages the construction and daily operations of wharves, and transfer of coastal line use.

Website: www.portshanghai.com.cn

Others

Shanghai Finance Administration (Local Tax Bureau)

The bureau is in charge of local public finance and budget plan, implementation of national fiscal policies, and collection and distribution of fiscal revenues.

Website: www.csj.sh.gov.cn

Shanghai News & Publication Bureau (Copyright Administration)
The bureau mulls development plans for the local publishing industry, examines and approves books, newspapers, magazines and electronic publications, and monitors subject selection of local publications.

Website: cbj.sh.gov.cn

Shanghai Statistics Bureau
The bureau collects, analyzes and provides statistical information on Shanghai's economic and social development conditions.

Website: www.stats-sh.gov.cn

JUDICIARY

Courts

The Shanghai municipal judiciary system consists of Shanghai High People's Court, two intermediate people's courts, subordinate courts in each district or county, and two special courts – a railway intermediate court and Shanghai Maritime Court. Civil and criminal cases can be heard in the normal courts and the party who loses the lawsuit may appeal in higher courts. Technically, China's Supreme People's Court has the final judgment. However, most cases are settled before they reach intermediate court or high court.

Website: www.hshfy.sh.cn

Procuratorate

Shanghai People's Procuratorate reports to People's Congress and its Standing Committee. Its main duty involves prosecution of government officials with corruption, embezzlement, assault and battery, and misconduct; prosecution of criminal cases; and supervision over court's judgments.

Website: www.shjcy.sh.cn

For contact information of other government agencies in Shanghai, please refer to the Directory at the back of this Guide.

Administrative Regions

Shanghai is made up of 19 administrative regions. As Nanhui and Fengxian were newly converted to districts in early 2001, the municipality now has only one county left, Chongming. Most of these districts have been developing quickly in recent years. Their development has fueled new momentum to the economy in the Yangtze River Delta and helped build a modern Shanghai with eco-friendly environment.

The opening-up and development of Shanghai is a part of the national strategy for economic reforms. This is also a major strategic decision in carrying on the social and political progress of China. The development of Special Economic Zones (SEZs) and Pudong New District of Shanghai leads the country in the innovation of administration system and upgrading of industrial structure. Among others, Shanghai will keep playing an exemplary role to the rest of the country.

PUDONG NEW DISTRICT

Pudong, literally meaning the east of Huangpu River, has been catching foreigner's eyesight since April 1990 - when the central government in Beijing announced to open up and develop Pudong New District.

The territory has a total land area of 522 sq km and a population of 1.65 million. In the past, due to the lack of bridges and tunnels, the economic development of Pudong lagged far behind those districts in the west of Huangpu River where the old downtown of Shanghai lies. With spectacular infrastructure, it is now fast becoming a most prosperous region of Shanghai in the 21st century.

Economic Development

Since 1990, Pudong has been playing a pivot role in creating new administrative systems, industrial upgrading and opening to the outside world. Its annual growth rate was about 20% in the 1990s, 8%

Land Area and Population of Shanghai Administrative Regions

Administrative Regions	Land Area sq km	Pupolation 000	Population Density per sq km
DISTRICT			
Downtown	289.44	6,282.4	21,705
Huangpu	12.41	661.8	53,326
Luwan	8.05	355.9	44,212
Xuhui	54.76	867.7	15,845
Changning	38.30	604.9	15,793
Jing'an	7.62	358.0	46,985
Putuo	54.83	842.7	15,370
Zhabei	29.26	708.3	24,209
Hongkou	23.48	803.6	34,225
Yangpu	60.73	1,079.5	17,775
Pudong New Area	522.75	1,651.4	3,159
Minhang	371.68	654.0	1,759
Baoshan	415.27	809.5	1,949
Jiading	458.80	486.4	1,060
Jinshan	586.05	530.1	905
Songjiang	604.71	495.5	819
Qingpu	675.54	458.9	679
Nanhui	687.66	690.3	1,004
Fengxian	687.39	504.2	733
COUNTY			
Chongming	1,041.21	653.6	628
TOTAL	**6,340.50**	**13,216.3**	**2,084**

Source: Shanghai Statistics Bureau, 2000 figures.

higher than Shanghai's average. In 2001, the GDP of Pudong reached RMB108.2 billion and total industrial output stood at RMB188.6 billion, up 16.1% and 20.1% respectively. It has undoubtedly become a key growth engine for the metropolitan Shanghai.

Map of Pudong New District

Economic strength of Pudong New District (2001)

Indicator	Shanghai	Pudong New District	Percentage
Area (sq km)	6, 340.5	533.4	8.4%
Population (m)	13.27	2.40	18.1%
GDP (RMB bn)	495.1	108.2	21.9%
Contractual FDI (USD bn)	7.37	2.0	27.1%
Export (USD bn)	27.63	11.02	39.9%

Airport

The Phase I development of the Pudong International Airport has been completed, with RMB12 billion invested and 32 sq km land area to be reclaimed. The airport, opened in October 1999, has an existing handling capacity of 20 million passengers and 750,000 tons of freight per year. The ultimate capacity will reach 70 million and 5 million tons respectively when four runways and 800,000 sq m terminals are all completed. With Hongqiao Airport in the west, Shanghai is the only city in China with two international airports.

Pudong International Airport

Land Transportation

Three bridges, namely, Nanpu Bridge, Yangpu Bridge and Xupu Bridge, are spanning over Huangpu River, connecting Pudong to the west side of the river. Inner Ring Road and Outer Ring Road also extend into Pudong.

The grand project of the magnetic light rail started early in 2001 and is now under trial operation since January 2003. The 35 km long line will connect Longyang Road, the Metro Line 2 and Pudong International Airport. People will then enjoy speedy, convenient and comfortable services as well as a great view of urban landscape along the track. Shanghai thus becomes the first city in the world with a magnetic rail system for commercial operation.

Expressway and elevated road leading to Pudong International Airport

Environment

Pudong area has long been encouraging environmental protection. By the end of 2001, the per capita green space had reached 12 sq m. About 35 % of the land in Pudong is now greenized. In October 1999, Pudong New District was honored as a "Garden City in China".

Green land at Lujiazui

Investment Climate

Pudong aims to become one of the international economic, financial and trade centers. It is also ambitious in establishing a modern industrial structure. A few state-level development zones with specific purposes have been allocated since the development of Pudong in the early 1990s. Noticeably, they include Lujiazui Finance and Trade Zone, Zhangjiang High-tech Park, Waigaoqiao Free Trade Zone and Jinqiao Export Processing Zone.

Investment in Pudong

Pudong constitutes a significant proportion of all FDI inflow to Shanghai. By the end of January 2001, over 70 countries and regions worldwide had established 6,684 projects in Pudong with total investment volume of USD35.07 billion. In 2000, 693 new projects were approved, with total contractual investment of USD2.88 billion, or 45.1% of the total of Shanghai.

To date, 108 of the Fortune Global 500 companies have invested in about 200 projects in Pudong. Among them, Shanghai General Motors, Huahong NEC and KRUPP all have investment above RMB 10 billion (USD1.2 billion) each.

In addition to the huge influx of overseas investment, Pudong also entices

Many MNCs have moved into Pudong's brand-new office buildings

a growing rate of domestic investors. By the end of 2000, there were 5,712 domestic projects signed in Pudong, with a total registered capital of RMB23.817 billion. Many prominent domestic enterprises are relocating their headquarters or regional headquarters to Pudong.

Human Resources

In 2000, 290,000 new jobs were created for local residents in Pudong. According to the official statistics, the registered unemployment rate was kept at 3%. An employment and social security network has been established at both the district and neighborhood level, providing services like employment guidance, job training, aid to low-income group, unemployment insurance and other social aid.

Pudong has 13 universities and colleges, such as China Europe International Business School (CEIBS), Shanghai Maritime College and Sanda University. Shanghai Traditional Chinese Medicine University and Shanghai Second Industrial University are now in the process of relocating to Pudong.

Website: www.pudong.gov.cn

CEIBS

URBAN DISTRICTS

Huangpu District

Huangpu District is located at the heart of Shanghai, right facing Pudong along the west side of Huangpu River. With a small land area of 12.85 sq km, the district is the most populous in Shanghai. Being an old town, it has accelerated the pace of reconstruction in the recent years, and has been actively focusing on tertiary industries such as finance, real estate, trade, tourism and information consultation service.

As the center of Shanghai, Huangpu enjoys great advantages due to its convenient location. Nanpu Bridge, Yan'an Road Tunnel, Yan'an Road, Inner Ring Road and North-South viaducts, and Metro Line 1 and 2 in all form an efficient three-dimensional land transport system. People's Square, a major sightseeing place cum transportation center of the city, lies in the district's territory. The main building of the municipal government and the magnificent Shanghai Grand Theatre is also located there.

Shoppers at Nanjing East Road

Huangpu District has long been known as a hub of commerce. Nanjing East Road and the newly developed Jinling East Road make the district a shopping heaven. Moreover, Beijing Road is famous for hardware shops and Fuzhou Road for bookstores and cultural antiques. Yuyuan Garden, with traditional Chinese architectural style, attracts numerous tourists there for shopping, gourmet tasting and sightseeing.

Many prestigious stores of specialties, which absorbed and assembled the quintessence and sophistication of the Shanghainese, were originated from Huangpu District a century ago. Among them are Heng Deli Clock and Watch, Cao Sugong Ink Stick, Shao Wansheng Groceries, Wu Liangcai Glasses and Zhang Xiaoquan Knives and Scissors. Tong Hanchun, Cai Tongde, Hu Qingyu Tang and Lei Yunshang, are the four big Chinese traditional medicine pharmacies in Shanghai.

Heng Deli, Wu Liangcai and Cai Tongde are three local famous brands

The Bund, famous for the display of international architectures with various genres, has attracted many world-class banks and other financial institutions.

The district is also strong in scientific and technical force. It has attracted a great many of professionals and thus sped up the development of high-tech industries, particularly, in fields such as electronic instruments, machineries, metrology technology and energy-saving technologies and products.

Website: hpq.sh.gov.cn

Luwan District

Luwan District lies to the south of Huangpu District. With a mere land area of 8.02 sq km and population of 355,900, it is also one of the most populous administrative regions in Shanghai. In the period of 1996-2000, its annual GDP growth rate averaged at 18.6%.

As a downtown district, Luwan also owns a highly developed service sector. In 2001, its value added reached RMB3.35 billion, up 17.2%, of which 86.2% was contributed by the tertiary industries. As its industrial structure is being upgraded, commerce and recreational business, with 1,600 such enterprises in the district, accounted for 46.4% of the tertiary sector.

Huaihai Middle Road, historically a hustle and bustle classic shopping street for rich people, showcases the esthetics and fashion of Shanghainese. Along the road, there are abundant star hotels like Jinjiang Hotel and Okura Garden Hotel, and giant shopping malls like Parkson, Shanghai Ninth Department Store, Pacific Department Store, Lippo Plaza, Hong Kong Plaza, Cyber Digital Square, Times Square Shanghai, Goldbell Plaza and Radisson Plaza. There is also a newly developed area for gourmets and tourists called Xintiandi, or New Heaven and Earth.

Currently, more than 400 FIEs have invested in Luwan with total FDI over USD1.1 billion. There are 42 Fortune Global 500 MNCs resident in the district, for example, IBM, DuPont, Bayer, Cisco, Pfizer and P&G. Exports by FIEs now account for nearly a half of the district's total.

As Luwan is undergoing redevelopment of urban infrastructure and dwelling districts, it will be a leading commercial area for Shanghai in the future.

Website: www.luwan.sh.cn

A skybridge connecting two towers of the Hong Kong Plaza over Huaihai Middle Road

Xuhui District

Xuhui District is located in southwest part of urban Shanghai. With an area of 54.76 sq km, or nearly one fifth of the downtown, it is one of a few urban districts that are still able to offer land for industrial purpose.

Xuhui is one of the fastest growing districts of Shanghai. In 2000, the value added of the district reached RMB5.245 billion, of which the tertiary sector took a bulk share of 78.6%. High-tech industries, with emphasis on information technology and biopharmaceuticals, are catching up quickly. Six parks have been started to develop Xuhui into an innovative technology-intensive area. These include the high-profile state-level Caohejing Economic

Pacific Department Store at Xujiahui

and Technological Development Zone, Xujiahui Technological Zone, Shanghai Jiaotong University Science Park, Xuhui Park, Huajing Industrial Park and East China University of Science and Technology Industrial Park. The Longhua Diamond Processing Zone is also under construction.

In 2001, 43 new foreign-funded enterprises were registered in Xuhui with total contractual FDI worth USD82 million. The utilized amount amounted to USD72.23 million.

The Grand Gateway will resume the construction of two towers on each side

The educational resources at Xuhui District are as strong. Shanghai Jiaotong University – the alma mater of the Chinese top leader Jiang Zemin, the Medical College of Fudan University, East China University of Science & Technology and Shanghai Chinese Medicines University are all located in the district.

Website: www.xh.sh.cn

Changning District

Changning District is situated in the western part of the city. It has built up a convenient transportation network combining airport, subway, expressway and viaducts. The area of Changning District measures 38 sq km, with a population of 604,900.

Hongqiao International Airport is located in the west of the district, linked to the city by Yan'an Road Viaduct. The airport used to be the only one for Shanghai in the past century and remains a key role in welcoming foreign guests to the metropolis. Hongqiao Economic and Technological Development Zone, a state-level development industrial park, forms an important foreign business area of Shanghai. The district tops in central Shanghai in terms of greenery coverage per capita. For the advantageous location and ecological living habitat, many foreign expatriates are now living in Gubei New Area nearby or along Hongqiao Road.

Carrefour Gubei store is home-care ad for expats in this area

Three economic clusters have been planned at district level to propel the local economy since the 1990s. These are Hongqiao Foreign Trade Center, Zhongshan Park Commercial Center and Hongqiao Airport Industrial Zone. As the district gives priority to the ambitious development of IT industry, the "Digital Changning" blueprint has been pinned on the area for the development of a comprehensive test field. Supporting institutions within Changning district include Donghua University, East China Institute of

Politics & Law, Shanghai Foreign Trade College and Shanghai Engineering University.

In the period of 1995-2000, the district had attracted FDI worth USD877 million; the value added of all industries reached RMB3.987 billion in 2000, an increase of 16.1% over 1999.

Website: cnq.sh.gov.cn

Jing'an District

Jing'an derived its name from Jing'an Temple, a Buddhist monastery originally built in 247 AD. The district is the smallest one in Shanghai in terms of size. However, it is the second most crowded district as to population density. The strategy of the district is to develop a "high-class business district and high-quality residential area".

Nanjing West Road is the heart of the district. Superb office buildings like Shanghai Mart and Shanghai Exhibition Center, and many elegant hotels such as Hilton, Portman Ritz-Carlton, J. C. Mandarin and Equatorial line up alongside this 2.9 km long road.

Highrise office buildings and five-star hotels stand along Nanjing West Road. From left to right, Shanghai Centre, Plaza 66, Citic Square, JC Mandarin.

Like other urban districts, the economy of Jing'an is largely dominated by the tertiary sector that accounts for 77% in its GDP. Commerce, real estate, and financial and professional services are the three vital components of this sector. The secondary sector is represented by a few urban light industries, such as garments, food processing, household appliances, and high-tech products such as telecommunication instruments, fine chemicals and bioengineering technologies.

By the end of 1999, 483 FIEs have established in the district. The total contractual and utilized FDI stood at USD3.2 billion and USD1.3 billion, respectively. Foreign-funded projects are distributed in various industries of real estate, entertainment, consultancy, property management, software development, IT services, chemicals, garments and medical appliance etc.

Website: www.jingan.gov.cn

Putuo District

Putuo District is the northwest gateway to the city of Shanghai. Shanghai-Beijing Railway, Shanghai-Nanjing and Shanghai-Jiading Expressway all run through its territory. With an area of 54.83 sq km, it is able to offer industrial land for new projects. In fact, Putuo has long been a traditional industrial base of Shanghai.

The district has several industrial parks, such as Changzheng, Xinyang, Changfeng and Taopu. Three science parks are supported by local universities and research institutes. As a lot of state-owned enterprises are located in Putuo, restructuring and fresh investment in these areas are much welcomed. Recently, Putuo becomes an emerging trade and distribution center of commodities for Shanghai. It also hosts the only silver spot transaction market in China. Local government encourages investment in urban industry, real estate, commerce, logistics and tourism services. Specifically, investments in paper packaging, IT, biopharmaceuticals, education, healthcare facilities and the establishment of regional headquarters are plausible.

In the 1996-2000 period, major economic indicators of Putuo grew at an average of 15%. The first half of 2002 saw GDP increased by 13.75% to RMB2.284 billion, largely contributed by the surge in real estate and construction.

Website: www.putuo.sh.cn

Zhabei District

Zhabei lies to the north of Suzhou Creek and hosts Shanghai Railway Station for passenger and North Station for cargo. It is the south end of Shanghai-Beijing Railway and is planned to build a terminal station for long-distance buses as well.

The district has an established structure of industry. Since February 2002, Zhabei has started the development of so-called metropolitan industrial zones intensively. There are two models now, namely, the North New Industrial Zone and Pengpu Town Industrial Park. The former, leveraging on Shanghai University, emphasizes on high tech developments in information technology and software; the latter has formed a combination of industries in electrical and electronic manufacturing, printing, engineering plastics, fireproof materials, mechanical processing and garment manufacturing.

Many MNCs and domestic enterprise groups have established subsidiaries in Zhabei, including Philips, Honeywell and Alcatel.

Website: zbq.sh.gov.cn

Hongkou District

Hongkou District is situated in the north of urban Shanghai and covers an area of 24.38 sq km. The population of permanent residents is 860,000.

Wholesale and retail, F&B and real estate form the mainstay of the tertiary sector in Hongkou. "Holiday economy" and chain stores have become the two new phenomena in the district's retail market. The manufacturing enterprises in Hongkou are mainly in the production of suitcases, garments, lamps, automotive spare parts and jewelry processing.

Sichuan North Road is one of the most famous shopping areas in Shanghai, known for its attraction for middle-class consumers. Dabaishu is a place where many specific markets cluster. Those markets deal with home electronics, steel products, decorative materials, furniture, kitchen and sanitary wares etc. Ace Group, the biggest suitcase producer, is now building a high-standard exhibition and trading center.

Being one of Shanghai's major education districts, Hongkou hosts Shanghai University of Finance and Economy and Shanghai Foreign Studies University.

In 2001, 46 foreign-funded projects were approved by the district government, an increase of 53.3% over the previous year; the contractual FDI amounted to USD140 million, an astonishing increase of 94.7% over the previous year. In the same year, with total registered capital of RMB3.11 billion, 2,952 domestic enterprises were established in the district.

Website: hkq.sh.gov.cn

Yangpu District

With its total area of 60.61 sq km and a population of 1.24 million, Yangpu District is the largest one among all nine urban districts. Located in the northeast of urban Shanghai, it is linked to its close neighbor of Pudong New District by Yangpu Bridge.

In 2001, the district's GDP reached RMB4.88 billion, up 13.3%; total industrial output stood at RMB4.66 billion, up 13.9%; total foreign trade amounted to USD385 million, up 10%; and contractual FDI amounted to USD121 million.

Yangpu is known for many prestigious universities and research institutions resident within its administrative region. These include Fudan University, Tongji University, and the Second Military Medical University. Altogether, 15 universities and over 100 research institutes with 110,000 students are located in Yangpu. There are nearly 200,000 professionals working there too, including 33 fellows of CAS (Chinese Academy of Science) and CAE (Chinese Academy of Engineering).

Yangpu has four major industrial parks, namely Wujiaochang High-tech Park, Tongji University Science Park, Fudan University Science Park, Fudan Software Development Center and Shanghai Yangpu Incubation Center. Yangpu is also famous for being one of the birthplaces of China's modern industry. Over 100 large and medium sized enterprises, such as Shanghai Mechanical Factory, Shanghai Diesel Engine Factory and Yangshupu Power Station all have originated in this place.

Website: ypq.sh.gov.cn

SUBURBAN ADMINISTRATIVE REGIONS

Shanghai administers nine suburban districts (including Pudong New District) and one county.

Major Economic Indictors of Shanghai Suburban Administrative Regions in 2001 (RMB billion)

Rank	Region	GDP	GDP per capita (RMB)	Retail sales of consumer products	Industrial output	Fiscal revenue
1	Jiading	19.10	39,262	6.41	60.60	1.47
2	Qingpu	14.43	31,443	5.24	41.05	1.77
3	Minhang	20.00	30,586	9.09	48.22	2.85
4	Songjiang	15.11	30,484	6.80	46.79	1.61
5	Pudong	33.84	20,494	23.30	36.09	3.68
6	Nanhui	13.67	19,799	5.88	33.01	1.00
7	Fengxian	9.68	19,199	5.12	26.20	0.92
8	Baoshan	13.12	16,211	8.41	26.95	2.05
9	Jinshan	8.01	15,101	4.97	17.37	0.99
10	Chongming	5.79	8,851	1.48	5.37	0.59
Total		147.00	21,200	70.70	360.68	17.76

Source: based on *Shanghai Economic Yearbook*, 2002. Pudong's statistics are of district-level. Ranking by GDP per capita based on population figures 2000.

Since 1990s, the suburban area of Shanghai has undergone rapid urbanization, with the ratio of township residents to total population raised from 28% in 1992 to 49% by the end of 2001.

Industries in the suburban districts have been developing at an alarming rate, particularly in IT, biopharmaceutical, chemistry, metallurgy, automobile and environmental protection technologies. In 2001, realized industrial value added of the suburb districts was RMB74.12 billion, up 12.78%; industrial output stood at RMB315.9 billion, an increase of 14.96%. The secondary sector now accounts for 57.2% of the GDP of all suburban regions.

Foreign investment has been the new growth engine for suburbs. An increasing number of investors have noticed the locational advantages and cost-effectiveness of those districts and shifted their businesses there. With newly approved 1,368 foreign-funded projects, contractual FDI influx surged by 110% to reach USD4.567 billion in 2001, which accounted for 60% of Shanghai's total.

Noticeably, nine municipal-level industrial parks have been the important industrial bases to power the suburban economy.

Investment In 9 Municipal-Level Industrial Parks (2001)	
Foreign-funded projects approved	1,107
Total FDI	USD8 billion
Number of Fortune 500 companies	58
Projects with investment that	
above USD5 million	149
above USD10 million	106
above USD20 million	112
Projects invested by domestic investors	339
Projects invested by Shanghai investors	404

The tertiary sector saw a moderate 2.9% growth in 2001, with its value added reaching RMB54.31 billion, or a proportion of 36.9% in suburban GDP.

Minhang District

Minhang District borders the urban area to the southwest, with Huangpu River cutting through it from south to north. As a suburban district, Minhang had an area of 372 sq km and a population of 680,000 at the end of 2001. It is Shanghai's southern gateway because Shanghai-Hangzhou Expressway, Shanghai-Hangzhou Railway and the Outer Ring Road all run across this area. Hongqiao International Airport lies just next to the district. Minhang is a key industrial base for the municipality. There are a couple of well-developed industrial parks in this region, such as the state-level Minhang Economic and Technological Development Zone, and industrial parks at Xinzhuang, Mindong and Minbei.

Minhang is the second largest economy among all 10 suburbs in Shanghai, next to Pudong. In 2001, local GDP achieved RMB20.0 billion, an increase of 12.5%. The ratio among the three sectors is 2.0:56.2:41.8. Total export in 2001 amounted to USD1.21 billion. By the end of 2000, 1,518 FIEs had been approved in Minhang with total contractual FDI of USD2.02 billion and investors from over 40 countries or regions worldwide. Year 2001 saw FDI surge dramatically in Minhang with 283 new FIEs approved, or up 42.2% from the last year. Contractual FDI increased 2.9 times to USD1.015 and utilized FDI went up by 94.4% to reach USD350 million, showing Minhang's great attraction for investors. MNCs such as Mannesmann, BASF, Itochu, Tomen, Hyundai and Alcatel Alsthom have established subsidiaries in Minhang.

Website: mhq.sh.gov.cn

Baoshan District

Baoshan District is located in the northern part of Shanghai where Huangpu River joins the Yangtze River. The total area of Baoshan is 424.4 sq km and the population was 1.23 million at the end of 2000. There are three container terminals, which makes up as much as 70% of the total handling capacity of Shanghai. Ships from Baoshan reaches over 400 ports worldwide.

Baoshan is famous for Baosteel Group, which is one of the largest iron and steel producers in China and a world-class conglomerate in this trade. In addition, the local government has been encouraging storage, transportation services, logistics, tourism, real estate and modern agriculture.

The west area of Baoshan has witnessed the gradual development of a new residential area. Baoshan is determined to develop the district into a garden city and an ideal place to live in. Changxing Island, famous for its clean water and fresh air, has been identified as an ideal manufacturing base for healthcare and green food.

In the period of 1996-2000, the average GDP growth rate was 13.8%. In 2001, local GDP reached RMB13.12 billion, up 12.8% from 2000, 48.9% of which was contributed by the second sector; total export of Baoshan was USD690 million, and the import was USD480 million.

There are a few industrial parks for investors to choose from. The 5 sq km municipal-level Baoshan City Industrial Park aims to be a manufacturing base for new materials, telecommunication, mechanical instruments and automotive parts. Shanghai University Nanometer Technology Park is a specific high-tech park for the commercialization of nano technology.

Website: bsq.sh.gov.cn

Jiading District

Jiading District, with a total area of 458.8 sq km, is in northwest region of the city. The population of residents was around 486,000. The State Council upgraded it from a county to a district in October 1992. The district has strong cultural heritage and was historically an established township in Shanghai.

Recently, the district's economy has been witnessing a healthy growth. In 2001, Jiading achieved a GDP of RMB19.1 billion, up 12.0%, of which the industry alone contributed more than 65%. In terms of GDP per capita, Jiading is the richest district among all 10 suburbs of Shanghai. Foreign investment in Jiading reached a record high in 2001 – 357 foreign investment projects were approved with total contractual FDI of USD800 million, up 56.8%, and total utilized FDI of USD282 million.

The district is also famous for its automobile industry. The Sino-German joint venture, Shanghai Volkswagen Co. Ltd., is located at Anting town. With annual sales of more than RMB30 billion, it ranked as the largest foreign joint venture in China for seven consecutive years. In fact, the automobile industry with related component manufacturing has become the mainstay of the district's economy. Besides, the district is also strong in the manufacturing of household appliances, textile, metal products, and high-tech products like optical electronics, microelectronics, new materials and software etc.

Led by the above automobile industry, the district has also built up its strength in trade, banking and finance and other services. Now, Jiading hosts the Anting Automobile Market, Shanghai Light Textile Market, Shanghai Decoration Market and Shanghai Dongfang Auto Components Market.

Shanghai Volkswagen

As for agriculture, the district is offering a great variety of vegetables, fruits and poultry, such as white garlic, grapes, strawberry, pigeon and black bone chicken. As the local government encourages environmental protection, some well-designed farms become great attractions for international tourists and domestic city people.

Jiading District has a well-developed infrastructure. In 1988, China's first expressway, Shanghai-Jiading Expressway, was completed here. Shanghai-Nanjing Expressway and Shanghai-Beijing Railway run through its southern part.

In the district there are over 10 high-level research institutes like CAS Shanghai Optics Fine Mechanical Institute and East China Computing Technology Institute. Shanghai University Jiading Campus and Shanghai Science and Technology Institute are also located here.

Jiading Industrial Zone is one of Shanghai's nine municipal-level industrial parks. There is also a Jiading Civil Technological Park, which consists of Jiading High-tech Park, Fuhua High-tech Park and CAS Shanghai High-tech Industrial Park. Many district-level parks are also available at towns like Nanxiang, Tanghang, Jiangqiao, Huangdu, Caowang and Malu. Most impressively, Shanghai International Automobile City is taking its shape at Anting town. Based on Shanghai Volkswagen and officially started in September 2001, the area is ambitious to become the "Detroit of China".

Website: jdq.sh.gov.cn

Jinshan District

Jinshan lies in the southernmost part of Shanghai. With a 586 sq km land area and a 23.3 km deepwater coastline, Jinshan enjoys great advantage in geography and location. The Jinshan branch of Shanghai-Hangzhou Railway and a couple of highways run through the district. A cross-sea bridge to Zhejiang is also under construction.

The district places heavy emphasis on industrial development. Nearly 5,000 enterprises, engaged in petrochemicals, mechanical, textile and garment, electronics, pharmaceuticals and automobile components, form the mainstay of its industry. In the first half of year 2002, the industry grew at a spectacular rate of 25%. The petrochemical sector is one of the most prominent. Shanghai Petrochemical, a conglomerate in China's petrochemical industry, is located there.

There are a few industrial parks in Jinshan with distinctive characteristics, including Jinshanzhui Industrial Zone, Jinshan No. 2 Industrial Zone, and Shanghai Chemical Industrial Park Jinshan Zone. In addition, Shanghai

International Garment Machinery City is located in Fengjing Town of Jinshan. Zhuhang High-tech Park is meant for pharmaceuticals and there is also a Jinshan International Small & Medium Enterprise Park in Tinglin Town.

Jinshan has also been a major agricultural base for Shanghai, supplying rice, edible oil, vegetables, poultry, pork, egg, milk and aquatic products.

In 2001, Jinshan's GDP reached RMB8.01 billion, or 12.4% over the last year. The first half of year 2002 saw FDI inflow to Jinshan reaching a historic high. Total 32 new foreign-funded projects were approved with contractual FDI of USD62.72 million, up 62.4%. Domestic investment rose even higher, by an increase of 188.1% to RMB1.43 billion in the same period.

Website: jsq.sh.gov.cn

Songjiang District

Songjiang claims to be the origin of indigenous Shanghainese as the establishment of Songjiang county can be traced back to 751 AD in Tang Dynasty. In 1998, Songjiang was transformed into a district under Shanghai Municipality's jurisdiction, with a territory covering 604 sq km and a population of 490,000.

As both Shanghai-Hangzhou Expressway and Shanghai-Hangzhou Railway run through its entire region, the district has attracted many investors and this inevitably causes land scarity. In this regard, a new town with planned area of 36 sq km is under construction to meet the increasing demand, and plans to accommodate 250,000 residents upon completion.

The first phase of Songjiang University City was completed in 2001. It has attracted a few universities and colleges with 5,000 students from the city, including Shanghai International Studies University and Shanghai Institute of Foreign Trade.

FDI in Songjiang doubled in 2000, reaching USD610.59 million, up 101.2%. In 2001, the GDP of Songjiang climbed up 15% to RMB15.1 billion.

The district contains the state-level Songjiang Export Processing Zone (EPZ) and a 20.56 sq km Songjiang Industrial Zone the first municipal-level industrial park of Shanghai. In addition, Songjiang Modern Agricultural Zone has been specified in the southwest part of the district to develop into a green agricultural base for the municipality.

Website: sjq.sh.gov.cn

Qingpu District

Qingpu is located in the conjunction area of Shanghai, Zhejiang Province and Jiangsu Province. With famous Dianshan Lake bestowed within the territory, the district is a beautiful place for tourism.

The district hosts a 16.16 sq km municipal-level Qingpu Industrial Zone. Textile, machinery and electronics, food processing, fine chemicals and modern agriculture are the five industries that are emphasized in the zone.

In 2001, Qingpu's export totaled USD1.36 billion, making it the third among all administrative regions in Shanghai. And its GDP, up 15% from the previous year, reached RMB14.43 billion. With per capita GDP over RMB31,000, it becomes the second richest district among the suburbs, only after Jiading district. The first quarter of year 2002 registered a vibrant GDP growth of 14.1% for Qingpu, showing a continued trend of economic development.

Website: www.shqp.gov.cn

Nanhui District

With an area of 688 sq km, Nanhui is the largest district in Shanghai and is also one of the two latest districts approved in 2001. It is located in the southeast part of Shanghai, bordering Pudong New District in the north. With Pudong International Airport Phase II and the grand Yangshan Deepwater Port project under construction, the district will seize great opportunities in its future development. In fact, Nanhui has already been designated as a key district in Shanghai for further opening.

In 2001, Nanhui achieved GDP of RMB13.67 billion, an increase of 14.2%. The ratio for primary, secondary and tertiary sector is 10:55:35. Contractual FDI in 2000 rose by 22% to USD90.27 million.

Nanhui has one municipal and three local industrial parks. The municipal-level 26.88 sq km Shanghai Pudong Kangqiao Industrial Park, mainly located in Nanhui, was founded in May 1992. Nanhui Industrial Park is another important industrial park in the district. A 6.23 sq km Huinan New Town Technological and Educational Zone has also completed its first phase in 2001.

Website: nhq.sh.gov.cn

The expanding capacity of Pudong International Airport will bring opportunities to Nanhui

Fengxian District

In January 2001, Fengxian was approved by the State Council to be the one of two latest districts of Shanghai. Located in the south of Shanghai, the district sits on the north side of Hangzhou Bay. It has become a new hot place to attract investment.

In 2001, Fengxian realized GDP of RMB9.68 billion, an increase of 13.6% over 2000. The total industrial output reached RMB27.88 billion, an increase of 18%, and contributed 63.8% to the district's economic growth. The industrial sector is mainly composed of enterprises specialized in manufacturing of electrical products, garments, suitcases, construction materials, chemicals, machinery, plastics and textile. The tertiary sector contributed 33.2% to the GDP. In the same year, Fengxian saw FDI inflow of USD220 million, up 93.2%, with 103 new FIEs approved.

The district owns Shanghai Comprehensive Industrial Development Zone (SCIDZ) and Shanghai Chemical Industrial Park Fengxian Zone (SCIPFX). Besides domestic investors from other part of China, foreign investors from over 50 countries or regions worldwide have already put in their stake in Fengxian, such as GE, Mannesmann, Pioneer and Fuji etc.

SCIDZ, formerly known as Shanghai Fengpu Industrial Zone, is a 20.8 sq km municipal-level industrial park. Strategically located in the center of the district, the industrial park has been growing very fast during the recent years. SCIZFPX, situated in the southwest corner of Fengxian, is a 23.5 sq km area fully dedicated to the chemical industry development. An ethylene project with investment of RMB25 billion was officiated already. Tianyuan PVC, Gaoqiao Petrochemical and Bayer's USD400 million chemical projects have all been started.

Website: fxq.sh.gov.cn

Chongming County

Chongming, with a total land area of 1,200 sq km, forms the biggest administrative region, however, the last county of Shanghai. Its population is around 650,000. Sitting in the middle of Yangtze River Estuary, Chongming Island is the third largest island in China, after Taiwan and Hainan.

In 2000, the county realized GDP of RMB5.40 billion, up 7.2%. Its primary sector made a contribution of 24.8%, reflecting Chongming's strengths in agricultural production. As a retarded economy, Chongming lags behind other districts in FDI absorption. However, with an amount of USD11.47 million received in 2000, it already showed an astonishing growth rate of 227%.

In October 2001, Chongming passed inspection on its development of a State Ecological Exemplary Zone which was first stated in 1996. This will be a milestone in the county's pursuit of a "green economy"- led by the tertiary sector, followed by the primary and secondary. Encouraged industries include ecological tourism, conference and exhibition, transit logistics, organic and ecological agriculture, biotechnology and export-oriented processing industries. A recycling economy with clean production is the direction for any development in the future.

Chongming Industrial Zone, established in 1996 with a size of 9.97 sq km, is one of the nine municipal-level industrial parks in Shanghai. Chongming Green Food Zone is a 321 sq km giant modern agricultural development zone to be built in the eastern part of this island.

Website: cmx.sh.gov.cn

Infrastructure

INTRODUCTION

The city of Shanghai, dubbed as the "Paris of the Orient", has always been exposed to Western influences. In the early 1990s, it finally reopened its doors to the rest of the world. As many foreign companies began to move in, the city took on a new lease of life. But this growth brought with it the inevitable problems of an outdated infrastructure being forced to cope with far greater amounts of traffic than it was designed for. The ensuing chaos led the municipal authorities to take the decision to adopt a solution which was gaining increasing credence across the world – to bulldoze its dilapidated infrastructure and replace it with a modern urban landscape, and to replenish its clogged streets with an interplay of broader, levitated and underground passages.

LAND TRANSPORTATION

Metro

Tickets for metro are sold manually or by machine

The subway in Shanghai, or called Metro locally, is one of the youngest in the world. It has an existing length of 65 km. The first line (Metro Line 1) was opened in 1995 as a north-south axis from Shanghai Railway

Shanghai Metro Route

Station to southern suburbs. The first 27.3 km section of Metro Line 2 followed four years later, running from Pudong to Puxi (west of the Huangpu River) and intersecting Line 1 at People's Square. A third line, the Pearl Line, has been developed out of a former ring railway, mainly elevated. It is planned to start from Baosteel in the north, turn to Shanghai Railway Station, and end at Caoxi Road in the south. The track has a total of 36 km in length consisting of 21 stations. Construction of the first 25 km with 19 stations between Caoxi Road and Jiangwan was completed in May 2000 and became operational since the end of the year. In September 2001, the number of trains running on the three lines was increased to 17 for Line 1, 10 for Line 2 and nine for the Pearl Line.

Travelling with Metro is still a crowded experience

Tips for trips

The metro starts operation as early as 5.30 am and 6.30 am, depending on which line and direction you are taking, with the last train leaving each terminal around 10:15 pm. Fares range from RMB1 to RMB4 for a single ride based on distance. Free transfer between Line 1 and Line 2 at People's Square is available. Pre-paid cards of RMB50 or RMB90 are obtainable from ticket booths.

Interval for each train:

- Metro Line 1: every 4.5-5 minutes
- Metro Line 2: every 7 minutes
- Pearl Line : every 11.5 minutes

The future development of infrastructure is drawn in the 10th Five Year (2001-2005) Plan, which includes the construction of a total of 181.5 km of new high capacity transit lines for Shanghai. The original plan for the east Line 2 was to extend to Pudong International Airport, however, in late 2000 China decided to build a 30 km long magnetic levitation railroad with German technology and design, from Longyang Road Station of Line 2 to the airport instead. It has been under trial operation since 1st January 2003.

Railway

Starting from Shanghai, railways reach almost every region of China except Hainan, Tibet and Taiwan, and stretch into Korea, Russia and other European states. Everyday Shanghai Railway Station dispatches 80 pairs of trains to major cities in the country. Centering around Shanghai, long-distance passenger trains depart Shanghai in the evening and arrive in other cities in the morning. In 2001, the railways in Shanghai transported 32.31 million passengers and 33.09 million tons of freight, representing a share of 6.6% and 51.1% of the city's total passenger and total freight throughput, respectively.

Shanghai Railway Station

Shanghai Railway Station is a large-scale passenger terminal. The passenger departure hall is on an elevated level with 16 air-conditioned lounges. The station has exits in the north and one in the south. There is a tunnel linked to the subway. Outside the station are terminals for public buses. Left-luggage Claim, ATMs, tourist information center, shops and restaurants can be found within the station premises.

Tips for trips

All Chinese express trains have four different types of seats and sleepers, namely, the soft sleeper, soft seat, hard sleeper and hard seat. The price varies according to the types of tickets you hold. Tickets are normally sold at the ticketing windows outside railway station and other outlets and representative offices in town. Some star hotels may provide the service as well. Reservations, especially for sleepers, should be made two or three days in advance. The most popular routes include Shanghai to Beijing (14 hrs 15 mins) and Shanghai to Nanjing (4 hrs). There is also a route scheduled on alternative days between Shanghai and Hong Kong (24 hrs) with three classes available: hard sleeper, soft sleeper and deluxe soft sleeper. Tickets for these routes could be purchased through China International Travel Service and China Youth Travel Service.

Journey Schedule (*day after departure)
(Effective on 21 Oct 2001 until further notice.)

STATION	Train No.			
	K99 (Shanghai-Kowloon)		K100 (Kowloon-Shanghai)	
Shanghai	12:25	depart	15:54*	arrive
Hangzhou East	14:13	depart	14:00*	arrive
Shaoguan	06:55*	depart	21:14	arrive
Guangzhou East	10:08*	depart	17:47	arrive
Dongguan	12:00*	depart	16:11	arrive
Hung Hom	13:10*	arrive	15:00	depart

(No stopover is allowed for this route.)

Shanghai - Kowloon Through Train (2002)

Destination	Train No.	Jan	Feb	Mar	Apr	May	Jun	Jul	Aug	Sep	Oct	Nov	Dec
Kowloon to Shanghai	K100	Even	Odd	Odd	Even	Even	Odd	Odd	Even	Odd	Odd	Even	Even
Shanghai to Kowloon	K99	Odd	Even	Even	Odd	Odd	Even	Even	Odd	Even	Even	Odd	Odd

*Odd - Odd number dates, e.g. 1st Dec, 3rd Dec, 5th Dec, 7th Dec etc.
Even - Even number dates, e.g. 2nd Dec, 4th Oct, 6th Dec, 8th May etc.

Ticket Fares for Kowloon-Shanghai Railway Ride (in HKD)

Station	Adult					Child (5-9 years old)				
	Deluxe Soft Sleeper	Soft Sleeper	Hard Sleeper			Deluxe Soft Sleeper	Soft Sleeper	Hard Sleeper		
			upper berth	middle berth	lower berth			upper berth	middle berth	lower berth
Shanghai	$1239	$1025	$708	$719	$730	$880	$727	$520	$531	$542
Hangzhou East	$1181	$985	$686	$696	$706	$838	$697	$504	$514	$525
Shaoguan	$704	$645	$480	$484	$487	$501	$457	$361	$366	$368
Guangzhou East	$500	$500	$390	$390	$390	$350	$350	$295	$295	$295
Dongguan	$400	$400	$340	$340	$340	$300	$300	$270	$270	$270

Remarks:

- *For Dongguan, Guangzhou East, Guangzhou and Shaoguan, the deluxe soft sleeper ticket will only be available 2 days before departure.*
- *For all the other classes of travel, e.g. soft and hard sleeper, the pre-sale period will remain as existing.*
- *Deluxe Soft Sleeper tickets for Shanghai to Kowloon are not for sale in Hong Kong.*
- *Child ticket is required for children aged five to nine. However, an adult tikcet is necessary for children aged ten or above. A child under five and accompanied by a fare paying adult may travel free, provided that the child does not accupy a seat.*
- *Advance tickets can be purchased up to 60 days in advance for Shanghai Station. For all the other stations, advanced tickets are only available 30 days in advance. Return tickets for Shanghai Station can be purchased in Hong Kong. For other stations, return tickets have to be bought at departure station. Return tickets are sold within 2 days of departure.*

Shanghai Railway West Station

From Shanghai Railway West Station, trains leave for Baotou, Yantai, Changchun, Hengyang, Guangzhou, Ningbo and Nanjing West Station.

Shanghai Railway South Station

It dispatches four trains daily to Hangzhou, taking less than two hours to arrive at Hangzhou East Station. Passengers may get tickets on board. The station is connected to Metro No. 1 Line.

Highway and Expressway

Shanghai has a convenient road system comprising highways and expressways that lead to other parts of the country. More than 130 cargo routes and 500 passenger lines to other cities and provinces are in operation. In 2001, the city's highway network transported 15.08 million passengers and 288.7 million tons of freight, up 17.6% and 1.8% respectively, which accounted for 23.8% and 57.4% of the city's total transportation volume respectively.

Well-developed expressway system in Shanghai

Shanghai-Hangzhou-Ningbo Expressway links Shanghai to Hangzhou, the provincial capital of Zhejiang, and Ningbo Port. It takes 4 hours to finish the journey on this four-lane expressway. The northeastward 1,262 km

Beijing-Shanghai Expressway, mainly four lanes but with six lanes on some stretches, opened to traffic in December 2000. It runs through Jiangsu, Shandong, Hebei, Tianjin and Beijing, the most developed regions of China. There are major 11 tollgates along its trunk line.

Long-distance bus

Different levels of comfort are available for long-distance (LD) buses from Shanghai's various LD bus stations:

- **North LD Bus Station -** 80 Gongxing Road: handles buses to Jiangsu, Zhejiang, Anhui, Fujiang, Hunan, Shandong and Hubei Provinces;
- **Tianmu East Road LD Bus Station** - 100 Tianmu East Road: serves similar destinations;
- **Hengfeng Road Bus Station**: has buses heading for Nanjing, Ningbo and Wuxi;
- **Xujiahui Bus Station** - Hongqiao Road: behind Grand Gateway, has departures to Nanjing and Yangzhou;
- Shanghai Tour Bus Lines leave from Shanghai Stadium to destinations primarily in the suburban districts. They are cheap and comfortable, providing the best choice for daily trips to the outskirts of town.

Reportedly, the city plans to spend RMB560 million (USD67 million) to build the largest long-distance bus station of 3.7 hectares in the downtown area. This station will be located near the north square of Shanghai Railway Station. All existing long distance bus stations in the area will be merged into the new one. The construction will begin at the end of 2002 and take three years. Upon completion, the station will be able to send 20,000 passengers every day on 1,000 trips scheduled.

Urban Public Transport

The public transport system, comprising buses, taxis and Metro, moved 2.68 billion people in 2001. Foreign visitors are suggested to avoid riding buses and minibuses unless they have a good understanding of Mandarin. Travel via Metro or taxi is much more amicable. Shanghai Transportation Bureau has been painstakingly seeking to develop an integrated and comprehensive urban public transport system, albeit overburdened by the city's breakneck expansion.

Bus

By the end of 2001, Shanghai had 991 bus routes and a fleet of 18,100 buses. It accounted for 70% of the city's total public traffic. City buses usually operate from 5 am to 11 pm and can be appallingly crowded during rush hours (6:30 am - 8:30 am and 5 pm - 7 pm). Flat fare of RMB1 (up to RMB3 for air-conditioned buses) is payable to the conductor. Routine routes are numbered, but suburban buses have only destinations written on. Minibuses operate on some fixed routes with a flat fare of RMB2 in town.

Taxis

There are 46,900 taxis strolling on road in Shanghai. Despite alarming steel cages protecting the drivers, Shanghai taxis are reliable, affordable and safe. However, travelers are advised to watch the meter carefully and ask for receipt before alighting. Taxis in Shanghai are almost ubiquitously Santana or Passat manufactured locally by Shanghai Volkswagen Co. Ltd. Fares are calculated at a rate of RMB10 for the first three kilometers with RMB2 per kilometer thereafter. During nighttime (11 pm - 5 am), it rises to RMB13 for three kilometers and RMB2.6 per subsequent kilometer. For foreign visitors, maps, written addresses or business cards in Chinese are the best tools to direct taxi drivers, because few are able to speak English. Taxi bookings are available at some big cab operators, such as Dazhong and Qiangsheng, both of which are recommended for high-quality services rendered. Tipping is not mandatory but of course appraisable. Some major taxi fleets

Volkswagen's Santana is the dominant model among Shanghai taxis

also offer limousine service with starting rates around RMB600 per day for an Audi.

Given the large number of taxis in Shanghai, traffic chaos and complicated road signs in Chinese, hiring a car is generally discouraged. Private cars are still not the mainstream in Shanghai, although the phenomenon is more visible than almost anywhere else in China. Drivers should also be reminded that there are many bicycles and pedestrians in the streets.

Leading Taxi Companies in Shanghai

Company	Fleet	Booking Number
Dazhong	7,000	82222, 62581688
Qiangsheng	6,000	62580000
Bashi	4,700	84000, 64312788
Jinjiang	3,600	62584584

CIVIL AVIATION

Currently, there are two international airports in Shanghai, both managed by Shanghai Airport Ltd, a Shanghai Stock Exchange listed company. In 2001, the two airports handled a combination of 194,100 aircrafts and 20.66 million passengers, up 20.9% and 16.8%, respectively.

Hongqiao International Airport

Hongqiao Airport was the principal airport of Shanghai in the past. It is situated about half an hour's taxi ride away from the city center. Due to limited capacity and constrained space, the new airport in Pudong gradually makes inroads into its predominance. Since 27 October 2002, all international (including Hong Kong and Macau) flights to and from Shanghai have been shifted to Pudong International Airport, leaving hongqiao to serve domestic airlines only. Facilities available at the airport, though a bit crowded, include bureaux de change, business center, banks, ATMs, post office, luggage lockers, car rental, duty free shops, cafés, restaurants, information center and hotel reservation services.

Shuttle buses depart every 30 minutes starting from 6 am to 9 pm. The fare is RMB4 to RMB7, with tickets sold on board. Transit buses to Pudong Airport are scheduled every 30 minutes from 6 am to 9 pm daily, with a one-hour journey and an RMB30 fare. Travelers are advised to hire taxis from the main taxi stand outside the domestic arrival hall to avoid touts. The average fare is about RMB65 to reach downtown Shanghai, including toll fees.

Pudong International Airport

The airport is located on the East China Sea coast, 30 km southeast to downtown Shanghai. It is about 40 km away from Hongqiao Airport. Officially opened on 1 October 1999, the 32 sq km Pudong Airport has become Shanghai's new international air hub. Its terminal, which takes the shape of a giant seagull fluttering its strong wings, is designed to accommodate 36 large aircrafts' landing simultaneously. The throughput of the airport is as high as 126,000 planes, 20 million passengers and 750,000 tons of cargoes per year. Since October 2002, the new aiport assumes all responsibilities to fly international passengers and passengers to Hong Kong and Macau. The second phase of the airport includes a 4,000 meter-long new runway to be completed by 2005. By then, its annual handling capacity will rise to 70 million passengers and 5 million tons of cargo, making Shanghai the largest air hub in China.

The terminal building hosts a shopping mall, duty-free shops and 11 restaurants and bars. It also provides hotel rooms for transit passengers. The airport broadcasts in three languages, Chinese, English and Japanese. It has eight ticket island booths. Passengers can arrive directly at the second floor of the terminal building by car and enter the departure hall that has 20 domestic and 25 international check-in counters. Passing through any of the 18 entrances, passengers can enjoy a panoramic view of 65,000 sq m of lawn through the inside glass walls while waiting to board.

Pudong Airport Business Center provides facsimile and computer facilities. Outside the arrival hall, shuttle buses depart every 30 minutes from 6 am to 9 pm to city with a journey estimated at 1 hour 20 minutes. Transit buses to Hongqiao Airport cost RMB22 and leave every half an hour from 8 am to 9 pm. The fare of metered taxis is about RMB170 to get to the city.

An RMB90 (for international flights) or RMB50 (for domestic flights) airport tax, or "construction fee", is payable in cash (Chinese currency only) at both airports; children under 12 years old are exempted. Luggage trolleys are now free to use but luggage bundling service is still chargeable at RMB10 per unit.

Tips for trips

Bus fare from Pudong International Airport to

Honqiao Airport	RMB22
Shanghai Exhibition Center	RMB19
Zunyi Road	RMB20
Shanghai Railway Station	RMB18

Flight information

From Pudong International Airport to

Beijing	1 hr 45 mins
Chicago	15 hrs
Frankfurt	11 hrs
Hong Kong	2 hrs 15 mins
Los Angeles	13 hrs
New York	17 hrs 30 mins
Osaka	2 hrs
Paris	11 hrs
Seattle	12 hrs
Seoul	1 hr 45 mins
Singapore	5 hrs

PORT

In terms of overall handling capacity, Shanghai is the world's third-largest port. Throughout 2001, a total of 14,438 vessels called at the port. However, the Huangpu River, with a maximum depth of eight meters, is currently incapable of berthing the 5th and 6th generation container vessels with a draught of about 15 meters. The ideal site for a deepwater port is set at the Big Yangshan and Small Yangshan Islands (currently under the administration of Zhoushan, Zhejiang Province) located some 20 nautical miles off Shanghai's Luchao Port.

The islands will be connected to the mainland by grand cross-sea bridges. As the Luchao site is an uninhabited flood plain, large-scale reclamation and major infrastructural works are necessary. The first phase, the resettlement of 80,000 residents from the present land, is timetabled for 2005. The second and third phase will meet deadline by 2020. The development of the ambitious project was already kicked off after detailed planning. In early 2000, a visiting delegation from the Netherlands expressed their interests in co-developing the deepwater port with the local authorities – as Rotterdam has one of the world's rare deepwater ports and extensive experience in land reclamation.

Yangshan Deepwater Port is expected to have a deepwater zone of 18 kilometers wide and 15 meters deep, and be able to accommodate 50 fifth or sixth-generation container liners. It is designed with an annual container handling capacity of 22 million TEUs, which may confer Shanghai a leading position in global transportation network. Upon the completion of phase one, the container handling capacity will immediately rise to 10 million TEUs.

Furthermore, Waigaoqiao New Harbor in Pudong, whose third and fourth phases are under still construction, would also enhance the capability of the New Shanghai Port. It has ample space to accommodate 49 10,000-tonnage berths and a number of small and medium-sized berths. The full annual handling capacity is planned to be 50.4 million tons of cargo.

URBAN CONSTRUCTION

Since the beginning of the 1990s when the Development of Pudong was announced by the central government, Shanghai has been focusing its urban construction on developing functional and hub infrastructures. In the past decade, it has invested more than RMB310 billion in various urban construction projects.

Cranes are busy working in Lujiazui, Pudong

Information Technology

The city has achieved remarkable advancement in the construction of IT related infrastructure. The primary part of Info Port project, featuring broadband, high speed and multi-functions, has already been completed. Integrated information pipeline, broadband IP urban network, data network, cable television-internet transformation, and broadband information exchange center have all been completed, too.

In recent years, Shanghai has increased investment on setting up software development and incubation centers, and set aside preferential policies to boost IT industry. The industry has developed so fast that it has allegedly replaced the automobile industry as the largest industrial cluster of the city. It has already formed a strong foundation consisting of software development and production, system application, microelectronics production and IT services.

Telecommunication

The availability and reliability of Shanghai's telecommunication facilities are ranked among the top in China. The population of telephone subscribers increased sharply since the opening, from less than a million in 1978 to 6.16 million in 2001. In the past decade, the number of mobile phone users increased even more dramatically, from a mere 1,000 in 1990 to 6.26 million in 2001 and for the first time surpassed the population of fixed line subscribers.

All choices of telecom services are available in Shanghai, such as IP phone, Internet and multimedia communication. The statistics of 2001 show that online time of IP phone calls increased while the time of long-distance calls dropped. The population of web surfers continuously expands. By the end of 2001, there were 3.1 million Internet users, an increase of 53.5% from 2000.

The administration of the telecommunication industry sees changes too. As China telecom market underwent reforms, in April 2000, the Shanghai Communications Administration was installed to supervise the telecom service providers in Shanghai. China Telecom, China Mobile, China Unicom, China Netcom, Jitong Telecom and SGM are competing in the local telecom market, with core businesses ranging from fixed line, mobile phone, IP phone, paging, internet, to broadband data transmission.

Housing

In the 1990s, more than 3,000 skyscrapers mushroomed in Shanghai, among which Jinmao Tower, the world's third tallest building, surrounded by 267 high-rises, created a brand new urban landscape for Shanghai. One-fifth of the world's cranes have been working on more than 20,000 sites in Shanghai. These cranes have also lifted away the housing problem that had plagued the city for several generations. Changes to the old houses in Shanghai almost took place over short periods.

On 27 December 2000, the municipal government announced that the renovation plan of 3.65 million square meters of shabby and dilapidated houses except those conservation buildings. The ten-year renovation work of old residential areas has benefited millions of local residents. According to Shanghai Construction Commission, the city had demolished 27.87 million square meters of houses during the period of 1990-1999, which was equivalent to the total residential area in 1949.

In the past ten years, more than 100 million square meters of new resident buildings were put up, housing millions of citizens. Some 80,000 expatriates have settled down in the city and increasing numbers of Taiwanese and Hong Kong people have also rushed in here for permanent residence.

Streets and Roads

The city's transport flows would have been clogged without the development of the viaducts. It is a two-way four-lane lifted road system above existing streets to enhance the capability of metropolitan traffic. It comprises the North-South viaduct, Yan'an Road viaduct, and Inner Ring Road viaduct, which resemble a "Shen" (the nickname of Shanghai) in Chinese characters.

Elevated roads in the city

With a width of 100 meters, the 4.2-kilometer Century Boulevard is a land transport artery of the Pudong New District. It forms a part of Shanghai's West-East Development Axis connecting Hongqiao Airport and Pudong International Airport. Its unique layout of asymmetric lanes and the integration of eight botanic gardens greatly reflect the 21st century urban planning trend. With a total investment of RMB1.35 billion, the boulevard opened to traffic at the beginning of 2000.

Exhibition Facilities

To enhance the "exhibition economy" in Shanghai, the city spares no efforts in building modern exhibition centers with up-to-date technologies applied. Complementary to the Shanghai Exhibition Centre, Shanghai International Exhibition Centre, Shanghai Everbright Exhibition Centre and Shanghai Mart, two new ones have been constructed in Pudong.

Shanghai Exhibition Centre

Worth RMB800 million, Shanghai International Convention Center (SICC) was completed in August 1999 on the riverside of Pudong. Much of its fame

came from the successful hosting of the Fortune Global Forum 1999 and the 2001 Shanghai APEC Summit. With a total construction area of 110,000 square meters, SICC has a 4,300 square meter multi-function hall that can host a 4,000 people conference, a 3,600 square meter press center, a conference hall with seat capacity of 1,200, a round-table conference hall for 200 persons and nearly 30 meeting rooms of different sizes.
www.shicc.net

A more spacious Shanghai New International Expo Center (SNIEC), located at Pudong's central, was open to exhibitors in October 2001. The completed USD99 million phase one project contains four halls, with exhibition space of 11,547 sq m each. Upon completion, SNIEC will own 17 such halls, totaling 200,000 sq m in size, and hotel, office building and convention center.
www.sniec.net

Shows at SNIEC

Urban Environment Protection

Shanghai has made remarkable progress in urban pollution control and environment protection. In 2000, the city cleaned Suzhou Creek which had been notorious for its stinking smell and stagnant water. After a series of dredging works done, the water quality of the Huangpu River also improved.

The city is running a program called the Shanghai Vehicle Inspection and Maintenance (IM) Program that helps minimize air pollution in Shanghai. This plan is a cooperative project between the United States Environmental Protection Administration and the Shanghai Environmental Protection Administration.

Urban Landscape

More public parks for leisure, more colorful plants for urban landscape and more meadows for better air quality are the local environmental authorities' priorities in greening Shanghai. In 2001, 1,374 hectares are added to the city's

New urban area in Pudong with planned green land

green area. Shanghai now boasts 125 parks, 5.56 sq m of green space per capita, and 23.82% green coverage of urban built area. It attempts to achieve the national standard of 6 sq m of green space for each resident. The major challenge for now will be stretching green belts along the downtown Yan'an and Huashan roads and the Xujiahui commercial area.

Water Supply and the Drainage System

Traditionally, Shanghai lacks quality drinking water – which contributed partly to the city's boom of all kinds of water-supplying businesses. Huangpu River, which supplies 80% of the city's drinking water, is nearing exhaustion. The city, therefore, has been exploring new sources from the Yangtze River and growing forests along it for water conservation. In 2001, daily water supply in Shanghai reached 10.48 million cubic meters. The quality of drinking water in Shanghai is set to meet EU standards by 2010. Public awareness of the serious water shortage problem has also been raised. In 2001, Shanghai saved 300 million cu m of water either from the readjustment of industrial structure or the employment of new technology. For example, the city will renovate its 600,000 family toilets to reduce their water per flush from 13 liters to 9 liters.

The Phase I of Lingqiao Water Plant in Pudong is already completed. The second phase will cost RMB200 million and increase water supply capacity to 200,000 cubic meters per day. According to plan, the plant will depend on Chenhang Reservoir where water comes from the Yangtze River.

Shanghai is also engaged in improving sewage treatment. At present, the city can only treat 44% of its 5.04 million tons of wastewater produced daily. To meet the total demand, 27 more sewage treatment factories are to be established with total estimated investment of RMB18 billion.

FOREIGN TRADE PERFORMANCE

Over the past decade, Shanghai has witnessed rapid and sustained expansion in its foreign trade, even during the Asian financial crisis. In the Ninth Five-Year Plan period (1996-2000), the cumulative foreign trade volume totaled USD163.4 billion, 150% higher than that in the previous five-year period. In 2001, Shanghai's foreign trade volume reached USD61 billion, a dramatic increase of 11.3% from the previous year. The city's exports amounted to USD27.6 billion, and imports USD33.3 billion, increments of 9% and 13.3% respectively. However, due to the shrinkage in global demands, imports of processing trade were increased by a mere 0.5%margin and steel exports dropped 23.2% to USD620 million.

Shanghai's Foreign Trade 1991-2001

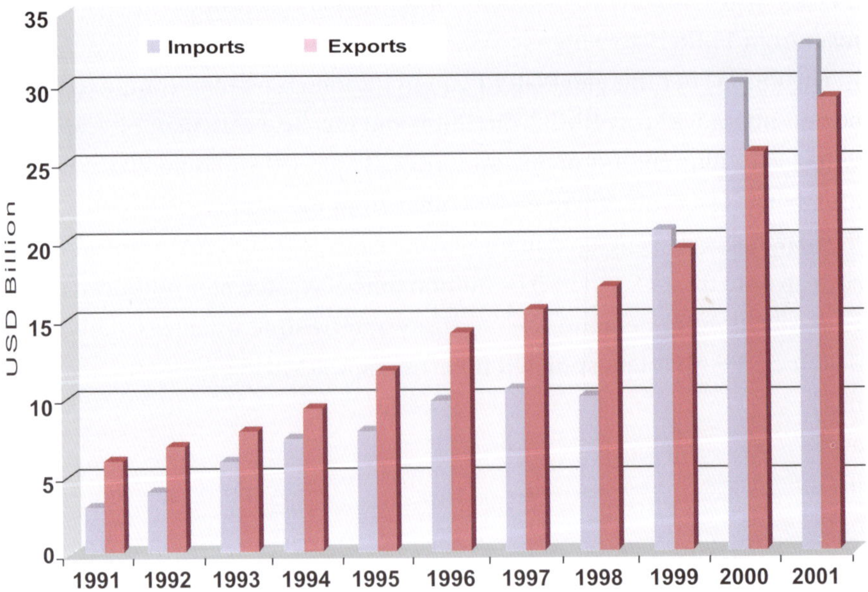

In recent years, Shanghai has upgraded its technological content in export products. In 2001, the exports of new and high-tech products totaled USD5.4 billion, up 12.9% over the previous year. These products made up 19.6% of the total exports. Mechanical and electronic products took the largest share in exports and imports in 2001. Their export value totaled USD14.2 billion, an increase of 17% over 2000; the proportion in the total exports rose from 47.9% in 2000 to 51.4% in 2001.

In 2001, exports of USD11.2 billion by state-owned businesses showed a 5.1% growth, while foreign-funded businesses managed an export increase of 11.9%, having reached USD16.0 billion.

Shanghai is the nation's largest foreign trade port. In 2001, the total throughput of Shanghai Port reached 200 million tons, an increase of 8.1% over the previous year. Containers handled reached 6.34 million TEUs, a yearly increase of 13%, which ranked Shanghai Port the largest in China and the fifth in the world.

FOREIGN INVESTMENT

Shanghai has emerged to be the prime choice for foreign direct investment in China since 1990s. After a three-year slowdown following the 1997 Asian Financial Crisis, it quickly rebounded in 2000. The cosmopolitan character, sophisticated and affluent consumers, highly educated and skilled workforce, plus the municipality's preferential policies and pro-business attitude, make Shanghai a huge magnet for overseas capitals. In addition, the city's established industrial sector makes investors feel at ease while seeking technological support or cooperative partners in related industries.

Shanghai's attraction to foreign investors of all sizes is clearly demonstrated in figures. So far, investors from 95 countries and regions have made their presence in Shanghai, with India, Sudan and Senegal newly added to the list. There are around 25,000 foreign invested enterprises in the city, the highest levels among the cities in Mainland China. During the Ninth Five-Year Plan period (1996-2000), the city approved 11,807 foreign-funded projects, involving USD42.2 billion in contractual capital and USD30.1 billion in actual utilized value.

New FDI Projects in Shanghai 1991-2001

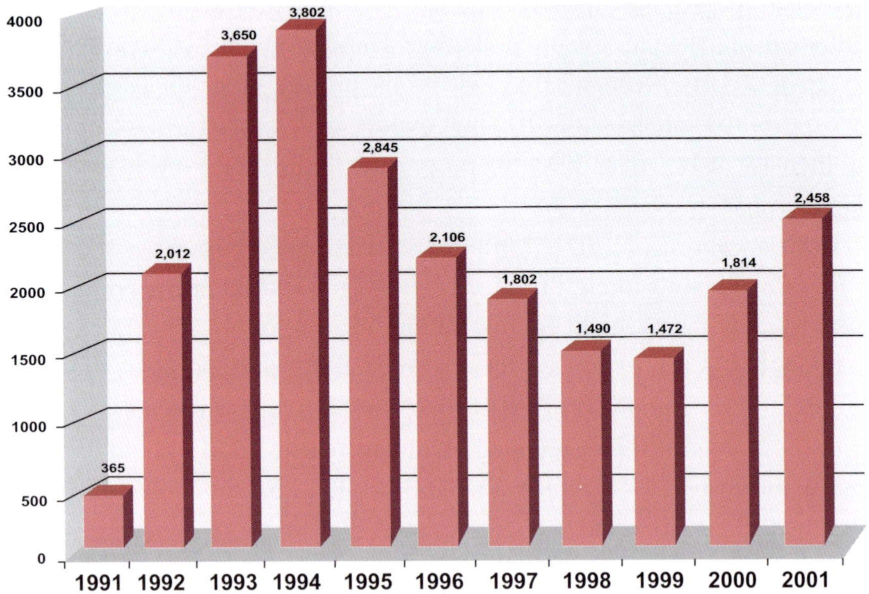

Contractual FDI in Shanghai, 1991-2001 (USD billion)

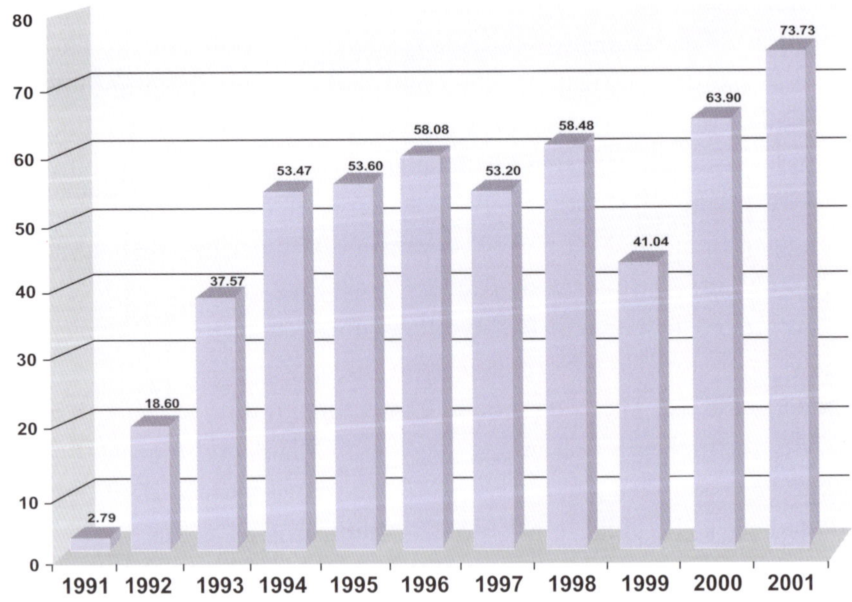

In 2001 alone, the city approved 2,458 foreign investment related projects, up 35.5% from year 2000; contractual foreign investment capital reached USD7.37 billion with actual utilization of USD4.39 billion, setting a new record. By now, more than half of the industrial output in Shanghai was generated by foreign-invested enterprises, many of which are manufacturing or distribution facilities of world leading consumer brands—from automobiles to household appliances and consumables.

Industrial Distribution of FDI in Shanghai 1991-2001 (USD billion)

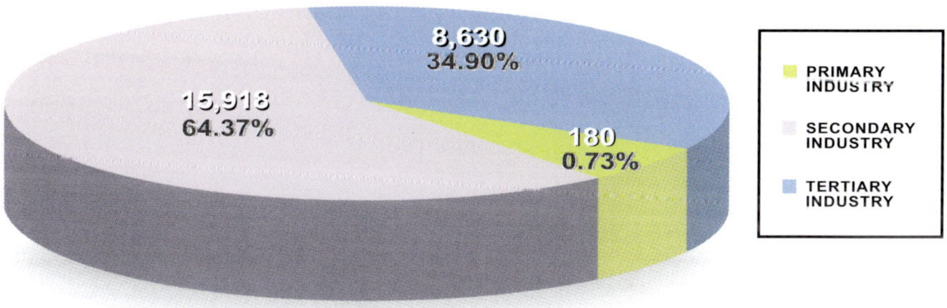

Industrial Distribution of FDI in Shanghai till 2001 (USD billion)

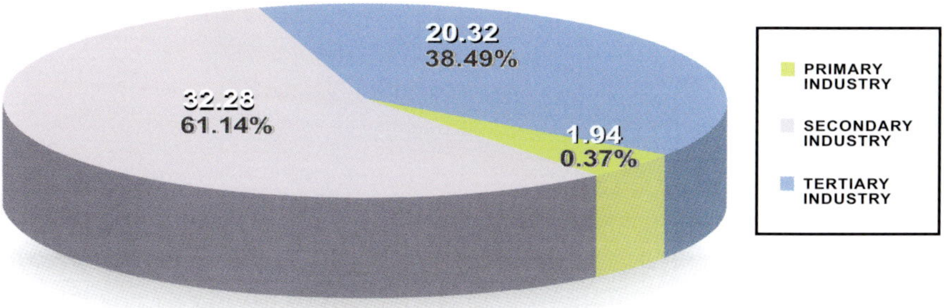

Total Contractual FDI : USD 52.79 billion

Characteristics of Foreign Investment

Previously, overseas capital was mainly invested into the commercial, financial, tourism, real estate and other service industries. In recent years, particularly after the development of Pudong New District, the city has seen a steady inflow of large international conglomerates and major industrial projects. In 2001, Shanghai approved 1,308 projects in industry sector with a total contractual value of USD5.5 billion, increasing 39.4% and 13.3% over the previous year respectively. Of this total, there were 158 projects with total investment value of more than USD10 million each, which accounted for 97% of the total contractual capital. These were projects that involve advanced technology with high export potential.

In terms of absorption of overseas capital, manufacturing projects take the lead. About 70% of overseas investment in Shanghai went to the manufacturing industries, especially so-called pillar or high-tech industries are heavily promoted in local industrial plans.

Industrial Distribution of Contractual FDI in 2001 (USD billion)

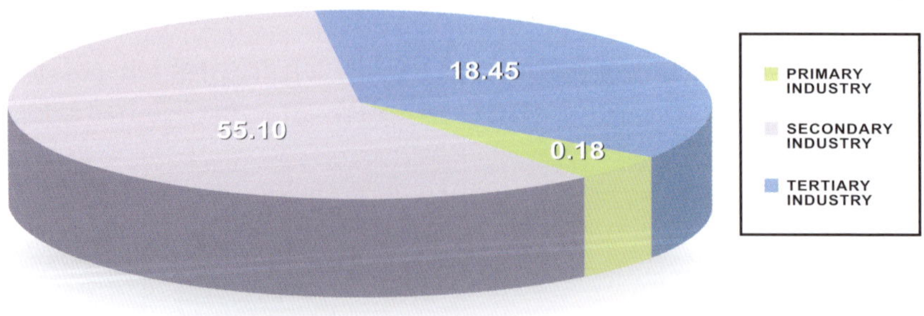

As a result of China's accession to the World Trade Organization and relaxation of certain regulations governing the tertiary sector, the number of foreign-invested projects in service industry is increasing. As Shanghai is always in the frontline in China economic reforms and experiments, industries such as financial services, education, telecommunication and tourism in Shanghai are able to receive foreign funds now.

The export volume of foreign-invested enterprises is having a continuous growth; many foreign-invested enterprises are either readily increasing investment or reinvesting their profits. These clearly indicate that the city's investment climate is in sustained improvement.

Most of foreign-funded enterprises in Shanghai reported good financial returns, thanks to their sound management and great endeavor in exploring the market. In 2000, these enterprises achieved total sales of RMB397.8 billion, with profits of RMB21.8 billion and foreign exchange balance of USD3.0 billion. The figures represented an increase of 33%, 110% and 21.6% respectively, over 1999.

Hong Kong, the US, Japan top in the overseas investors' list of Shanghai, followed by Virgin Islands, Singapore, Germany and Taiwan. To date, equity joint venture (EJV) remains the most popular form of foreign direct investment. However, wholly-owned foreign enterprises (WOFE) keeps gaining its popularity – almost 35% of foreign-funded enterprises in Shanghai currently take the form. It is expected to be the dominant form of new investments in the future.

Contractual FDI in Shanghai by Country till 2001 (USD billion)

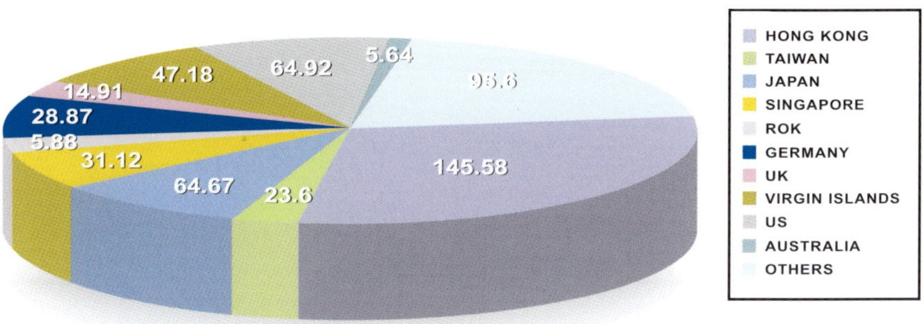

FDI Projects of Different Modes in Shanghai till 2001

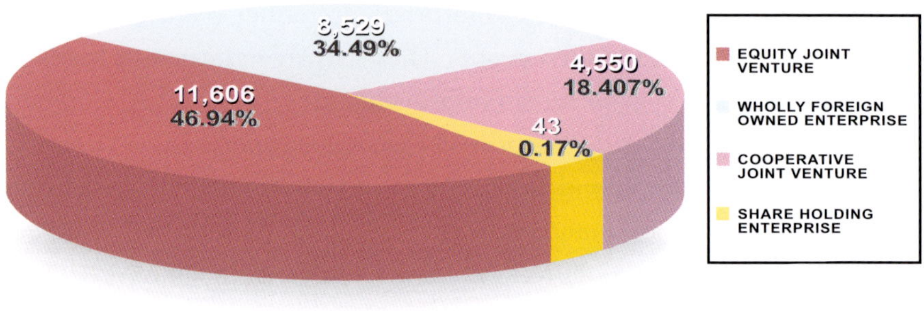

Foreigners in Shanghai

THE FOREIGN COMMUNITY

With a population of 14.2 million permanent residents, Shanghai is one of the largest metropolitan areas in the world. When the feudal Qing Dynasty was forced to open the door to foreign nations about 150 years ago, they allowed Western investors to plant their feet on the coast of Shanghai. The British, French, American, and Japanese traders followed on each other's heels and rapidly built fortunes on silk, tea and opium businesses there; many parts of the city became a special foreigner's enclave immune to Chinese laws and administrations.

The revolution in 1949 kicked out the colonizers with their money, but the western influences, both physical and psychological, remained an essential element of Shanghai. Their nostalgic European architecture displays similarity to very old western movie scenes.

Shanghai is one of the most forward-thinking and unorthodox Chinese commercialized cities. Enjoying double-digit economic growth over the past two decades and having absorbed billions of dollars of overseas investment, Shanghai is, unquestionably, the first choice for foreigners who wish to do business in China. To date, Japanese citizens account for one third of foreigners in Shanghai, while Americans come second with a proportion of 11%. The numbers for Koreans, Singaporeans and German are about 6% each. Recently, a growing number of Malaysians are chosing to work in Shanghai too.

About 95% of the foreign citizens employed in Shanghai have received university education with most of the rest being chefs in hotels. In fact, 8 out of 10 foreigners working in Shanghai are holding senior management positions, such as CEOs, general managers and accountants, or technical posts like engineers and IT professionals. At the same time, around 81.9% of foreigners are employed by foreign enterprises, and a 5% are working for state-owned enterprises or in the growing private sector. A good example is Shanghai Eastern Airlines who has employed 90 stewards from Japan, France, Germany, the United States, Spain and Korea to improve face-to-face communications with overseas passengers on board.

With a growing number of foreigners working in Shanghai, bars, beauty salons, and restaurants serving Japanese food, Argentina-style roast meat and French food, have mushroomed in town. Along the busy streets in Shanghai, people have long enjoyed KFC, MacDonald's, Starbucks, Haggen Daz and Hard Rock Café. Foreign boutiques and cosmetics are also readily available in Shanghai.

Hard Rock Café at Shanghai Centre

Sipping a cup of coffee at Starbucks along Nanjing Road

Foreigners entering Shanghai in 2001	
Total customs entries in Shanghai	2,042,637
Foreigners	1,469,694
Overseas Chinese	46,784
Hong Kong and Macau Residents	206,245
Taiwanese	319,913

Foreigners in Shanghai holding various visas in 2001	
Population of foreign residents	50,586
Foreign businessmen and officials	6,608
Foreign staff in FIEs	33,069
Teachers	943
Professionals	2,231
Foreign students	4,113
Others	3,622
Total number of foreign visas	111,339
increase over 2000	6.3%

CHINESE HOLIDAYS

Foreigners will find that China has her own set of commemorative dates. For example, March 8 is for women, June 1 for children, August 1 for servicemen and September 10 for teachers. The anniversary of the founding of the Communist Party of China, which originally took place in Shanghai, is on July 1. Important holidays include National Day on October 1 and Labor Day on May 1, both celebrated with a seven-day-long "Golden Week" to promote domestic tourism. For Chinese, Spring festival is the most important traditional holiday. The first day, or Chuyi in Mandarin, falls on different dates in January or February, as based on the lunar calendar. The whole festive season usually lasts for two weeks. Foreign businessmen are advised to avoid this period as many Chinese organizations and companies are closed or in partial operation. In Shanghai, a general cleanup of the city begins two weeks before October.

EMPLOYMENT PERMITS

Foreigners who wish to work in Shanghai need to obtain an Employment Permit before they apply for a z-type (for work) visa to enter China. The person must summit to Shanghai Municipal Labor and Social Security Administration a Chinese resume, photocopies of academic qualification, a letter from employer and company registration certificate for processing. It normally takes five days. With the approval letter, the Shanghai employer can, on behalf of the employee, proceed to Shanghai Foreign Trade and Economic Cooperation Commission for relevant visa application. The permit certificate is valid for six months and renewable upon application. Foreign employees must get the Employment Permit in person within 15 days after arrival in Shanghai.

Shanghai Municipal Labor and Social Security Administration
Block A, 865 Zhongshan South Road, Shanghai 200011
Tel: 833666 (enquiry); 86-21-63650095 (complaint)
Office hours: 9:15-11:15 (Mon~Fri), 13:30~16:30 (Mon~Thu)
Website: www.sh.lss.gov.cn

Shanghai Foreign Trade and Economic Cooperation Commission
Tel: 86-21-62752200
Pudong Office
Tel: 86-21-58788388

According to the official statistics, there are about 60,000 people from 120 nations and regions working in the city. The administration issued 25,224 such permits to foreigners in 2001, a 14.5 % year-on-year increase. A total number of 6,733 foreigners obtained their employment permits in Shanghai in the first quarter of 2002, up 30% over the same period of the previous year. The administration also received 33,801 employment applications from Taiwan, Hong Kong and Macau people.

CHINESE VISA

Type	Applicants	Validity
L (Tourist)	Tourist	30 days
F (Business) Businessmen with invitation	Multiple entries	within 3-6 months
D (Resident)	Family members of expats	-
G (Transit)	Individuals in transit to other countries	Overnight stay
X (Student)	Students with invitation from accredited Chinese institutions	-
Z (Work)	Foreigners working in China	6 months renewable

For Z and D Visa application

Foreign Entry and Exit Permit Division, Public Security Bureau

333 Wusong Road, Shanghai

Tel: 86-21-63577925

For Z, X and D Visa holders' physical exam

Shanghai Entry and Exit Inspection and Quarantine Bureau

1701 Hami Lu, Shanghai

GREEN CARDS

Shanghai has started to issue so-called "green cards", or permanent residence permit, to more than 240 overseas residents since its recent inception of the practice to attract overseas investors and talent. The green card allows the holder to engage in scientific research activities, to start a business, to send his/her children to school under the same conditions as locals, and to enjoy preferential taxation treatment. This has been recognized as a breakthrough in the city's bid to attract domestic and overseas talent.

According to the official report of Shanghai Personnel Administration, about 90% of the green card holders are returned Chinese students, many holding US green cards concurrently. The rest are foreign nationals and overseas Chinese from Taiwan, Hong Kong and Macau who have passed through the strict scrutiny.

SETTLING DOWN

The whole of Shanghai is in a transition. An increasing number of foreigners have chosen Shanghai as the place to settle down and start their businesses.

Getting Around

Although Shanghai is an immense city, the layout of its streets and the prominence of new landmarks make it relatively easy to get around. It is advisable to travel with a map. Shanghai offers commuter buses and Metro, both inexpensive. But first-timers are recommended not to ride on public bus unless for challenging experience.

Foreigners may be amazed by the fact that bicycles are the most commonly used method for commuting. However, bicycle theft is also common and mountain bikes usually fall prey. On the other hand, taxis are the most convenient means of travel in Shanghai, and they are economical. Foreigners who aren't proficient in Mandarin should bring along addresses written in Chinese, since taxi drivers hardly speak English, let alone other foreign languages.

Driving in Shanghai

Those who choose to drive can obtain a Driver's License by surrendering their existing foreign or international licenses, which will be held until they leave the country. In this regard, they must undergo a physical examination and purchase third-party insurance, and Shanghai residence is a prerequisite. There are numerous traffic rules and one-way lanes which foreigners may not be comfortable with. Besides, drivers must be aware the many bicycles, motor scooters and jay-walk pedestrians will make driving experience considerably different from most countries. The wisest choice, however, may be hiring a local driver to avoid the frustration of dodging bicycles and pedestrians.

Steps to getting a local driver's license

- Get two application forms, which must be duly filled in Chinese, at Department of Automobiles, 1101 Zhongshan North 1 Road (Tel: 86-21-65168168 ext. 5332);
- With completed forms and RMB150, applicants must obtain a health checkup at the Foreigners' Section, Huadong Hospital, 221 Yan'an West Road (Tel: 86-21-62483180);
- Translate the original driver's license at Shanghai International Studies University, Dalian West Road (Tel: 86-21-65422912 , 65311900 ext. 2360);
- With all documents and four passport-size photos, RMB20, and a copy of company's Business License, applicants must pass a written test (in English) at the Department of Automobiles;
- Those with less than 3 years' driving experience must take a road test;
- Pick up the license one week later.

Expatriate Housing

Suitable housing for foreigners is not only difficult to find, but also costly, compared to other parts of China. Rents may range from USD500 to USD15,000 per month, depending on location, type of the house, quality, property management and incorporated facilities and amenities. The prevailing rental rates are estimated at USD20 per sq meter per month, based on gross floor area. Recent trend shows that due to the strong demand in high-end properties, rents for the mid-to-upper market register an average increase of 6%. The average vacancy rate for all types of expatriate housing properties is currently at a level of 30%, though varying in locations.

According to Colliers International Shanghai, the rents for major housing areas are estimated as follows:

Area	Bedroom	Sq m	USD/month
Hongqiao House/Villa	3	200-300	6,000
	4	250-400	6,500
	5	450-800	9,000
Downtown Apartment	1	80-120	1,500
	2	90-150	2,500
	3	150-250	2,000-6,000
	4	250-350	4,000-6,000
Pudong House/Villa	3	250-300	5,800
	4	300-400	8,000
	5	400-500	9,000

Source: Colliers International, Shanghai

The Portman Complex

Although there are many property agencies in the city, it is best to deal with qualified ones. Generally speaking, rental contracts are for minimum one year and the price for the second year is usually negotiable. Rental is usually paid in quarterly installments, and a security deposit equivalent to three months is often required. Commission for the agent, if any, typically equals to one-month rental.

Popular residences in Shanghai include the

Portman Complex, Green Valley Villas, Longbai Serviced Apartments, Silver Tower Apartments, Ascott Apartments and Equatorial Serviced Apartments. There are also many new housing developments that are nearing completion, including President Mansions and those in the Gubei New Area.

Rentals of Selected Apartments

Location	Size/Type	Monthly Rental
Da An Plaza Yanan Zheng Lu *One hour to Airport*	134 sqm, 2br, 2baths 198sqm, 3br, 3baths	USD 4800 USD 6000
Da De Apartment Jiang Ning Lu *One hour to Airport*	160 sqm, 2br, 2baths 179sqm, 3br, 2baths	USD 3500 USD 4200
Pearl Building Gubei Area *45 minutes to Airport*	200sqm, 3br, 2baths	USD 5000
Cypress Villas Hong Qiao Lu *5 minutes to Airport*	260 sqm, 4br, 2baths 361sqm, 4br, 3baths 402sqm, 4br, 2baths	USD 6000 USD 9000 USD 10000

Due to unfamiliarity, most foreigners stay in hotels until they manage to find suitable accommodations. Shanghai offers numerous hotels with prices to suit almost any foreigner or traveler, from the budget conscious to the busy executives. Most offer business centers, tennis, squash, gymnasiums, beauty salons and international food and beverage outlets. However, only recognized tourism hotels, usually given stars in rank, are able to accept foreigners.

Healthcare

Foreigners in Shanghai should be vaccinated against hepatitis A and B, typhoid, tetanus and polio. They should also avoid drinking tap water, and use boiled or distilled water instead. Mineral water is widely available, as are a wide range of water purifiers and distillers. Vegetables should be thoroughly washed in water that contains a drop of iodine.

Shanghai is home to a number of well-equipped hospitals that have special foreigner departments. Some hospitals also formed joint ventures with organizations from Hong Kong, Australia and Japan, and this has improved the level of services and skills they offer. At the same time, they are trying to enhance their ability to provide international standard emergency treatment. Famous hospitals in Shanghai include Huadong Hospital, Zhongshan Hospital, Shanghai No. 6 People's Hospital, Huashan Hospital, Shanghai No. 1 People's Hospital and Xinhua Hospital. In Shanghai, foreigners are familiar with World Link Medical and Dental Centers, whose international team of medicals and dental professionals provide primary healthcare, pediatrics, OB-GYN, and a full range of dental services. Pemier members even have 24-hour access to physicians.

Places of Worship

Shanghai is home to a number of places of worship for all beliefs. There are mosques on Xinle Road, while Xujiahui Cathedral and Shanghai Community Church at Hengshan Road serve the Catholic and Protestant Masses respectively. Buddhists may choose to go to the Jade Budda Temple at Anyuan Road, Longhua Temple at Longhua Road, and Jing'an Temple at Nanjing West Road, which are also attractions for sightseers. A 780-year-old Confucius Temple is located in Jiading District of Shanghai, where people may show their respect to the greatest philosopher and educationist of ancient China.

Shopping

Shops and department stores in Shanghai are among the most well stocked in China. They boast a wide variety of stylish local and foreign goods. The three major shopping streets are Nanjing Road, Huaihai Middle Road and Sichuan North Road. To experience the incredible bargaining pleasure, shoppers may also patronize Xiangyang Market near Huaihai Road, Dongtai Road Market and Fuyou Road Market, where branded products of different qualities and antiques can be found.

Foreigners may easily locate foodstuffs and household goods at chain supermarkets and convenient stores all over the city, including Carrefour, Tops, Metro, Hualian, Lianhua, Watson's and Wellcome. They can also take advantage of free home delivery services, such as City Supermarket, which offers foodstuffs ranging from fresh meat and seafood, vegetables, wines and liquors, bread, to pet food.

Leisure

Nightclubs, pubs, discos, and karaoke lounges for all styles and tastes abound throughout the city. As one of China's cultural centers, Shanghai offers a wealth of entertainment options, from theatre and Chinese opera, ballet and symphony, to museums. Gourmets will appreciate the city as it is also home to a variety of restaurants, be it German, Italian, Spicy Sichuan or Crude Cantonese.

Health-conscious foreigners will find an abundance of health clubs, mainly in the city's large hotels. Most are well equipped with the latest gym apparatus, and supervised by trained professionals. Facilities include swimming pools, squash and tennis courts, and aerobics rooms. Memberships are available, but prices could be expensive and services vary. Some leading clubs for foreigners include Shanghai International Club, Portman Health Club, Holiday Inn Health Club and Hilton Health Club.

Visitors are encouraged to use their own imagination to enjoy exciting city life in Shanghai. Taking a cruise drifting down the Huangpu River at night or having a family picnic at Dianshan Lake in the suburbs are just two of the many pastime options.

Education

CHINESE EDUCATION

The Chinese education system usually divides education into primary school, middle school, and college and university. The compulsory nine-year education consists of six-year primary and three-year junior middle school schooling. After that, students may choose to go to vocational or technical school education to acquire skills for jobs, or to continue senior schooling to prepare for higher education.

Shanghai is one of Chinese education centers where over 50 universities and colleges are located. A bachelor degree normally requires four-year full time studying on campus, and the two- to three-year colleges only offer diploma programs. Graduate may pursue higher degrees by passing a general graduate registration examination and being enrolled as a postgraduate student. Full time students can usually expect their master's in three or less years and another three years for doctorate.

Chinese mandarin is used as the only medium in Chinese maintream schools except some language courses. Shanghainese, a branch of Wu dialect, however, is occasionally popular after class.

INTERNATIONAL SCHOOLS

For foreign children accompanying their parents coming into Shanghai, it is recommended that they first consult an international school in order to continue their schooling compatible with the home curriculum.

In recent years, an increasing number of international schools have emerged to meet the ever growing expatriate population in Shanghai. These include Shanghai American School, Shanghai Singapore International School, Yew Chung Shanghai International School, Concordia International School Shanghai, Shanghai Changning International School, French, German and Japanese Schools.

Shanghai American School

Originally established in 1912, Shanghai American School (SAS) is the first international school in mainland China. As the largest international school in Shanghai, SAS offers pre-kindergarten through grade 12 classes to more than 1,700 students from about 50 nationalities, most being Americans, Koreans and Taiwanese. It offers American curriculum on two campuses in Puxi (elementary through high school) and Pudong (pre-kindergarten through grade 8).

Fully accredited by the Western Association of Schools and Colleges (WASC), SAS is an independent non-profit school owned by the SAS Parent Association. The annual school fees for 2002-2003 range from USD11,500 for pre-kindergarten to USD20,000 for grade 9 though 12.

Website: www.saschina.org

Kids playing on SAS's Puxi campus

Shanghai Singapore International School

Founded in 1996, the Shanghai Singapore International School (SSIS) offers a balanced curriculum in line with the educational policies of Singapore. Located in Zhudi town of Minhang district, SSIS is near to Shanghai American School's Puxi campus. Besides a bilingual educational system, SSIS enables its pupils to access authentic Singapore-produced textbooks and learning materials. Offering pre-school (aged 3 to 6), primary school (aged 7 to 12) and secondary school (aged 13 to 16) education, SSIS maintains competitive rates in tuition. Full day program for pre-school is between USD7,000 and USD8,000, and ranges from USD8000 to USD12,000 for primary and secondary school per year.

Website: www.ssischool.com

Shanghai Singapore International School is based on SAS's former campus

Yew Chung Shanghai International School

First established in Hongqiao by the Hong Kong-based Yew Chung Education Foundation in 1993, Yew Chung Shanghai International School now boasts its other two campuses in Gubei and Pudong. It also has its sister schools in Hong Kong, Beijing, Yantai and Chongqing.

Yew Chung offers an international curriculum based on the National Curriculum of England together with a bilingual approach. It provides programs for 1 to 2 years old up to secondary school students. For instance, the Infant and Toddler Learning Program is priced at USD4,000-USD11,000 per year, depending on days per week; Kindergarten (K3 and K4), Primary (Year 1 to 6), Secondary (Year 7 to 13) schools are at USD17,000, USD17,500 and USD18,000 per year, respectively, all excluding miscellaneous charges.

Website: www.ycef.com

Yew Chung Gubei Campus

BUSINESS SCHOOLS

Lured by the expanding community of business executives in the area, many of Shanghai-based universities have been actively offering MBA or Executive MBA (EMBA) programs. These include the national "key universities" of Shanghai Jiaotong, Fudan and Tongji, and other universities and institutes too.

CEIBS

China Europe International Business School, or CEIBS, however, is not attached to any universities. Started from a bilateral education cooperative project between China and the European Union in 1984, which was the first ever MBA program in China, it was upgraded to a joint venture between the two parties ten years later in 1994. As a non-profit organization, CEIBS still receives financial support from the municipal government of Shanghai and the EU.

CEIBS is widely recognized as a leading business school in China by its world class faculty and teaching quality, westernized management, international exposure, program size and coverage, authenticity and methodology. In 2002, its MBA and EMBA programs are ranked the 3rd and 2nd in Asia, or among the world top 100 and top 50, respectively, by the Financial Times. Its Executive Education Program is also ranked the 1st in Asia, which makes it the only Asian School among the world top 50 by Financial Times. Located in Pudong with a new campus designed by Pei Cobb Freed & Partners, CEIBS now enrolls two classes of MBA students and eight classes of EMBA students (including three in Beijing) a year. In 2002, it also trains over 5,000 senior executives for companies operating in and outside China with both open programs and specific programs customized for client companies.

Though the tuition fee is by no means inexpensive - RMB120,000 for a 17-month full-time MBA and RMB238,000 for a 23-month part-time bilingual EMBA program - the entry requirements are stringent. MBA candidates must have passed GMAT and an exam designed by CEIBS before they can be considered for an interview. Besides, proficiency in foreign language is necessary as all courses are taught in English. As a result, the ratio of enrolment to applicants remains at 1/6 for MBA and 1/4 for EMBA.

The school has a strength of 30 permanent full time faculty, over 200 visiting faculty and about 160 staff. The size of each class should not be exceeding 64 as limited by the number of seats in all classrooms. Though majority of the students are those who wish to update and broaden their management knowledge and expertise or for a better career, some are sponsored by their foreign employers in China. Among the 127 new MBA students in 2002, there are 18 overseas students from the US, Korea, Singapore, Taiwan, Israel and Mexico. More than half of the EMBA students are general managers, presidents or CEOs from local or foreign-invested companies. Short-term executive education programs are also available all year round, covering topics of general management, marketing strategy, leadership, advanced financial management, supply chain and entrepreneurship. There is also one multi-module course tailored for expatriates in China.

Website: www.ceibs.edu

Information center of CEIBS

Aetna School of Management

Aetna School of Management (ASM) is the business school of Shanghai Jiaotong University. Restored in 1984, the school changed its name in appreciation of the Aetna Insurance who donated USD10 million in 1998. The school is among the first batch in China approved to offer MBA programs. ASM now has 1,200 registered MBA students and just started EMBA enrolment in December 2002.

A two-year full-time IMBA program with English as the medium at ASM costs RMB80,000. And full-time or part-time MBA program is priced at RMB60,000. However, the 20-month-long part-time EMBA program costs RMB218,000.

As Shanghai Jiaotong University has extensive cooperation and exchange programs with many world-renowned universities, ASM also offers a wide range of options like UBC-MBA of Canada, NTU-MBA of Singapore, City University MBA of Hong Kong, China-Germany International MBA (IMBA), and Rutgers-EMBA, etc.

Website: www.asom.sjtu.edu.cn

Exhibitions & Trade Events

Shanghai is fast emerging as a popular venue for international conferences and exhibitions. In the past years, Shanghai has successfully hosted numerous international events, the most prominent being the 1999 Fortune Global Forum, Shanghai Five Nations Summit and the 9th Asia Pacific Economic Cooperation (APEC) Summit in 2001.

OVERVIEW

Intensive infrastructure investment and urban redevelopment in the past decade have laid an essential foundation for Shanghai to organize and host high-level international exhibitions. In early 1980s, the city had only one suitable site for large-scale exhibitions – the Shanghai Exhibition Center (SEC), which accommodated 10 to 20 major events per year. Since 1990, large and modern conference and exhibition venues have been built up to meet the increasing demand. These include the Shanghai International Exhibition Center (INTEX), the Everbright Conference and Exhibition Center, Shanghai Mart, the Shanghai International Conference Center (SICC), and Shanghai New International Expo Center (SNIEC).

With the capacity expanded, the number of large regional and international events held in Shanghai has been increasing by nearly 20% annually. According to official statistics, the city approved 278 applications for international conferences and exhibitions in 2001, of which 172 were successfully held with total transaction volume of over RMB55 billion and ticket sales and direct income of RMB1.8 billion.

In recent years, more and more exhibitions and trade fairs have converged on five hot topics, that is, automobile, information technologies, construction, environment protection technologies and products, and biopharmaceuticals. These altogether account for over 30% of the total events.

With 300 hotels (including 14 five-star hotels) and over 500 hostels, Shanghai is fully capable of accommodating a large influx of visitors. In addition, there are over 100 professional exhibition and conference organizers and logistic service providers.

In December 2002, Shanghai beat other four contestant cities in bidding for hosting the World Expo 2010. This magnificent show, expected to have profound impact on the city's urban construction in the coming years, will be held in 1st May to 31st October 2010, under the theme of a "Better City, Better Life".

Looking forward to World Expo 2010

MAJOR EVENTS

Shanghai International Industry Fair

Shanghai International Industry Fair (SIF), held every November in Shanghai, is the largest one of its kind in Mainland China. Currently, SIF is jointly sponsored by eight government organs, including the State Economic and Trade Commission (SETC), Ministry of Foreign Trade and Economic Cooperation (MOFTEC), Shanghai Municipal People's Government, Ministry of Science and Technology (MOST), Ministry of Information

Technology and innovation are the theme of SIF

China Mobile and SAIC's booths

Industry (MII), Ministry of Education (MOE), Chinese Academy of Science (CAS) and China Council for the Promotion of International Trade (CCPIT).

SIF showcases advancement in high technologies and industrial equipments. Based on the past events, around 20% of those frequent exhibitors were MNC giants, including Microsoft, IBM, Lucent, Siemens, GE, Volkswagen,

Roche, Johnson & Johnson, Emerson, 3M, Dow Corning, Daewoo Motor, Alcatel, Motorola, FAG, Volvo, Philips, ABB, Epson, Hewlett Packard, Delphi Systems, Intel, SOLAIC, Alps and Omron; 40% were from domestic leading enterprises in China, for example, Sinopec, Sinochem, Baosteel Group, Anshan Iron and Steel, Changhong Group, Shanghai Automobile, Shanghai Electrical, Wuhan Iron and Steel etc.

The third session of SIF was successfully held at SNIEC between 22nd-27th November 2001, with total exhibition area of 50,000 sq m, skyrocketed from 15,000 sq m in the previous year. SIF 2001 attractted a total of 1,192 overseas

MNCs are now actively participating in Shanghai's trade fairs

and domestic exhibitors and over 505,000 visitors. Total transaction volume over the show exceeed RMB31.3 billion, or over 60% of the total amount achieved in all trade fairs in Shanghai around the year. Of this figure, RMB13 billion came from products, RMB8.3 billion was spent on technical projects, and RMB2.5 billion went for property rights.

SIF 2002 was held at SNIEC between 22nd-27th November 2002, with an increased exhibition area of 61,000 sq m and a total of 2,700 booths. In line with its four key functions of "Display, Transaction, Evaluation and Forum", SIF 2002 was held in nine professional halls featuring IT and network, bioengineering and pharmaceuticals, new materials, electrical equipment, automobile and components, household electrical appliances, environmental protection technologies, energy and technological innovations. In addition, SIF 2002 released a large number of projects for foreign investment and introduced venture capitalists to enterprises both at home and abroad.

Shanghai International Industrial Fair 2002 was held at SNIEC, Pudong.

Business Division of Shanghai International Industry Fair
Tel: (86) (21) 62560100, 62586398, 62586638
Fax: (86) (21) 62561068, 62586630
Email: sif@jtpc.com.cn
Website: www.sif-expo.com

East China Fair

The East China Fair (ECF), held every 1st to 7th March in Shanghai since 1991, is co-sponsored by nine provinces and cities in East China, namely, Shanghai, Jiangsu, Zhejiang, Anhui, Fujian, Jiangxi, Shandong, Nanjing and Ningbo. Delegations from other 20 plus provinces, municipalities and autonomous regions attend the fair.

ECF has shifted from the previous exhibition concentration on five main industries – textile and garments, light industry and crafts, electric equipment and machinery, pharmaceutical and chemical industry, husbandry byproducts and foodstuff – to focus on textile garments, arts and crafts, and light industrial products.

ECF 2002, the 12th such fair, was for the first time held in SNIEC, occupying 57,500 sq m exhibition area and containing 2,850 standard booths in 5 exhibition halls. Among them 46.7% is for textile and garments (1,330 booths), 11.8% for arts and crafts (338 booths), 37.3% for light industries (1,062 booths), and 100 booths were specially designated for overseas enterprises. The total transaction volume of ECF 2002 amounted to USD1.7 billion, increased by 10.3% over the previous year. International guests, from 154 nations and regions attended the fair, totaling 13,646. When 64.8% of them came from Asia, guests from North America, Europe and Latin America accounted for 5.52%, 5.61% and 1.69%, respectively.

By now, more than 100,000 guest and exhibitors have attended ECP, with accumulated transactioins worth USD20.2 billion. The 13th ECP will be held in 1st-7th March 2003 in SNIEC.

East China Fair Permanent Office

Tel: (86) (21) 62560100

Fax: (86) (21) 62561068

Email: shitpc@sh163.net

Website: www.east-china-fair.com

Forms Of Investment

INTRODUCTION

There are three main types of foreign direct investment in China, namely, the equity joint venture (EJV), the cooperative joint venture (CJV) and wholly-owned foreign enterprise (WOFE). Collectively, they are referred to as "foreign invested enterprises (FIEs)".

By definition, joint ventures (including EJV and CJV) are jointly invested and established by one or more Chinese business entities or individuals together with one or more foreign business entities or individuals in accordance with the Equity Joint Venture Law and Regulations or the Cooperative Joint Venture Law and Regulations. The fundamental feature of a joint venture in China is that the foreign party or parties hold 25% or more in the ownership of the joint venture. In contrast, a WOFE refers to a separate legal entity with limited liability status set up in China based on the Wholly Owned Foreign Enterprise Law and Regulations. In such an entity, the foreign investors hold 100% ownership.

Apart from the above three, other forms of foreign investment are also available, such as:

- Foreign Invested Holding Companies
- Foreign Invested Joint Stock Companies
- Build-Operate-Transfer (BOT)
- International Leasing
- Compensation Trade
- Processing and Assembling

MAJOR FORMS OF FOREIGN INVESTMENT

Equity Joint Venture vs. Cooperative Joint Venture

EJVs are legal persons under Chinese law and may own assets, sue and be sued. In other words, equity joint ventures operate in the form of a limited liability company, which means that the personal wealth and property of the shareholding partners are shielded from corporate loss. In addition, the liability of the partners is limited to their contribution to the company's registered capital.

In comparison, CJVs can choose to acquire or not to acquire a legal person status. In other words, a CJV with non-legal person status is allowed to set up, which is legally equivalent to a partnership establishment. It does not enjoy limited liability protection, but the advantage of a non-legal person CJV is that the profit of a CJV can be distributed among the parties before submitting tax and still enjoy tax preferential treatment. This is quite a good point in some cases as it offers foreign investors the flexibility to plan their tax to their benefits under their home country's tax laws. In practice, the majority of cooperative joint ventures are set up as limited liability companies.

The most significant difference between EJV and CJV is the allocation of profits and liabilities. In an EJV, profits and liabilities are allocated according to the ratio of the capital contributions made by the partners. It simply means that if one party contributes 30% of the capital investment, they will be rewarded 30% of the total profits and required to take up 30% of the liabilities.

CJV allows for greater flexibility in the agreement between the joint venture parties. In a cooperative joint venture, profit sharing is generally prescribed by the joint venture agreement between the parties. In practice, the foreign party generally receives a higher percentage of profit in the early years of the CJV while their Chinese partner will become the owner of the fixed assets of the CJV at no cost after termination of the joint venture.

Wholly-Owned Foreign Enterprises

Since the introduction in 1986, WOFEs had only been an alternative to joint ventures in certain specific sectors for a long time. However, in October 2000, the country amended its Wholly Owned Foreign Enterprises Law and removed the restrictions imposed on WOFEs in areas such as foreign exchange balance, export obligation, priority of domestic sourcing, and the reporting requirements for production and operation plans. Due to a more liberalized and transparent regulation system, WOFE has already overtaken JVs in recent years to become the most popular form for foreign investment.

Export obligation

Under the revised law, WOFEs no longer have to export all or the majority of their products. According to the original law, enterprises with foreign capital shall be established in such a manner to help promote the development of China's national economy and they shall adopt advanced technology and equipments, and market all or most of their products outside China. But the amended laws state that foreign enterprises are "encouraged" (not "shall") to market their products outside China and use advanced technology. This change gives a greater degree of autonomy to WOFEs to sell their products in China's domestic markets.

Sourcing

According to the past regulations, WOFEs should purchase their production equipments and raw materials in domestic markets. The revised law now stipulates that when purchasing raw materials within the permitted scope of its operation, an FIE "may purchase the goods in China and may also buy them in the international markets." With these new amendments, WOFEs in China can enjoy greater freedom in purchasing.

Foreign exchange

The original regulation on WOFE requires a WOFE to achieve the balance of foreign exchange income and expenditure. If a WOFE is unable to achieve the balance of its foreign exchange income and expenditures on its own, it may, in accordance with State provisions, apply to relevant authorities for assistance. In the current amendments, the provisions on "foreign exchange balance" requirement for WOFEs have been removed.

- Filing system for reporting production and operation plans to relevant authoritie.
- According to previous regulations, WOFEs are required to submit

their production and operation plans to the authorities for filing. This requirement has, to a certain extent, impeded the daily operation and management of WOFEs. The revised laws on Foreign Capital Enterprises and Sino-foreign Equity Joint Ventures have deleted this item. WOFEs now have greater autonomy in operation.

On the other hand, the industrial restrictions on WOFE have also been gradually lifted. According to the 2002 Industrial Catalogue promulgated by Ministry of Foreign Trade & Economic Cooperation (MOFTEC), wholly owned foreign enterprises can be set up in all the "Encouraged" and "Restricted" sectors except those specified as "exclusive for joint ventures". Compared to the previous edition, the newly released Industrial Catalogue 2002 liberalized more industry areas from "Prohibited" to "Restricted" or "Encouraged" categories.

Currently, the areas in the "Encouraged" category exclusively reserved for joint ventures are considered strategic or of great importance to the nation's social and economic development and security:

- Construction and operation of municipal light railways;
- Construction and operation of civic airports;
- Construction and operation of nuclear power plants;
- Exploitation and mining of copper, lead, zinc and aluminum;
- Repairing, designing and manufacturing of special type or high quality ships;
- Manufacturing of nuclear power units (more than 600 megawatts);
- Construction and operation of comprehensive water irrigation systems;
- Construction and operation of trunk railway line networks;
- Airlines;
- Postgraduate level education institutions;
- Manufacturing of air transportation control network equipment;
- Designing and manufacturing of civilian airplanes and airplane engines;

- Designing and manufacturing of satellites for civilian use; and
- Designing and manufacturing of rocket launchers for civil purposes.

The areas in the "Restricted" category exclusive for joint ventures are:

- Development and production of grain, cotton and oil seeds;
- Processing of wood from precious trees;
- Exploration and mining of special and rare types of coal;
- Printing of publications;
- Smelting and separation of rare earth;
- Manufacturing of automobile cranes with capacity under 50 tons;
- General services (used in areas such as photography, mineral exploration and industries)
- Development of large tracts of land;
- Medical facilities;
- Senior high schools; and Construction and operation of cinemas.

NEWLY EMERGED INVESTMENT FORMS

In addition to setting up EJV, CJV or WOFE, other forms are also available for foreign investment. Since 1995, foreign investors can set up holding companies and foreign invested joint stock limited companies in China. These two new forms of investment are expected to become popular with the Chinese government's relaxation of the laws and regulations in accordance with WTO entry agreement.

Foreign Invested Holding Companies

Foreign invested holding companies (FIHCs) refer to those EJVs or wholly-owned subsidiaries engaging in direct investment activities set up in China by foreign investors. They are set up as separate legal entities with limited liability status and independent from enterprises in which they invest (i.e. their subsidiaries).

In terms of business activities, FIHCs are restricted to engage only in direct investment activities. Since 31st May 2001, FIHCs can also act as a promoter or shareholder of a joint stock company in China.

Unlike foreign manufacturing and trading enterprises, which are restricted to carry on business only in the place of its business registration, FIHCs are able to invest in projects all over China without the need for further registration in the location of project.

However, there is capitalization requirement for FIHCs. An FIHC is required to have registered capital of at least USD30 million. The total loan amount that a foreign invested holding company can borrow shall not be more than four times its actual paid-up registered capital unless approved by MOFTEC. This is clearly different from the case of the general forms of Foreign Investment Enterprises where the limit of debt financing is determined by the total investment of the relevant foreign invested enterprises.

Foreign Invested Joint Stock companies

A foreign invested joint stock company refers to an enterprise or a legal person that meets the following conditions:

- Its capital consists of shares of equal denomination;
- The liabilities of its shareholders are limited to the respective subscription of shares by such shareholders;
- Its liabilities are limited to the value of all its assets;
- The shares are held by Chinese as well as foreign shareholders and the foreign investors together hold more than 25% of total shares.

A foreign invested joint stock company is considered as a type of foreign investment enterprise. With regards to foreign investment in China, all laws and regulations are applicable. In other words, it would be legally impossible to set up a foreign invested joint stock company in the industrial sectors that are prohibited to foreign investment.

The minimum capitalization requirement for registering a foreign invested joint stock company is at least RMB30 million, of which foreign investors must subscribe and contribute more than 25%.

FORMS OF INDIRECT FOREIGN INVESTMENT

BOT

BOT (Build-Operate-Transfer) refers to the cooperative pattern in which the government signs contract with the project company of a private department (in China, it refers to overseas entity), who will, according to the contract, collect funds and construct infrastructure projects. Over an agreed period of time, the project company will own, operate and maintain the project while reclaiming investment and making reasonable profits by charging fees. When the contract period is over, the ownership of the project will be transferred to the government. BOT is mainly adopted in developing infrastructure projects such as toll road, power plant, railway, wastewater processing facilities and subways etc.

International Leasing

Primarily, there are three kinds of leasing trade called financial lease, operating lease and comprehensive lease. Under financial lease, long-term credit is extended by a leasing company to its client, that is, the leasing company will first pay for the purchase of the equipments selected by the client and then lease it to the client. In the course of use of the equipments both parties shall not arbitrarily terminate the contract; the lender shall retain the ownership of the equipments while the client shall possess the right to use it. The client is responsible for the maintenance of the equipment and the leasing company shall collect rents from the client. Upon expiry of the lease, the client may require an extension of the lease or purchase the leased equipment at a negotiated price.

Under this method, the leasing company will provide equipment needed by the client and be responsible for the maintenance and repair of such equipment while the client shall pay rents according to the lease contract and return the equipment upon termination of the lease. The comprehensive lease is a method whereby lease is combined with equity or contractual joint ventures, or lease is combined with inward processing and compensation trade. However, the method of combining lease with equity or contractual joint ventures shall be the portion outside the registered capital of the joint venture.

Compensation Trade

On the basis of credit, the foreign party provides the Chinese party with capital or equipments, technology and raw material, and undertakes to buy a certain quantity of products from the Chinese party. The Chinese partner compensates in installments to the foreign party directly or indirectly by using the products manufactured with the equipment and technology provided by the foreign party or other products agreed upon with the foreign party to repay in installments the equipment and interest. Inward Processing and Compensation Trade, or "san lai yi bu" in Chinese, have been very popular since the beginning of the reforms.

Processing and Assembling

The foreign investors provide raw material, auxiliary material, parts, components or drawings, while the Chinese partner processes them or assembles them into finished products which are then returned to the foreign party for marketing, and the Chinese party charges a fee for the processing; alternatively, the foreign party provides production equipments with or without a price and funds for building the plant premises where the Chinese party collects a processing fee. The cost of production equipments purchased by the foreign partner shall be transferred to the Chinese party in installments using the processing fee.

LAND USE RIGHTS IN SHANGHAI

Various types of foreign investment have been adopted in Shanghai, but the main forms of FDI remain Sino-foreign EJV, Sino-foreign CJV, and WOFE. Inevitably, setting up business involves land use. In China, the ownership of all urban land belongs to the State. Land transactions only involve the land use rights and do not affect ownership of land. Underground natural resources, minerals, and objects buried or hidden in the land shall not form part of the transfer of land use right for valuable consideration.

Currently, investors may acquire land use right through grant or assignment from the government. The maximum terms for granting of land use right are as follows:

- Residential purpose – 70 years
- Land for industrial purpose – 50 years
- Land for the purposes of education, scientific research, culture, public health and sport – 50 years
- Land for commercial, tourism and recreational purpose – 40 years
- Land for comprehensive purpose or other use – 50 years

Unless otherwise stated in the grant contract, or disallowed for planning reasons, the term may be extended on application by the grantee. Unless otherwise stated in the grant contract, land use rights may be assigned or mortgaged by the grantee. Land use rights may also be inherited. Grantees that are FIEs shall not pay ground rent as stipulated in "Measures of Shanghai Municipality for Administration of Land Use by Joint Ventures Using Chinese and Foreign Investment. "Whoever conducts economic activities on the granted land shall, according to regulations concerned, apply to the relevant department of Shanghai Municipality for approval, business registration and tax registration".

Foreigners intending to invest in Shanghai may first consult People's Republic of China's embassies or consulates stationed in their respective country or region for the right procedures. Or you can directly contact the Shanghai Chapter of China's Council for the Promotion of International Trade, Shanghai Foreign Investment Service Center, or the overseas offices of Shanghai Foreign Investment Board, regarding specific issues related to doing business in Shanghai. You may request for an invitation letter by stating the purpose of visiting, proposed dates of stay, and the intended investment projects. Upon receiving a letter of invitation, you can proceed to the nearest embassy or consulate to apply for an entry visa to China.

SETTING UP JV OR WOFE IN SHANGHAI

Before doing business in China, foreign investors need to produce required documents in order to go through the process smoothly. The procedures and required documents for direct investment vary in the forms of business entity, such as Joint Ventures (JVs) and Wholly-owned Foreign Enterprises (WOFEs). In general, there are some basic procedures that FIEs have to follow.

Letter of Intent (LOI) or Memorandum of Understanding (MOU)

This stage is only for those who wish to establish a joint venture in Shanghai. They need to reach a preliminary understanding with their Chinese partners in the form of LOI or MOU. These documents provide a basic description of the project, planned equity distribution among the partners and the amount of planned capitalization. The latter will determine to which level the project approval application will be directed. Although LOI or MOU does not serve any legal binding effect on both parties, it should nevertheless expressly provide provisions concerning exclusivity and confidentiality.

Investment Procedures for Establishment of JVs and WOFEs

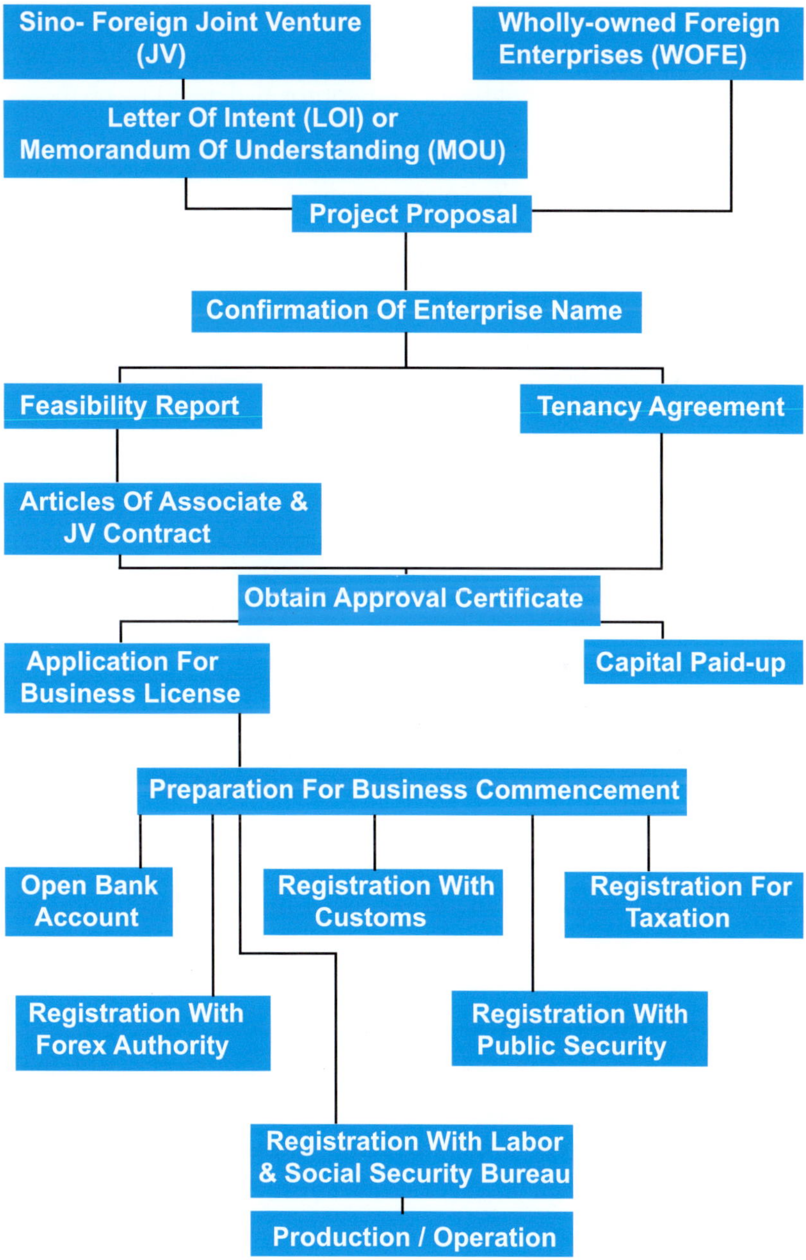

The preliminary agreement is attached to a project proposal to be submitted by Chinese partner(s) to one of the authorities – MOFTEC, Shanghai Development and Planning Commission (SDPC), Shanghai Foreign Economic Relations and Trade Commission (SMERT), or the Shanghai Foreign Investment Board – for approval, depending on the scope and scale of the project.

Project Proposal

For JVs, the next stage is the submission of a project proposal for preliminary scrutiny. Chinese partner(s) should be solely responsible for preparation and submission of the proposal.

For WOFEs, to draft a proposal is the first step to set up the business. It should be prepared by the foreign investors and submitted directly to the authorities in Shanghai. The foreign investor may appoint a local agent to liaise with the government. The foreign investor should thus sign an authorization letter stipulating the agent's scope of services, responsibility and fees.

Generally, the authority shall give an official reply, whether approve or not, within 20 days upon receipt of the proposal and other relevant if required. The approval or disapproval letter will be issued to the foreign investor, if a WOFE, or to the Chinese partner, if a JV. The foreign party in a JV should thus request a copy of this document from the Chinese partner to confirm that the approval is consistent with the agreed terms of the project.

Having received a favorable reply, the Chinese party of a JV or the foreign investor in a WOFE shall apply to Shanghai Industrial and Commercial Administration for company name registration.

Feasibility Study Report

Once the preliminary approval on the project proposal is obtained, a feasibility study shall be prepared. This involves all investing parties. A feasibility study is indeed a more detailed and expanded version of the previous project proposal, however, it must include:

- A general description of the project and the parties involved in the venture;
- Production plans and basic market research;
- Location of the project and reasons for the selection;
- Description and explanation of purposes of equipment and technology to be utilized;
- Organizational structure of the enterprise;
- Environmental protection, employment, construction plans and timetable;
- Capital sources;
- Attachments such as certificate of incorporation and business license, financial reports of the investing company, background information of legal representative, etc.

One important issue in drafting the feasibility study is the "scope of business" for the enterprise. The scope of business should be carefully defined, as it will likely be repeated in the JV contract, articles of association and on the enterprise's business license. The scope of business on a Chinese business license delineates what activities the company is authorized to conduct; the language is usually narrowly construed. Therefore, investors must make sure that the scope of business covers all categories of business activities planned for the enterprise. However, Chinese authorities will reject overly broad or vague language and narrowly interpret those broad or ambiguous words, so the scope must be described in precise terms. This might prevent the enterprise from engaging in business activities that the investor might have believed that they were authorized.

Another key issue to be addressed in the feasibility study is capital contributions. Chinese authorities have a series of guidelines that must be followed with respect to the minimum amount of capitalization for each type of FIE. Specific amount should be confirmed with local agencies and it normally involves no less than USD200,000. There is also a timetable, based on the size of investment, for foreign partners to fulfill commitments for capital contributions. In addition, investors should be aware of the maximum ratio of debt to equity allowed for a JV. There are also regulations requiring audits to confirm the valuation of state-owned assets to be counted as the Chinese partners' contributions to capitalization. Finally, foreign investors' contributions in kind need appraisals from Chinese import and export authorities.

The feasibility study is to be approved by MOFTEC, SDPC, SMERT, or the State Council, depending on the amount of investment; usually, investment more than USD30 million requires state-level approval. However, due to the recent decentralization, those projects that fall in "encouraged" category of the industrial catalogue may be approved by Shanghai government.

Contracts, Articles of Association

For JVs, the next step is the completion of contract, articles of association and the application for formal approval. While the feasibility study is under review, JV partners can work out the actual contract and articles of association. The contract incorporates all understandings and terms from the preliminary agreement, project proposal and feasibility study, though there may be some modifications. Chinese law views the joint venture contract as the fundamental document for the establishment of joint venture. The contract must meet the conditions in China's joint venture law (for equity JVs) or cooperative enterprise law (for cooperative JVs). The feasibility study and preliminary project approval document are included as attachments when the contract is submitted for formal approval.

As WOFEs involve no contract, the documents include a written application for the establishment of the WOFE, a feasibility study report, the articles of association, a list of board directors, an authorization letter of legal representatives, the foreign investor's certificate of incorporation and evidence of credit standing, the written approval of the project proposal and other necessary documents.

For both JVs and WOFEs, the articles of association must be drawn up and submitted as part of the formal application. Under Chinese law, the articles of association are viewed as the code of company governance – similar to the company by-laws or memorandum of association in other legal jurisdictions. Chinese law (JV regulations) contains detailed provisions regarding issues that must be addressed in the joint venture contract and articles of association. It should includes basic information about the enterprise: the enterprise's name and address, scope of business, total capital and organization chart. The JV regulations require that the JV contract and articles of association be written in Chinese. However, a foreign language version of the documents is frequently prepared and the parties may agree that both language versions have equal validity.

Generally, the authority that examines such application shall give a reply (approval or disapproval) within 30 days on receipt of the feasibility study report, contract and the articles of association. After this approval, the Chinese party of a JV or the foreign investor of a WOFE shall apply for the approval certificate. Shanghai Foreign Investment Board will issue the approval certificate within three days upon receipt of the application.

Business License

After obtaining the approval certificate, the WOFE or JV shall register with Shanghai Industrial and Commercial Administration (SICA) and apply for a business license within 30 days after receiving the approval certificate. SICA will issue the business license within 10 working days to projects that have passed the examination. The enterprise is deemed as established on the date when the business license is issued.

Having acquired the business license, the enterprise must register with the State Tax Bureau, the Local Tax Bureau and the Customs House and within a month, and must seek approval from the People's Bank of China in order to open a foreign exchange account or an RMB account with banks in Shanghai. FIEs are also required to register with Shanghai Public Security Bureau to obtain residence permit for foreign personnel and approved family members; and to approach Shanghai Foreign Service Co. Ltd. for the recruitment of local staff.

Preparation of Documents

Apart from the key documents like project proposal, feasibility study report, contract (if any) and articles of association, a number of forms and documents need to be prepared. In the case of a WOFE registration, before submission, documents required include:

- Company registration application form;
- Application for company name;
- Appointment letter of directors;
- Name list of directors;
- Registration form of the legal representative (chairman of Board);
- Environment Impact Report;
- Letter of authorization in case the investor wishes to appoint a representative to handle the registration matters relating to the company in Shanghai;
- Lease agreement with local landlord (foreign investor should enter into a tenancy agreement before processing the registration);
- Certificate of incorporation of the investing company;
- Board resolution that approved the investment in Shanghai;
- Original copies of bank reference;
- Brief resume and photocopies of passports of directors, general manager and assistant general manager.

SETTING UP REPRESENTATIVE OFFICE IN SHANGHAI

An overseas enterprise that wishes to establish a Representative Office (RO) in China may entrust a local agency to handle the issue and submit application on its behalf. Approving authorities may vary in respect to industries:

Approving Authorities for Representative Office Set-up*

Industries	Approving Authorities
Trading, manufacturing, forwarding agency	MOFTEC
Finance, insurance	People's Bank of China
Shipping and agency	Ministry of Communications
Airfreight	Civil Aviation Administration of China
Others	Relevant ministries in accordance with their nature of operations

***In Shanghai, most RO applications are filed with SMERT.**

Preparation of Documents

The applicant shall complete the form of "application for registration of foreign enterprises' permanent office in China" made by Shanghai Industrial and Commercial Administration (SICA), and prepare the following documents:

- The original Application letter, stating scope of business, trading history with China and reasons for RO establishment, etc;
- Brief introduction of the company. This document should include the company's registered capital, turnover, business scope, staffing, and business setups in other part of China;
- Certificate of incorporation certificate, photocopy is acceptable;
- A bank reference letter regarding the capital, transactions and credibility of the company;
- The Letter of Authorization of the chief representative. In the case that chairman of the board is the chief representative, other two directors should sign. In the case that general manager is the chief representative, signatures of the chairman and other two directors are necessary; board resolution is not compulsory but definitely appreciated;

- A brief resume, passport-size photographs, photocopies of identity card and every page of passport of the Chief Representative;
- The Letter of Attorney by appointed chief representative to authorize relevant consulting firms to handle application on behalf of the foreign company.
- Original rental agreement with local landlord. The original title deed and permit of RO of the property must be produced for verification upon submission of the application.

The foreign company should note that offices for ROs are pre-designated by SMERT and mostly located at CBD area in Shanghai. As Chinese regulations regard registered office as the same as the one of operating office, one office premise is allowed to register one company or RO only. Furthermore, Chinese translation shall be provided throughout the documentation if the original documents are in foreign languages. However, Chinese versions produced by those appointed translation houses, often under SMERT, are acceptable.

Examination and Approval

The foreign company or its appointed consulting agent should complete and submit all the relevant documents to SMERT. SMERT will examine the RO application of overseas enterprises, and, if satisfactory, issue approval certificate within 30 days after receiving the application.

Registration with Other Authorities

After receiving the approval, the foreign representative office need to further register with various government bodies before official opening:

- Registration with the SICA to obtain a registration certificate as well as a representative card;
- Registration with the Public Security Administration and preparation of company stamp;
- Registration with the Quality & Technical Supervision Administration to obtain a special identification number;

- Registration with the Authority for Foreign Exchange and opening a foreign currency account with the Authority;
- With approval from the Authority for Foreign Exchange, opening foreign and local currency account with banks in Shanghai;
- Registration with Local Tax Administration;
- Registration with State Tax Administration;
- Registration with the Customs House;
- Registration with Shanghai Foreign Service Co. Ltd. and completing proper formalities for hiring local employees;
- Application to the Labor and Social Security Administration for employment permits for foreign employees;
- Application to the Public Security Administration for residential permit and visas for foreign employees.

The entire registration process will probably take two months. The RO approval certificate would be valid for three years. The registration of the Representative Office is only valid for duration of one year and has to be renewed annually.

EMPLOYMENT PERMIT, EXPERT CERTIFICATE & RESIDENCE CERTIFICATE

A foreign invested enterprise, which is intending to employ foreigners, is required to apply for the employment permit for the foreigners at the Shanghai Labor and Social Security Administration with the following documents:

- business license,
- approval certificate for setting up enterprise,
- application letter,
- the employees' personal information.

After receiving the employment permit, the enterprise may apply for professional visa notification at SMERT, which is authorized by the Ministry of Foreign Affairs. Alternatively, the foreign employee can apply for a professional visa to enter China at a local Chinese embassy or consulate with the fax copy of professional visa notification. After entering China, the foreign employee can apply for employment certificates at Shanghai Labor and Social Security Administration with the following documents: professional visa, employment permit, employment contract, health certificate and photos of the foreign employees within 15 days. With the employment certificate, the foreign employees can apply for residence certificate at the Exit and Entry Division of Shanghai Public Security Administration.

The appointed Shanghai agent of a foreign company can apply for professional visa notification on behalf of the chief representative and representatives. After receiving the professional visa notification, the chief representative and representatives may apply for professional visa at a local Chinese embassy or consulate. Upon entering China, they can apply for employment permit certificate at SICA.

Import & Export

Enterprises that wish to engage in import and export either for "foreign trade" purpose or for "self operation" need to apply for Import and Export Rights at the authorized foreign trade and economic cooperation commission (department or bureau) of all provinces, autonomous regions, and municipalities or specially designated cities where the enterprises are located. In the case of Shanghai, Shanghai Municipal Foreign Economic Relations and Trade Commission (SMERT) has the approving authority.

FOREIGN TRADE COMPANIES

Foreign trading companies may import and export all kinds of products and technology, except those specified as prohibited by MOFTEC. The applicants must meet the following requirements:

- The enterprise must have legal person status with at least one-year history and valid business license;
- Registered capital no less than RMB5 million (or RMB3 million for those in central and western China);
- The enterprise has tax registration and passes the tax audit exercised by relevant taxation authorities;
- Qualified legal representative.

Application materials include:

- Formal application letter produced by the enterprise;
- Certified copy of corporate business license;
- Photocopy of certificate of tax registration;
- Photocopy of the legal representative's identity card; and
- Other relevant documents.

As the final decision is made at state level, SMERT will transfer the application to MOFTEC for approval. Upon receiving the documents,

MOFTEC will check and reply within 10 working days. After receiving approval letter from MOFTEC, SMERT will issue the certificate of import and export enterprise qualification within 5 working days.

The Customs Building in Pudong

IMPORT AND EXPORT FOR SELF OPERATION

Enterprises that wish to import machinery, components and materials for own production purpose or export goods of their own need to have the following qualifications in order to apply for an import and export permit:

- The enterprise has valid business license;
- Registered capital no less than RMB3 million (RMB2 million for those in central and western China, and RMB1 million for research

institutes, high-tech enterprises and enterprises that engaged in machinery and electronic products);

- Tax registration;
- Qualified legal representative.

Application materials include:

- Formal application letter produced by the enterprise;
- Certified copy of corporate business license;
- Photocopy of certificate of tax registration;
- Photocopy of certificate of identification number issued by the Quality & Technical Supervision Administration;
- Photocopy of the legal representative's identity card;
- For high-tech enterprises or enterprises that engaged in machinery and electronic products, relevant certificates are required; and
- Other relevant documents.

Upon receiving of complete documents, SMERT will give its official reply within 10 working days and issue the certificate for approved enterprises.

Usually, the applicants will be asked to produce official approval letters from local customs house and local foreign exchange administration, and reference letter from banks indicating the enterprises' performance in the last three years.

Application forms can be downloaded from the following website:
www.lbn.trade.sh.cn/banfa/biaoge.htm

OTHER MATTERS

According to SMERT's regulation in March 2002, enterprises registered in Pudong New District that apply for import and export rights can enjoy certain privileges with regard to application procedures and qualifications:

- For enterprises wishing to engage in foreign trade business, the requirement for the minimum one-year business history is waived;
- The registered capital can be as low as RMB1 million for applicants for foreign trade business;

- For enterprises that wish to import and export for own operations, the registered capital minimum requirement could be RMB500,000.

After receiving SMERT's approval and certificate, the enterprises need to proceed to other authorities to complete formalities, such as Shanghai Industrial and Commercial Administration, tax bureaus, customs, quality supervision, foreign exchange administration etc. They are also required to send certain number of staff to learn the latest regulations on foreign trade and economic cooperation.

Every year from 1st January to 30th April, those enterprises are subject to SMERT's annual routine examination. Failure in participating or passing the examination will result in being unqualified to continue their import and export business and not able to reapply for the certificate within one year. All enterprises are required to submit reports indicating that they were not ever fined in the past year by local customs house, foreign exchange administration, taxation administration and other related authorities. For enterprises that had changes in enterprise's name, legal representative or registered capital, they have to apply for renewed certificates.

In order to enhance the efficiency and to simplify the procedures, the 2002 annual examination adopted the E-registration. Eligible enterprises could choose to go through the application by filling forms on a website (**www.lbn.trade.sh.cn**). For those not eligible for direct internet application, they could authorize Shanghai Foreign Trade Enterprises Association for registration on their behalf.

Shanghai Foreign Economic Relations and Trade Commission
New Hongqiao Plaza, 55 Loushanguan Road
Shanghai, P. R. China 200335
Tel: (86)(21) 62752200
Fax: (86)(21) 62704708
Website: www.smert.gov.cn
Email: smert@online.sh.cn
Office hours: 9:30-11:30, 13:30-16:30 (Mon, Wed); 9:30-11:30 (Fri)

SHANGHAI PORT

Shanghai Port handles 99% of Shanghai's foreign trade. Its annual passenger traffic and cargo throughput ranks the first in China. The Yangtze River links Shanghai port to inland provinces. The position at the midpoint of China's coastline brings Shanghai convenient access to all seaports in the country. It is a comprehensive and multipurpose commercial port and China's most important port for foreign trade.

Due to the port's limited water depth and overwhelming demand, Beilun Port of Ningbo in Zhejiang Province helps accommodate larger container ships. A crossing-sea bridge is under planning to shorten the distance between Shanghai and Ningbo to just an hour's ride.

To encourage import and export, Shanghai Port is undertaking further expansion and innovation. New berths have been built at Waigaoqiao in Pudong. Luojing Coal Terminal Project involves construction of two discharge berths for ships up to 35,000 tons and four loading berths for ships not exceeding 20,000 tons. A deepwater port for third and fourth generation container ships has also been completed at Jinshanzui in the south of Shanghai. In addition, the grand Yangshan New Port will be built up miles off Shanghai's southeast coastline.

Shanghai Container Terminals (SCT) is a joint venture set up by Shanghai Port Authority and Hutchison Whampoa Ltd, which owns and operates all container facilities in Shanghai.

Taxation

Tax incentives serve as one of the most important factors to be considered by foreign investors while making decisions to invest in China. Currently, the major taxes applicable to foreign invested enterprises (FIEs) include enterprise income tax, value-added tax, consumption tax, business tax, personal income tax, resource tax, land appreciation tax, stamp tax, tax on urban real estate, tax for vehicle usage and license, resources tax, customs duty and vessel tonnage tax. Various tax concessions or breaks are available to foreign invested enterprises (FIEs) under certain circumstances.

TAX APPLICABLE TO FOREIGN INVESTED ENTERPRISES

Over the past 20 years, China has made significant progress and has gained more experience in its tax legislation, in particular, those related to foreign invested enterprises. While China continues to use preferential tax treatment as an important means to attract FDI, it has shifted its emphasis from the amount or quantity of foreign investment onto the quality of foreign investment, believing that will help promote the country's overall and sustainable economic development. It is widely perceived that, with China's

Major Tax Applicable to Foreign Invested Enterprises

	On Business Transactions	On Income	On Property & Behavior	On Natural Resources
Levied By Tax Bureau	• Value-added tax • Consumption tax • Business tax	• Enterprise income tax • Individual income tax	• Urban real estate tax • Vehicle usage and license tax • Stamp duty • Land appreciation tax	• Resources tax
Levied by Customs	Customs duty			
	Vessel tonnage tax			

WTO accession, tax incentives will be focused on encouraging investment in specific industries (e.g. high-tech industries) and specific locations (e.g. Western China).

Enterprise Income Tax (EIT)

So far, China maintains two sets of EIT laws, one for domestic enterprises and the other for FIEs. For domestic enterprises, the EIT is 33%, while for FIEs, the EIT is 30% plus 3% local surtax when no preferential tax treatments are applicable. In fact, there are quite a lot of tax incentives available to FIEs tailored to the specific industries and locations.

For those foreign enterprises who do not have an establishment in China but derive profits, interests, rents, royalties or other income from sources in China, or those who have an establishment or a few establishments in China but their income is not effectively connected with those establishment, has to pay a withholding tax of 20% on such income.

If an FIE is terminated before the prescribed ten-year period, the amount of income tax exempted or reduced shall be repaid to the tax authorities.

In addition, for an FIE engaged in the building of municipal infrastructure with its business period of over 15 years, the EIT can be exempted for the first five years after making profits, and the EIT can be reduced by 50% for the second five years. For an FIE carrying on building infrastructure in Pudong New District, the EIT rate is 15%.

Those who reinvest their profits to set up or extend export enterprises or technologically advanced enterprises with business period no less than five years shall get a full refund of enterprise income tax paid on the reinvested amount.

Individual Income Tax (IIT)

- Individual income tax shall be levied on the following categories:
- Income from wages and salaries
- Income from production or business operation derived by individual industrial and commercial households

Preferential EIT rate for FIEs in Shanghai

<table>
<tr><th colspan="3" rowspan="2">Tax</th><th colspan="2">Tax Rate</th></tr>
<tr><th>Areas other than state-level development zones</th><th>Pudong New District & state-level development zones</th></tr>
<tr><td rowspan="7">Enterprise Income Tax</td><td colspan="2">In a normal year</td><td>Manufacturing enterprise 24%</td><td>Manufacturing enterprise 15%</td></tr>
<tr><td rowspan="2">Tax exemption and reduction period</td><td>1st and 2nd years after making profit</td><td colspan="2">Income tax is exempted for FIEs of a productive nature that are scheduled to operate for more than 10 years</td></tr>
<tr><td>3rd, 4th, 5th years after making profit</td><td>24%*0.5=12%</td><td>15%*0.5=7.5%</td></tr>
<tr><td colspan="2">Extension of tax exemption and reduction period</td><td>Technologically advanced enterprises enjoy tax reduction by 50% for three more years</td><td>Tax rate for technology or knowledge intensive enterprises during their whole period of operations</td></tr>
<tr><td colspan="2" rowspan="3">Tax reduction in a specific year</td><td>24%*0.5=12%</td><td>10%</td></tr>
<tr><td colspan="2">The enterprise can enjoy 50% tax reduction in the year when its export value reaches 70% or more of its total output</td></tr>
<tr><td>24%*0.5=12%</td><td>10%</td></tr>
<tr><td rowspan="4">Local Sur-tax</td><td colspan="2">In a normal year</td><td>3%</td><td>Tax exemption</td></tr>
<tr><td>Tax holidays</td><td>1st and 2nd years after making profit</td><td colspan="2">Tax exemption</td></tr>
<tr><td colspan="2" rowspan="2">Tax exemption in a specific year</td><td colspan="2">Export-oriented enterprises</td></tr>
<tr><td colspan="2">Tax can be exempted in the year when the export value of the enterprise reaches 70% or more of its total output</td></tr>
<tr><td colspan="3">When sending products abroad</td><td colspan="2">Free of tax</td></tr>
</table>

- Income from contracted or leased operation of enterprises or institutions
- Income from remuneration for personal service
- Income from author remuneration; income from royalties
- Income from interest, dividends and bonuses
- Income from lease of property
- Income from transfer of property
- Contingent income and other income specified as taxable

Income from wages and salaries is taxed at nine progressive rates, ranging from 5% to 45%. For foreign taxpayers, the monthly deduction is RMB4, 000 (RMB800 for domestic employees). Income from compensation for personal services, royalties, interest, dividends, bonus, lease of property, transfer of property, contingent income and other kinds of income shall be taxed at a proportional rate of 20%.

Individual Income Tax rates (applicable to Monthly Salaries)

Grade	Monthly Income Taxable (RMB)	Tax Rates (%)
1	The part less than 500	5
2	The part from 500 to 2,000	10
3	The part from 2,000 plus to 5,000	15
4	The part from 5,000 plus to 20,000	20
5	The part from 20,000 plus to 40,000	25
6	The part from 40,000 plus to 60,000	30
7	The part from 60,000 plus to 80,000	35
8	The part from 80,000 plus to 100,000	40
9	The part exceeding 100,000	45

Note: The Monthly Income Taxable refers to the remaining sum of an individual's monthly income after RMB800 or an extra deductible sum is deducted as stipulated by Article 6 of the Law on Individual Income Tax. With regard to foreigners, it refers to the remaining sum of his monthly income after RMB4, 000 is deducted.

Value Added Tax (VAT)

There are three kinds of rates for VAT:

- For taxpayers selling or importing goods, or providing services of processing, replacement and repairs, the tax rate is 17%.
- For taxpayers selling or importing grains, edible vegetable oil, coal gas, natural gas, coal or charcoal products for household use, books, newspapers, magazines, chemical fertilizers, agricultural chemicals and agricultural machineries etc., the tax rate is 13%.
- For taxpayers exporting goods, except otherwise stipulated by the State Council, VAT is exempted.

For enterprises and individuals engaged in production or providing taxable labor service with annual sales volume less than RMB1 million, those engaged in wholesale and retailing with annual sales volume less than RMB1.8 million, and those designated by the tax authority as small VAT payers, the tax rate is 6% on a tax-in price basis.

Business Tax

Business tax shall be levied on the organizations and individuals supplying taxable labors, transfer of intangible assets and sale of real estate. The rate of business tax is 3% for communications and transportation, civil construction, post and telecommunications, culture and sports industries; 5% for banking and insurance, service, transfer of intangible assets, real estate sales industries. The business tax rate for entertainment industries is 5% - 20%. Generally, the tax is applicable to companies in service industries.

Resources Tax

Foreign enterprises that exploit mineral and natural resources within the territory of China are subjected to resources tax.

Land appreciation tax is levied on the income from the transfer of state-owned land use rights, buildings and their attached facilities. The appreciation amount shall be the balance of proceeds received by the taxpayer on the transfer of real estate after deducting the following items:

Resources Tax

Description	Unit	Tax quantum
Crude Oil	Ton	RMB 8-30
Natural Gas	Per thousand m^3	RMB 2-15
Coal	Ton	RMB 0.3-5
Other non-metallic mine crude ore	Ton	RMB 0.5-20
Ferrous metal mine crude ore	Ton	RMB 2-30
Solid salt	Ton	RMB 10-60
Liquid salt	Ton	RMB 2-10

Land Appreciation Tax

The portion of the appreciation amount	Tax Rate %
not exceeding 50% of the deductible amount	30
between 50% to 100% of the deductible amount	40
between 100% to 200% of the deductible amount	50
exceeding 200% of the deductible amount	60

- The sum paid for the acquisition of land use rights;
- Cost and expenses for land development;
- cost and expense for the construction of new building and facilities, or the assessed value for used properties and buildings;
- The taxes related to real estate transfer;
- Other items as stipulated by the Ministry of Finance.

Stamp Duty

Activities involving purchases and sales, processing, contracting, leasing, transportation, storage, loan lending, property insurance, technology contract and property transfer vouchers, business account books and licenses are subject to stamp duty. The minimum rate is charged at 0.005% and the maximum is 0.1%.

Stamp Duty in Detail

Item	Taxable Amount	Tax Rate %
Purchasing and sales contract	Purchasing and sales amount	0.03
Processing and contracting contract	Income from processing	0.05
Construction project, exploration and survey and design contract	Fee collected	0.05
Building and installation project contract preparation	Sum from the lease	0.03
Property leasing contract	Sum from the lease	0.1
Goods transportation contract	Transportation fee	0.05
Storage and preservation contract	Fee collected	0.1
Money lending contract	Sum lent	0.005
Property insurance contract	Income from insurance fee	0.1
Technology contract	Sum specified	0.03
Property right transfer contract	Sum specified	0.05
Business account book	Each account book	RMB5

Consumption Tax

Consumption Tax shall be levied on sale of goods. Entrusted processing, organizations and individuals within China that import the consumer goods listed in the Detailed Rules for the Implementation of the Interim Regulations of the People's Republic of China on consumption tax, the consumption tax consists of 11 taxable items and 25 tax rates (for details refer to the rules for the Implementation of Interim Regulations of the People's Republic of china on consumption tax), with 3% as the minimum and 45% as the maximum. The tax on the goods used in production process shall be levied on the basis of the price of the goods, whereas the tax levied on yellow rice wine, gasoline and diesel shall be on the value per unit quantity basis. Consumption tax shall be exempted for the taxable consumer goods exported by the taxpayers, except those taxable consumer goods subject to export restrictions imposed by the Government.

Vehicle Usage and License Tax

The rate for vessels and vehicles is assessed on the basis of weight capacity and their types or number of seats if they are passenger vehicles. The tax payable for passenger vehicles with no more than 10 seats is RMB55 each per six months; for those with 11-30 seats, the tax payable is RMB65 each per six months; for those with 31 seats or more, the tax payable is RMB75 each per six months. The tax payable for vehicles is RMB24 per net ton per six months; for small motorcycles, it is RMB10 each per six months; for general motorcycles, it is RMB18 each per six months; and for motor tricycles, tax payable is RMB24 each per six months.

Customs Duty

After China's entry into WTO, the aggregate import duty was lowered to about 12%. According to a notice given by the General Customs Administration at the end of 2001, 7,316 items are still taxable. However, tariffs are categorized into four groups, namely, most favored nation rate, conventional tariff rate, special rate and normal rate.

Imported goods are taxed on its normal C.I.F. (cost, insurance and freight) prices. Customs has the authority to determine the taxable price if the goods' C.I.F. is not quotable. The tariff rates are set in a detailed checklist. For some special imported goods, tariff is exempted. For specific imports, the rates are checkable at Shanghai Customs' website (www.shcus.gov.cn).

Export commodities produced by the FIE itself, except those prohibited from export by the State and those subject to other State regulations, shall be exempted from export tariff.

The necessary import goods, such as raw materials, fuel, parts and components, accessories or packaging materials for FIEs to produce export products, are regarded as bonded goods and are supervised by customs.

TAXATION ADMINISTRATION

The Law on Taxation Administration is the basic law on taxation and is also a procedural law. All enterprises, no matter domestic or foreign, are treated equally under this law.

Taxation Authorities

Shanghai Municipal Finance Administration (SMFA) is the department of the municipal government in charge of fiscal revenue and expenditure, financial and tax policies and state-owned capital funds of the municipality. It also combines the functions of Shanghai Municipal Administration of State Taxation and Shanghai Municipal Administration of Local Taxation.

SMFA provides operational guidance to district and county bureaus of finance and exercises vertical administration over all taxation establishments within the municipality.

Tax Registration

Joint ventures, wholly-owned foreign enterprises (WOFEs), representative offices and other similar organizations in China are required to register with tax authorities within a limited time prescribed in the relevant regulations. In general, this has to be completed within 30 days after the business license is issued. Registrations have to be filed with both the State Taxation Administration and Local Taxation Administration. The two administrations have their own tax jurisdictions. To be qualified as an ordinary VAT payer and be able to issue VAT invoices, a taxpayer has to undertake VAT registration as well.

Upon completion of the tax registration, the tax authorities will issue a tax registration certificate that must be renewed every year. During the registration process, you should discuss with the tax officers and confirm the basis for tax calculation and filing. The consequence of late registration involves a maximum penalty of RMB10,000 or even the repeal of your business license. Any changes in business license or operating office require re-registration with the tax authorities.

Taxation Control

The tax year is the calendar year, i.e., from 1 January 1 to 31 December. If a foreign enterprise experiences difficulties in computing its taxable income on the calendar-year basis, it may apply to the tax authorities to adopt its own financial year as the tax year. For an enterprise that commences business within a calendar year or has operated for less than 12 months in a calendar year, the actual operating period will be treated as the tax year.

An FIE is required to file its annual tax returns, audited financial statements and the auditor's report to the tax administrations within four months after the end of the year. The application for deferring the filing of the above documents should also be submitted within this period of time. The penalty for failure to file the above documents within the prescribed time limit is calculated on 0.2% per day on the tax amount overdue.

Any taxpayer or withholding agent who fails to perform tax registration procedures, fails to set up accounting system and fails to keep its business records within a prescribed time limit is required to redress these within a prescribed period. Any failure to redress will be subject to a fine of up to RMB 2,000; if the violation is serious, a fine up to RMB10,000 will be imposed.

Any taxpayer or withholding agent who fails to file tax returns within the prescribed time limit is required to redress this and fine RMB 2,000. A fine over RMB2, 000 but under RMB10,000 will be imposed if the taxpayer or withholding agent fails to meet the due date the second time.

The fine for tax evasion which involves such unlawful activities as forgery, falsifying or concealing relevant information, fraud, or failure again to pay tax within the prescribed time period is up to but not more than 500% of the tax due. In most of the above cases, serious offenders will be prosecuted.

Tax Audit

The tax authorities have the power to carry out tax audits to examine taxpayer records, relevant documents and information. Refusal of tax examination will be subject to a maximum penalty of RMB50, 000. In general, tax authorities shall provide an enterprise a written notice about the impending tax audit. You should adopt a cooperative attitude, but do not forget to check with the tax officers on the exact scope of audit and ensure that they show you their staff identity cards.

Tax Reporting and Payment

Different taxes have different reporting periods and payment due dates. In general, Foreign Enterprise Income Tax is paid on a quarterly basis, VAT and Business Tax are usually on a monthly basis, and IIT is on a monthly basis too. Tax authorities will not send you tax returns. Instead, you should collect blank tax returns from tax offices, complete them and file accordingly.

Acceptable ways of submission differ from place to place and depends on the nature of the tax. For some locations, reporting via mail is acceptable, while at some other locations, submission must be made in person. Shanghai has recently launched electronic filing. Maximum penalty for late filing of tax returns is RMB10,000 plus 50% - 500% of the tax involved. Late payment of tax will involve a fine of 0.05% a day on the tax owing. Withholding agents who fail to observe these obligations will be subject to a maximum penalty of 500% of the tax involved. Under the tax regulations, you may apply to the tax authorities for deferred tax filing and payment.

PREFERENTIAL TAX POLICIES IN PUDONG NEW DISTRICT

- The income tax of foreign-invested manufacturing enterprises shall be levied at a reduced rate of 15%.
- Foreign-invested enterprises scheduled to operate for a period over 10 years shall be exempted from income tax in the first two years starting from the profit-making year and be granted a 50% reduction in the next three years.
- High-tech projects invested by foreign investors in Pudong New District may enjoy 10% income tax rate for another three years after the period of tax exemption and reduction. Export enterprises with foreign investment shall pay their income tax at a reduced rate of 10%when their annual export sales value amounts to more than 70% of the annual sales value.

- The income tax of foreign-invested enterprises in the field of ports, energy and transportation shall be levied at a reduced rate of 15%. If the operation period of the above-mentioned enterprises is over 15 years, the income tax shall be exempted for the first five years starting from the first profit-making year and entitled to a 50% reduction for the next five years.
- The buildings or houses built or purchased by foreign investors for their own uses shall be exempt from property tax for five years, starting from the transaction date.
- Foreign financial institutions, such as foreign banks and JV banks, with its paid up capital over USD10 million in Pudong New District or its operating fund as a branch allocated by its headquarters over USD10 million, after approval, may enjoy a reduced income tax rate at 15%. Starting from the first profit-making year, the abovementioned institutions can enjoy income tax exemption for one year and 50% income tax reduction for another two years.

Accommodation

HOUSING MARKET IN SHANGHAI

In July 2001, the municipal government of Shanghai made an official announcement on the merger of the two residential markets – the overseas-selling market and the domestic-selling market. Before that, two tiers of land price system prevailed, in respect of developer's nationality. Usually, overseas developers were charged at a much higher price than their Chinese counterparts even for the same piece of land. Therefore, with development cost brought up, those properties labeled "overseas-selling" were unnecessarily expensive.

After the merger, the property market in Shanghai is open and all the previous restrictions for purchase and lease to both foreigners and locals have been removed. Unlike in Beijing, foreigners may now live wherever they choose in Shanghai, whether in local housing, serviced apartments or star hotels. The only legislative requirement is that foreigners need to register at the Foreign Affairs division of Public Security Administration within 72 hours after signing a lease agreement.

HOUSING AREAS

The types of houses available in Shanghai vary but could be mainly categorized as Old Houses, Grade-A Apartments, Serviced Apartments, Budget Apartments and Villas. Everyday, an increasing number of foreigners are in search for a new home with a certain budget in mind. To avoid frustration and disappointment, foreigners should keep their expectation in line with their budget. Once a property of choice has been located, the inevitable negotiations will begin, and this is why having an experienced agent working on your behalf becomes crucial. Although often neglected, foreigners should be particularly aware of the Residential Contract of the property. Finally but most importantly, foreigners should ensure that the agency they choose offers satisfactory follow-up services so that assistance will be available throughout the whole process.

The urban area of Shanghai can largely be divided into three main areas, namely, Puxi (old town), Hongqiao and Gubei New Area, and Pudong.

Hongqiao and Gubei New Area, a large newly built residential area to the west of downtown, used to be a prime choice for expatriates living in Shanghai. The gregariousness was largely due to its proximity to the Hongqiao International Airport and relative convenience in commuting to the city – both within a 15-20 minutes' ride by taxi. Facilities catering to foreigners include international schools, restaurants and supermarkets like Carrefour, making settling down a relatively easy process. Housing, in the form of apartments, serviced apartments and villas are plentiful and often of the highest quality in town – most have their own gardens and playing grounds for kids. Although the area's popularity has been partly compromised by newly emerged residential properties across the municipality, the area remains attractive to new arrivals, particularly those with families. It is a suitable place where one may enjoy the peace and tranquility.

Usually the house rental in this area ranges from USD20-30 per sq m monthly, with property management and furniture included. Approximately, the rental for a 3-bedroom house is USD4,500 per month, and for a 5-bedroom one, it often requires USD7,000 or higher.

Pudong has recently emerged as a hot place for foreigners who want to be in closer touch with Shanghai's latest developments. With the establishment of Pudong International Airport along with the maturing Lujiazui Finance and Trade Zone, this area is set to become the new settlement for foreigners in Shanghai. In fact, housing in Pudong boasts green surroundings and fresher air which are precious in the industrialized metropolis. The constant improvement in infrastructures, enhanced accessibility and establishments of many MNCs in Pudong have promoted the demand for housing in this area. Most of the houses there are new and well designed. Large open spaces, luxurious gardenized habitat, less traffic,

Changning Equatorial Serviced Apartments

deally located in downtown Changning listrict, the apartments offer easy access to hopping centers, banks and restaurants, s well as to the Metro (Zhongshan Park tation). Overlooking Zhongshan Park, he 16-storey serviced apartments offer a reath-taking view with its 126 units of vell-furnished, comfortable and private ccommodation. Managed by an nternational hote management group, Changning Equatorial Serviced Apartments ffer high quality hotel comfort and usiness services

Changning Equatorial Serviced Apartments
889 Changning Road, Shanghai 200050
Tel: 86-21-62100889
Fax: 86-21-62109008
Email: rsosha@public9.sta.net.cn

subway and bridges add additional merits to its living environment as well as lift up cost of living.

Rental in Pudong is now comparable to that in Hongqiao and Gubei. A 3-bedroom apartment can easily cost the lessee a sum more than USD4,000 per month. For two to three-storey villa, the price can be as high as USD9,000. Puxi area, literally means west to the Huangpu River, is Shanghai's old town. It is currently still undergoing an urban redevelopment. Most of Shanghai's shopping centers, commercial streets, service providers and municipal-level government bodies are located there. Living in downtown ensures convenience to work, public transportation, bars, restaurants, and business partners. However, noise, air pollution and traffic congestion also coexist. Districts like Xuhui, Luwan, Huangpu and Jing'an have been foreigners' favorites as these areas are often equivalent to prosperity, elegance and nobility of Shanghai. A large number of architecturally aesthetical old houses and villas are set back from major roads and lie quietly in peaceful lanes and alleys, adding much character to the city landscape of Shanghai. Many foreigners find that old houses in Puxi area are the perfect choice in trying to find "a home away from home". Surprisingly, despite lack of green space and all-too-often traffic jams, demand for these properties far exceeds supply; most of such properties that become available will only appear in the market for a few days. Of course, brand-new condominiums are also numerous in town, providing extended choices for expatriates and their family members.

Monthly rental in Puxi may be as low as USD1,200 for a one-bedroom apartment for singles, with a space measured between 80-120 sq m. Normally, unit rent hardly exceeds USD20 per sq m per month unless tenants ask for very high-end facilities or amenities. With a monthly budget of USD3,000, expatriates are able to lead a decent and comfortable life in the heartland of Shanghai.

HOTELS

As Shanghai grows into one of the world's most expensive cities in terms of expatriate living expenses, hotels in Shanghai maintain fairly reasonable prices and services for overseas visitors who need a short-stay in the city.

The hotel business was among the first sector of China opened for foreign investment. International leading hoteliers and foreign funds have been flooding Shanghai since the early 1980s.

Five-star hotels' lobbies are usually luxurious and tastefully decorated

In China, only tourist hotels are able to accept foreign guests. Under the China National Tourism Administration (CNTA), most of them are star-rated hotels. By the end of 2001, Shanghai had 300 such hotels with an average occupancy rate of 67.5%. With China's entry into WTO, Shanghai's high-end hotels are facing great potentials, but fierce competition too. To date, there are 16 five-star and 26 four-star hotels in Shanghai, among which are many of the international renowned chains of hotels, such as the Marriott, Four Seasons, Sofitel, Novotel, Hilton, St. Regis, Holiday Inn and Shangri-La. Most of them manage to maintain an occupancy rate at above 70%. Jin Jiang, the largest hotel management in China and Shanghai's local brand, now manages 53 hotels nationwide; in Shanghai, four five-star hotels, five four-star hotels and 10 three-star hotels are under its brand name, including Jin Jiang Hotel, Jin Jiang Tower, Huating Hotel, Peace Hotel and Park Hotel, most situated at the city's premier locations.

Room rates vary in locations and the rank of the hotel. A comparison of published rates of selected hotels in Shanghai are shown as follows:

	Grand Hyatt	Sofitel Hyland	Novotel Atlantis	Novotel Yuanlin
Location	Pudong	Nanjing Road	Pudong	Botanic Garden
Rooms	555	400	303	223
Stars	Five	Four	Four	Three
Room rate (USD)				
Superior	320	150	160	100
Deluxe	365	170	180	-
Suite	510	300	240	160
Villa	-	-	-	200-300

With the ever-growing power of web community, discounted rates, often involving substantial savings, are readily available for budget-conscious travelers to check out for wiser bookings in Shanghai.

Local Talents

TALENTS IN SHANGHAI

Talent is a fundamental factor for corporate development. Its importance looms larger as many foreign enterprises in China are localizing workforce and even management team.

Currently, Shanghai is home to 50 universities and colleges. On the top of the list are Fudan University, Shanghai Jiaotong University, Tongji University, East China University of Science and Technology, East China Normal University, Shanghai International Studies University, Shanghai University and Shanghai University of Finance and Economics. The total enrollment of students at these institutions is more than 250,000. Fudan University and Shanghai Jiaotong University are two key universities greatly promoted by the central government.

List of Universities and Colleges in Shanghai
1. Fudan University (www.fudan.edu.cn)
2. Tongji University (www.tongji.edu.cn)
3. Shanghai Jiaotong University (www.sjtu.edu.cn)
4. East China University of Science & Technology (www.ecust.edu.cn)
5. Donghua University (www.dhu.edu.cn)
6. East China Normal University (www.ecnu.edu.cn)
7. Shanghai International Studies University (www.shisu.edu.cn)
8. Shanghai University of Finance & Economics (www.shufe.edu.cn)
9. Shanghai University (www.shu.edu.cn)
10. Shanghai Polytechnic University (www.sust.edu.cn)
11. Shanghai Engineering Technology University
12. Shanghai Fisheries University (www.shfu.edu.cn)
13. Shanghai Second Medical University (www.shsmu.edu.cn)
14. Shanghai Traditional Chinese Medicine University (www.shutcm.edu.cn)

15. Shanghai Normal University (www.shtu.edu.cn)
16. Shanghai Marine Transport College
17. Shanghai Electric Power College
18. Shanghai Applied Technology College
19. Shanghai Foreign Trade College
20. East China College of Politics & Law
21. Shanghai Sports Education College
22. Shanghai Music Academy
23. Shanghai Opera Academy
24. Shanghai Sanda College
25. Shanghai Customs Institute
26. Shanghai Medical Equipments Institute
27. Shanghai Publishing & Printing Institute
28. Shanghai Electrical Machineries & Technology Institute
29. Shanghai Tourism Professional Institute
30. Shanghai Lixin Accounting Institute
31. Shanghai Finance Institute
32. Shanghai Police Institute
33. Shanghai Commerce Institute
34. East Sea Professional Skills Institute
35. Xinqiao Professional Skills Institute
36. Shanghai Second Industrial University
37. Shanghai Electronics & IT Skills Institute
38. Shanghai Xinjian Professional Institute
39. Shanghai Jiguang Professional Skills Institute
40. Shanghai Transportation Professional Skills Institute
41. Shanghai Industrial & Commercial Professional Skills Institute
42. Shanghai Maritime Professional Skills Institute
43. Shanghai Municipal Administration Professional Skills Institute
44. Shanghai Jianqiao Professional Skills Institute
45. Shanghai Science & Technology Professional Institute
46. Shanghai Top Information Technology Professional Institute
47. Shanghai Bond Professional Skills Institute

48. Shanghai Agriculture & Forestry Professional Skills Institute
49. Shanghai Jianfeng Professional Skills Institute
50. Shanghai Zhongqiao Professional Skills Institute

Universities are also luring investments

With an area of 550 square kilometer, Pudong New District alone has almost two million permanent residents and the figure is estimated to reach three million by 2010. A large part of the number is non-Shanghainese, who have migrated to this city from other regions of China since the 1990s. With its attractiveness, Shanghai has announced "Implementation Measures on Attracting Domestic Outstanding Persons to Shanghai" so as to expand its base of human resources. Since its economic reforms, Shanghai has received more than 17,000 Chinese students back from overseas, nearly one fifth of all students having returned to the motherland. These returnees have set up over 900 enterprises with total investment of USD250 million.

Currently, Shanghai has 1.13 million professionals and researchers in different fields of expertise, accounting for 19% of the city's employees. In accordance with the development strategy, the municipal government pays special attention to attracting talents in fields like information technology, microelectronics, finance and insurance, venture capital, biotechnology, pharmaceutical, agriculture and international law. This may help Shanghai become more competitive.

OVERSEAS CHINESE SCHOLARS & STUDENTS

In the 1930s, the Chinese government encouraged and sent students abroad for studies. In the 1950s and 1960s, the first and second generation of Chinese students came back, most having completed studies under government sponsorship or scholarship offered by western nations.

Approximately, 400,000 Chinese students went aboard for studies in 103 countries in the last two decades, making China the world's largest source of students studying overseas. To date, one in every three students who have completed their studies has come back to the motherland. More than 130,000 Chinese with educational and working experience in developed countries have returned. They took up key roles in domestic organizations and foreign invested companies, set up their own businesses, and formed a new growth engine of the economy. A new phrase of "hai gui pai", or returned overseas generation, is now included in the latest published Chinese language lexicons.

The number of returnees shows a growing trend, with an increase of 13% every year. Many regard Shanghai as their foothold to develop their career in China. They have been making remarkable contributions to the city's economic development and social progress. After China's entry into the World Trade Organization (WTO) in December 2001, together with rigorous foreign investment inflows, the return of Chinese from overseas will hit an unprecedented high level.

The municipal government of Shanghai has implemented policies and measures to provide these students much flexibility to start their businesses and a more conducive living environment. Among others, it introduced a residence scheme on 15 June 2002, similar to the permanent residence status in the US, to attract talented foreigners or domestic citizens from other Chinese cities to take up residence in Shanghai. Under this scheme, the new migrants do not have to renounce their original nationalities or residence registration while enjoying the same benefits as local Shanghainese.

ADVANTAGES IN HUMAN RESOURCES

Shanghai has clear advantages in human resources vis-à-vis other cities of China:

- Employees who have received at least secondary school education account for 11.4% of the total workforce, ranked 2nd in the nation.
- The population of technical professionals is more than 200,000.
- Shanghai's educational system consists of elementary and secondary education, vocational skill training, higher education and adult education. Apart from universities and colleges, it also has 467 senior high schools, 533 junior high schools and 1,021 primary schools. There are also over 200 vocational and technical schools.
- Shanghai has a mature human resource market and a complete regulation system to attract national and local talents. It is also one of the regions where the most returned Chinese students converge.
- Shanghai is one of China's educational centers that produce high-end degree holders. The city has generated more than 60,000 doctorate and master's degree holders from its universities and institutes since 1978.

Postgraduates Graduated in Shanghai (1990-2001)

Year	Doctorate	Master	Undergraduate		
			Enrolment	Studying	Graduated
1990	300	2,746	3,127	9,568	3,322
1991	342	2,739	3,019	8,969	3,256
1992	343	2,124	3,668	9,855	2,526
1993	368	2,489	4,282	11,045	2,884

1994	442	2,363	5,130	13,090	2,859
1995	606	2,742	5,301	14,713	3,355
1996	627	3,233	6,507	16,835	3,860
1997	890	3,585	6,725	18,460	4,475
1998	1,090	3,552	7,874	21,162	4,642
1999	1,323	4,288	9,413	24,420	5,611
2000	1,307	4,546	12,652	30,614	5,868
2001	1,487	5,330	15,826	39,043	6,817

- So far, more than 811,000 professionals and technicians are working in various industries in Shanghai. An increasing number of them have shifted from the state-owned organizations to private or foreign enterprises.

Professionals and Technicians in Shanghai 2001 (a breakdown by industry)

Industry	Non-State-owned (1,000)	State-owned (1,000)
Engineering	37.8	166.8
Agriculture	3.1	2.9
Healthcare	18.1	91.5
Scientific Research	0.1	16.4
Education	1.1	163.5
Economic Research	19.4	101.2
Accounting	23.1	73.6
Statistics	2.5	7.0
Media	-	5.8
Translation	-	2.0
Arts	-	3.8
Others	9.3	62.3
Total	114.5	696.8

TALENT HUNTING

The Foreign Enterprises Service Co. Ltd. (FESCO) acts as a personnel department for all foreign companies in Shanghai and offers recruitment services. In most cases, FIEs are not able to deal with the very complex Chinese social security system. It is preferable for foreign employers to pay a monthly service fee (normally at RMB200 per staff) to let FESCO handle the social security fees on their behalf. In addition, all representative offices of foreign companies in Shanghai are legally obliged to employ their staff through FESCO.

Established foreign companies may also appoint Chinese HR agencies and many consulting firms, chambers of commerce and headhunters in Shanghai to locate qualified personnel for them. Direct recruitment from universities is also viable, but foreign employers must meet the October/November deadline every year when graduating students are still looking for jobs. In fact, this is the best way for many reputable MNCs in building up their local workforce as the brightest students in Shanghai are longing for employment with high profile foreign companies at reasonable expected remunerations.

Alternatively, job fairs, career websites and local publications provide complementary options for recruitment. However, foreign companies in Shanghai are advised to consult experienced agencies or other established FIEs to avoid unnecessary frustrations and trouble during the procedure.

Office Space

OFFICE PROPERTY MARKET IN SHANGHAI

Prior to the 1997-98 Asian financial crisis, office buildings were in great shortage as many multinationals and domestic companies from other provinces swarmed into this international metropolis. Strong economic growth has fueled the office property market and Shanghai's office supply has soared over a short period. The rental cost of the offices in some key areas once surpassed that of Hong Kong and Tokyo. Shanghai Center on Nanjing West Road, for instance, charged USD3 per sq m per day in 1996.

But as many construction projects were completed and came to the market couple with demands slowed down, the cost of office rental fell gradually. In the first half of 2000, rentals had dwindled to less than half of what it previously had been. But the recovery of the global economy since 2001 and China's entry into the WTO re-boosted Shanghai's real estate market. More foreign companies are now inspired to set up their offices in Shanghai than anywhere else in China. It is expected that the vacancies will drop to as low as 3% from its peak of nearly 50% in 1998.

Office buildings in Puxi need facelifts

In year 2001, demand for office space in Shanghai grew strong. According to the research report of Global Office Occupancy Costs by DTZ Debenham Tie Leung in January 2002, the costs of office space in Shanghai Pudong and Shanghai Puxi had already increased by 26.39% and 4.98% respectively. That was a sharp contrast with the tendency in most major cities in North America, Europe, Japan and other nations. The growth rate of office rental in Pudong ranks 2nd in the world, after Detroit whose growth rate was 28.26%.

PREMIUM AND GRADE-A OFFICES

Currently, there is still an abundance of office space in Shanghai for business people to choose. Besides size and quality, location is always a key determinant in defining Shanghai's Premium and Grade-A office buildings. According to DTZ (Shanghai) Research, the vacancy levels edged down to 12.4% in the 3rd quarter of 2002, with 12.8% in Puxi and 11.5% in Pudong. Rental averaged at USD0.61 per sq m per day, with USD0.58 in Puxi and USD0.7 in Pudong. Total rental growth for Premium and Grade-A offices was about 11% in 2001 and is forecast to be 5% in 2002. The total stock of Grade A office space in Shanghai was estimated at 3.18 million sq m by the end of September 2002.

Brand new office building in Lujiazui

The preferred locations in the city include the Lujiazui Finance and Trade Zone, Huaihai Middle Road and Nanjing West Road.

Annual Rents of Offices in Asia Pacific

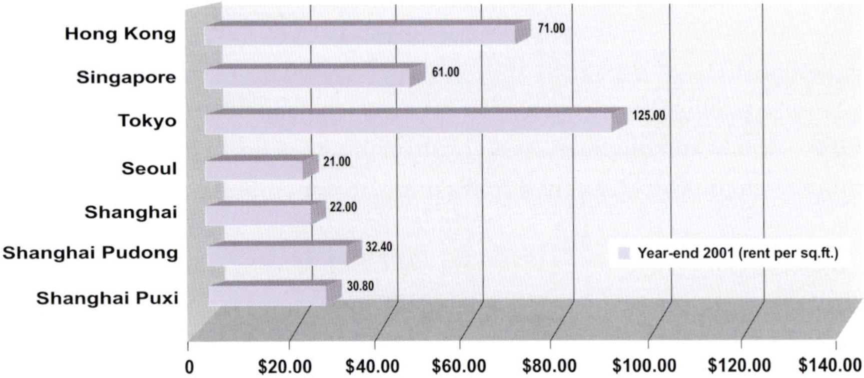

Source: DTZ Debenham Tie Leung

Grade A Office Rents: May 2002

District	Achievable Rent			Change From (USD)			
	USD/Sqf/Yr	Euro/Sqm/Yr	RMB/Sqf/Mth	Last Mth	3 mths ago	From Bottom (Q1/00)	Peak (Q4/95)
Grade A	26.39	328.62	18.18	2.5%	5.3%	45.9%	-67.6%
Hongqiao	19.84	247.06	13.67	2.2%	5.0%	24.8%	-70.6%
Central Puxi	26.84	334.31	18.50	2.7%	4.2%	45.5%	-66.9%
Lujiazui CBD	33.42	416.18	23.03	3.8%	7.4%	49.9%	-40.9%

Strata-Title Office Values: May 2002

District	Asking Price (Gross)			% Change From			
	USD/Sqf	Euro/Sqm	RMB/Sqf	Last Mth	3 mths ago	12 mths ago	Peak 97/Q1)
Prime	218	2,713	19,393	2.3%	3.8%	4.3%	-20.4%
Puxi	240	2,992	21,384	0.4%	0.4%	2.6%	-21.0%
Lujiazui	213	2,647	18,918	8.7%	9.2%	9.3%	-12.8%

Major Office Buildings in Shanghai

Location	Office Buildings
Lujiazui Finance and Trade Zone	Jinmao Tower, ICBC Tower, China Shipping Tower, New Shanghai Int'l Plaza, Huaneng International Plaza, Lucky Plaza,

	Shanghai Securities Plaza, HSBC Tower, Tomson Financial Center, Sinopec Tower, Times Plaza, The Merchants Tower, Zhongcheng Tower
Nanjing West Road	Shanghai Center, Plaza 66, CITIC Pacific Plaza, New Times Plaza, Kerry Center, Southern Securities Plaza, East Sea Plaza
Huaihai Middle Road	Hong Kong Plaza, CP Tower, Yongxin Plaza, New Hualian Tower, Radisson Plaza, Central Plaza, Lippo Plaza, Shanghai Plaza, Goldbell Plaza, Shui On Plaza

Alternatively, cost-conscious or large office space seekers may consider locating their offices in some secondary office areas around Shanghai, for example, along Yan'an East Road.

(From left) Yu An Mansion, Tomson Financial Center, Huadu Mansion in Pudong

SIGNING A LEASE

It is a prerequisite that any foreign investors enter into a tenancy agreement with local landlord before they submit the application for establishing a business entity in China. Often given short time span, foreign businessmen need to take additional caution in hastily signing a lease.

Under the Chinese law, one office unit can only accommodate one business registration, that is, you cannot register two companies or representative offices under the same address. The landlord is not allowed to lease one unit to two businesses concurrently as the original title deed needs to be produced for verification upon the submission of application to the relevant authorities.

Moreover, only those specifically designated office buildings are able to accommodate foreign companies' establishments in Shanghai. A list of those offices buildings is obtainable from Shanghai Municipal Foreign Economic Relations and Trade Commission (SMERT) or readers may refer to Business Directory at the back of this Guide.

Upon signing the lease agreement, tenants must be aware that the agreement needs to be a standard government-issued lease that is mandatory to process the registration of business. Other things require extra notice including:

- the typical lease term is 2 years with or without the option to renew for another term;
- though rents are frequently quoted in USD, they are payable either in USD or in RMB;
- under the Chinese law, sub-leasing is not allowed as one must obtain a leasing license prior to finding lessees. Tenants are not able to apply for such license simply because they do not have the title deed;
- subject to negotiation, tenants may ask for a rent-free fitting-out period between 1 to 3 months;
- depending on landlords, tenants can expect facilities like suspended ceiling, lighting, sprinkler system and air conditioning upon handover;
- as the Chinese is the only official language in China, Chinese version of the agreement has legal status. However, it is suggested that the agreement be written in both English and Chinese.

DTZ Debenham Tie Leung 戴德梁行
International Property Advisers

The article is contributed by DTZ Debenham Tie Leung Shanghai.

OVERVIEW

Immediately preceding the first anniversary of China's entrance into the WTO, Shanghai was awarded an honor of its own: being named the host city for World Expo 2010. With this grand event also comes the realization of promises for infrastructure and other urban investments. The successful bid will only buttress Shanghai's property markets further as the city promotes itself to a global audience.

Year 2002 saw the industrial property market in Shanghai strengthen dramatically. Average rentals from the major industrial development zones increased over 8% to a range of 0.55-0.96 RMB per sq m per day. At RMB 1,700-3,013 per sq m, industrial property sales values rose slightly from its Q4 2001 level of RMB 1,600-2,961 per sq m.

Recent developments in Shanghai's industrial property market include:

- The 1st Shanghai Industrial Real Estate Expo was held at Shanghai International Convention Center between 23rd-25th November 2002. DTZ was the Sole Professional Consultant.
- The Foreign Investment Service Center in Minhang Development Zone was set up to better service its clients.
- Waigaoqiao Free Trade Zone entered into an agreement with SHMC to setup a Citywide network, an Administration MIS network, and a Logistic Business network in Waigaoqiao.
- Zhangjiang New Development Science Park was inaugurated in Zhangjiang, Pudong, which covers around 3.7 sq km.

Meanwhile, MNCs kept making their investment commitments in Shanghai:

- Unilever established its international procurement center in Shanghai.
- Volvo Construction Equipment Group committed to establish its China Headquarters in Shanghai.
- WMGS, a subsidiary of Wal-mart group, kicked off its business in Waigaoqiao Free Trade Zone and indicated that a procurement center of Wal-mart will soon be set up.
- HSBC Group Service Center, a back office processing unit, became fully operational on June 14 in Shanghai, which makes HSBC the first foreign bank to set up such operations in Shanghai.
- In June, Japan's Toppan Printing, manufacturer of Visa, MasterCard and other creidt cards, planned to invest USD167 million to build a color filter factory in Shanghai to be open by 2005. It will be built in Shanghai Zizhu Science Park and become the first factory of its kind in China.
- In April, Telecommunication giant Alcatel and leading Chinese venture capital company NewMargin Ventures formed a joint venture with a USD18 million seed fund – T-Fund – to support innovation in telecommunication. Alcatel expects to spend 15% of its worldwide budget on R&D in Shanghai.

INDUSTRIAL FACILITIES

The lull in newly constructed premises that Shanghai experienced in Q3 2002 ended as developers rushed to finish their projects before the end of the year. The 235,772 sq m of newly completed properties is more than twice the amount completed in the last quarter, but a 15% drop from the same period last year. While the new supply increased dramatically, take-up instead decreased by 19%. This is expected as companies survey the new buildings and finalize their leases and does not represent a trend.

The huge influx of new supply increased the vacancy rate by 1 percentage point and also created a negative pressure on rents manifested in a drop of RMB0.03. This decrease in asking rentals comes from higher-priced zones - Caohejing, Jinqiao, and Waigaoqiao. This indicates that other zones are becoming more competitive as they gain experience. However, the drop in asking prices does not necessarily represent a drop in sales prices; it is merely an adjustment to reflect the real value of the property.

Industrial Premise Rental Index

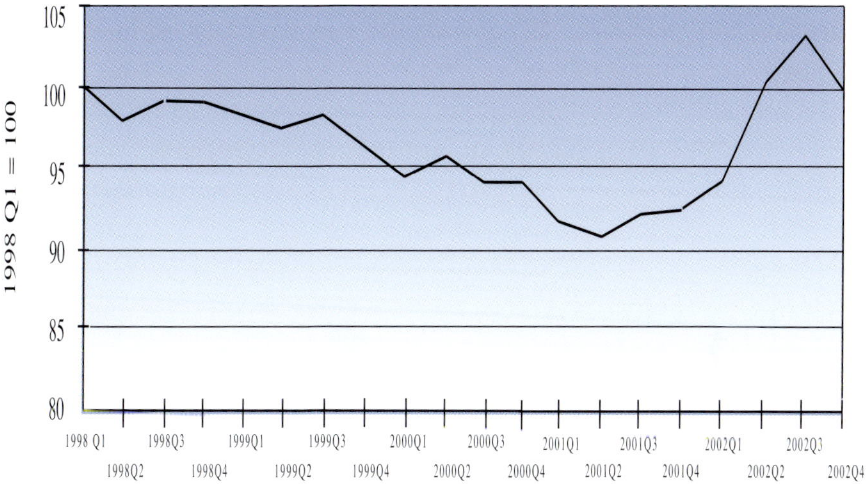

Source: DTZ (Shanghai) Industrial

Rentals in Shanghai Industrial Development Zones

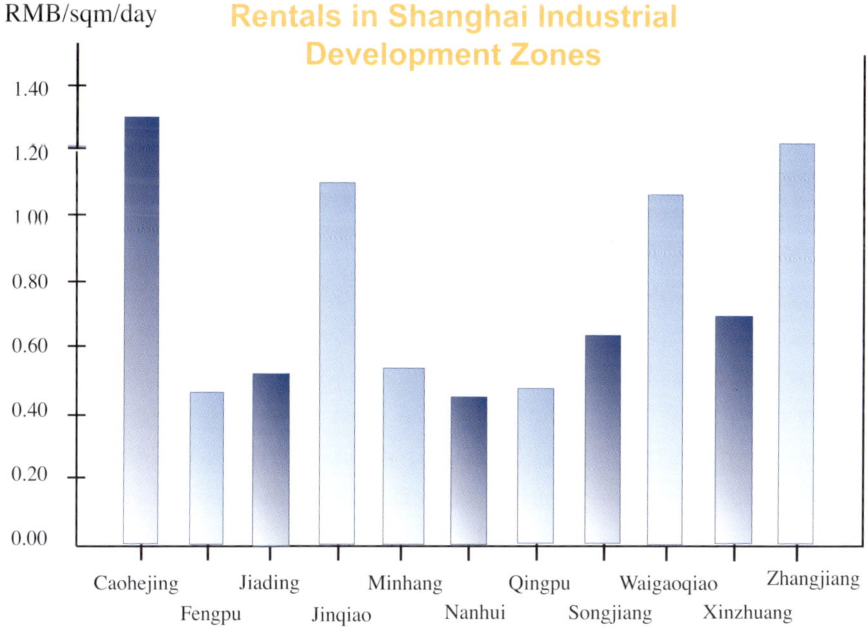

Source: DTZ (Shanghai) Industrial

Zhangjiang, Qingpu, and Songjiang completed 45,000 sq m, 30,000 sq m, and 25,000 sq m of new industrial facilities, respectively. This pushed up vacancy rates by 350% and 133% in Zhangjiang and Qingpu, respectively. Songjiang had no vacancy last quarter, but now has 32,000 sq m of empty facilities.

Vacancy Rates of Industrial Properties

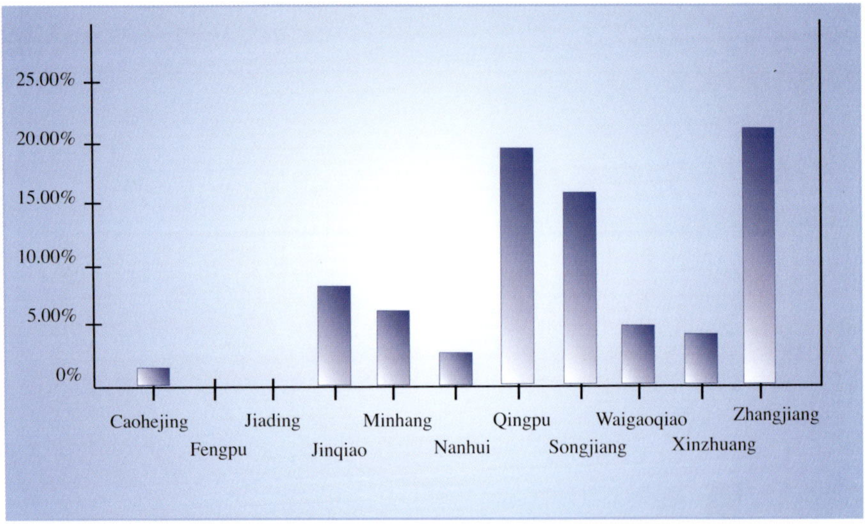

Source: DTZ (Shanghai) Industrial

LAND

The land price of Shanghai's 11 premier industrial development zones remained almost unchanged at USD53.4 per sq m, except for a slight increase in Nanhui and a slight decrease in Waigaoqiao. It stayed for unchanged in every other zone. Caohejing is still the most expensive industrial estate, with its land price over USD160 per sq m. Jingqiao, Waigaoqiao and Zhangjiang, all state-level industrial parks, are on the second tier with price close to USD100 per sq m. Smaller or relatively less prominent industrial zones, such as Fengpu, Jiading, Nanhui, Qingpu and Songjiang, offered their land at a significantly lower level, sometimes under USD25 per sq m. However, investors must be aware that the size of the project, the amount of

the registered capital, negotiating strategies and investment positioning may have tremendous influence on the actual selling price of the land.

Industrial Land Asking Prices as at Q4 2002

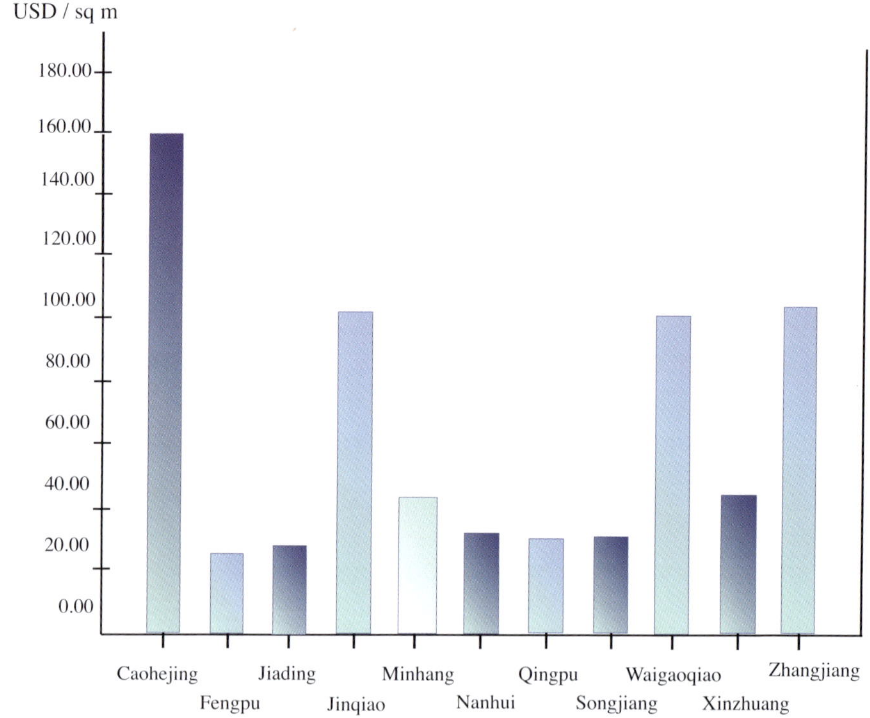

Source: DTZ (Shanghai) Industrial

Selected Industrial Property Transactions in Q4 2002

Company	Location	Space (m^2)	Industry
Metal	Waigaoqiao	5,000 (g.f.a)	Metal Processing
Arvin Meritor	Waigaoqiao	2,100 (g.f.a)	Auto System
Bearing Points	Shanghai Pudong Software Park	5,000 (g.f.a)	Software R&D
TOWA	Zhangjiang Hi-tech Park		IC Packing and Testing

Sigma	Fengpu	20,000 (Land)	Auto Accessory
SPX	Fengpu	33,000 (Land)	Valves

Source: DTZ (Shanghai) Industrial

FORECAST

The effects of China's WTO membership have begun to surface in Shanghai's industrial property market. The government continues to fund infrastructure and other investment projects; more international companies are moving their operations to Shanghai; many domestic companies are also flooding into Shanghai. These factors ensure that the demand for industrial properties will still increase steadily in the next eight months or more. However, due to Shanghai's increasing land costs, some companies are relocating their manufacturing facilities to other cities. The governments of neighboring cities like Suzhou, Hangzhou, and Wuxi, are attempting to grasp the opportunity by improving the quality of their property as well as business environment.

Financial Services

In the 1930s and 1940s, Shanghai was the financial center of the Far East. Now, Shanghai's financial industry is being rejuvenated again. A complete financial market system, with the central bank as its leader, big state-owned banks as its mainstay and various Chinese non-state-owned and foreign financial institutions incorporated, is in a formation process.

Altogether, China's banking system consists of the central bank, namely, the People's Bank of China (PBC), 3 wholly state-owned policy banks, 104 commercial banks, and a large number of urban and rural credit cooperatives. The three policy banks are China Development Bank (CDB), Export-Import Bank of China (EIBC) and Agricultural Development Bank of China (ADBC). The four big wholly state-owned commercial banks are Industrial and Commercial Bank of China (ICBC), Agricultural Bank of China (ABC), China Construction Bank (CCB) and Bank of China (BOC).

Most of major Chinese banks have set up branches in Shanghai. In addition, a large number of local and foreign banks, with transaction networks scattered all around Shanghai, offer a diverse range of banking services and great convenience for business and daily lives in Shanghai.

Bank of China Tower (left) and Bank of Commnication Financial Building (right) in Pudong

BANKING AND FINANCING

Banking Service

Generally, banks operate from Mondays to Fridays, from 9 am until 5 pm. Foreign banks have slight difference: Japanese banks tend to close at 4:30 pm, and Americans at 6 pm. Half days are the rule on Saturdays. Chinese banks in the tourist areas are often open on Sundays so that travelers can convert their foreign currencies.

For foreigners working in Shanghai, it is advisable not to keep all their money in the local currencies, typically, enough to maintain themselves for 2 to 3 months. Once foreign exchange is converted to Chinese currency, it is troublesome to convert it back to your home country's money. To do this, one must present the original receipt issued when converting the money at beginning. Except BOC, other Chinese banks only accept US dollar, Japanese yen and Hong Kong dollar.

Generally, most foreigners living in Shanghai do not have accounts with Chinese banks. Money is typically deposited overseas and cash is accessed at Automated Teller Machines (ATMs) around Shanghai by using their credit card. The main banks offering this service are Bank of China (daily limit of RMB2,500), Industrial and Commercial Bank of China (daily limit of RMB3,000) and Citibank. ATMs using the Cirrus (toll free 800-424-7787) and Plus networks can be easily found throughout the city. You will receive the official bank exchange rate on all transactions and may be charged a withdrawal fee by your home bank. In addition, credit cards are becoming more popular and acceptable at most of the department stores, airlines and hotels.

To open a multi-currency account in a local bank, for example, Bank of China, you should take your passport and Residential Card. You may open a passbook account in either US dollars or Chinese currency. Accounts are interest bearing. To withdraw cash, you need to visit the bank with your passbook.

Financing Issues

China implements a highly regulated system of foreign exchange control and strictly monitors foreign debt levels. FIEs are free to take foreign currency loans from foreign banks under certain conditions. However, when borrowing from overseas parties (including offshore branches of foreign banks and other parties such as foreign shareholders) or from foreign banks in China (such as mainland branches of foreign banks or joint venture banks), FIEs are required to undertake foreign debt registration at State Authority for Foreign Exchange (SAFE). Failure to do so may cause penalties to the borrower and the inability to remit money or to repay the debt.

FIEs can also seek Chinese currency financing, especially when foreign exchange controls were tightened and exchange rate risks were high. Chinese currency financing is available from Chinese banks and, subject to some geographical and other restrictions, from licensed foreign banks in China. When lending to FIEs, banks usually require credit support. The most common forms include guarantees from foreign shareholders, bank guarantees with standby letters of credit (particularly in RMB borrowings), and mortgages over real estate and equipment. Security given by FIEs in favor of foreign banks (including mainland branches of foreign and joint venture banks) must be registered at SAFE.

Foreign-funded enterprises in China are permitted to apply for loans from Chinese domestic banks with overseas assets of the foreign partners as mortgages. Inter-company loans (i.e. loans between Chinese domestic companies) are not permitted except through a financial intermediary. Foreign-funded enterprises are permitted to apply for A- or B-share issues. Insurance services may be provided to foreign investments in some areas.

SHANGHAI PUDONG DEVELOPMENT BANK

Shanghai Pudong Development Bank (SPDB), incorporated on 9 January 1993 with the approval of the People's Bank of China, is a shareholding commercial bank headquartered in Shanghai. On 23 September 1999, SPDB launched a 400 million A-share on the Shanghai Stock Exchange. The biggest shareholder remains to be the Shanghai Municipal Finance Administration.

By the end of 2001, the bank's total assets, outstanding balance of all deposits, and outstanding loans of all deposits, reached RMB173.7 billion, RMB148.3 billion and RMB97.2 billion, respectively, increasing sharply by 33.9%, 39.7% and 39.0% respectively over 2000. After-tax profits totaled RMB1.1 billion. The bank has set up branches in Shanghai, Beijing, Tianjin, Chongqing, Hangzhou, Nanjing, Guangzhou, Shenzhen, Kunming, Zhenzhou, Dalian, Ningbo, Suzhou, Wenzhou and Wuhu etc, with a network of 240 outlets in total. In 2001, Shanghai Pudong Development Bank was ranked 321st in the world's top 1,000 banks by UK's Banker Magazine.

SPDB's premises, No.12 the Bund, used to be the headquarters of HSBC in the past

SPDB provides retail and commercial banking services, such as taking deposits from the public, providing short-term and long-term loans, handling domestic and overseas settlements, discounting bills and notes, issuing financial bonds, acting as an agent for issuing, cashing and underwriting of government bonds, trading government bonds, conducting inter-bank financing, trading in, and acting as an agent for foreign exchange trading, providing letter of credit (LC) services and guarantees, acting as agent for accounts receivable and payable, acting as agent for insurance, providing safe box services.

Currently, SPDB is expanding its loan services. People who wish to travel but are temporarily short of money can apply for loans of up to RMB50,000. The maximum loan term is one year.

FOREIGN BANKS IN SHANGHAI

Many foreign banks have established either branches or representative offices in Shanghai. Those heavyweights are now playing increasingly important roles in Shanghai's financial sector.

Foreign banks are prosperous in Shanghai

By the end of 2001, there were 69 foreign financial institutions in Shanghai, of which 53 were foreign banks. Most of them are among the top banks in the world. Of these foreign-invested banks, 45 are the branches or representative offices of foreign banks and the rest are foreign-invested but local-registered banks. The total assets of these foreign banks reached USD23.6 billion, which accounted for more than half the foreign financial institutions assets in China. In Shanghai's financial market, foreign banks have already snapped an 11% share in foreign currency deposits and 48% in foreign currency loans.

By the end of May 2002, the total number of foreign banks operating in Pudong alone has risen to 37, 18 of which were authorized to conduct Chinese Renminbi (RMB) business. Foreign currency deposits and loans with the banks totaled USD1.63 billion and USD9.71 billion respectively. Four of the banks are from North America, while 18 are from Europe and 15 from Asia. Their assets totaled USD12.9 billion.

So far, the major businesses of foreign banks remain at financing large joint-venture projects and serving foreign customers who need access to western banking services. With China's accession to WTO, foreign banks in Shanghai are expected to gain more rights to offer retail banking services for the Chinese people.

Foreign Banks in Shanghai 2001

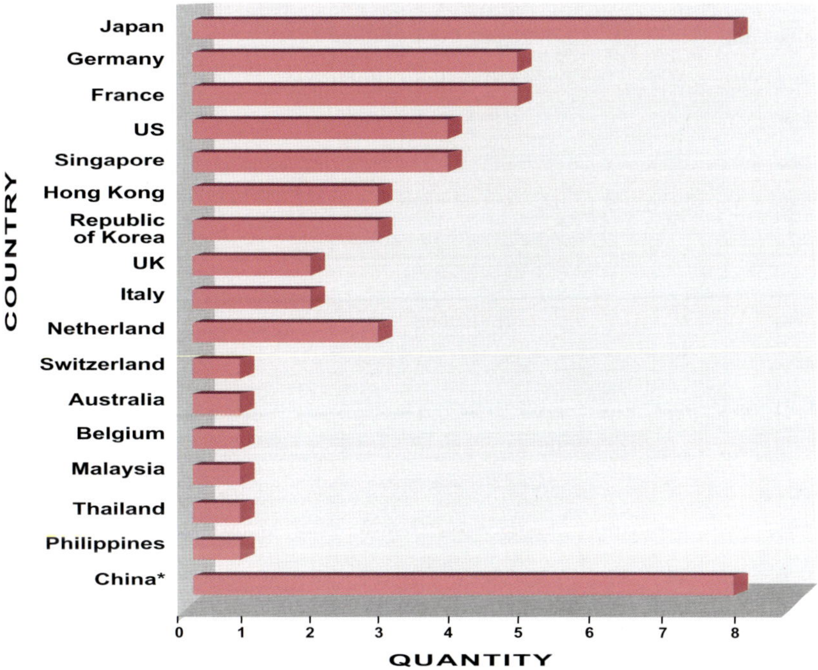

* Foreign-invested but China-registered banks.

Major Foreign Banks in Shanghai

Country of Origin	Bank Name	Establishment Date
Australia	ANZ Banking Group Limited	21 Jun. 1993
Belgium	Kredietbank N.V.	30 Nov. 1996
France	BNP Paribas	16 Dec. 1996
France	Societe Generale	18 Dec. 1994
France	Credit Lyonnais	07 May. 1991
France	Credit Agricole Indosuez	23 Apr. 1991
France	Natexis Banque	10 Jul. 1995
Germany	Bayerische Landesbank Girozentrale	17 Mar. 1998

Germany	Deutsche Bank AG	30 Nov. 1998
Germany	Commerzbank AG	17 Jul. 1994
Germany	Dresdner Bank AG	10 Apr. 1993
Germany	Westdeutsche Landesbank Girozentrale	17 Mar. 1998
Hong Kong	Hang Seng Bank Limited	26 Jun. 1997
Indonesia	PT Bank International Indonesia	30 Nov. 1998
Japan	Dai-Ichi Kangyo Bank	30 Dec. 1991
Japan	Industrial Bank of Japan	13 Apr. 1991
Japan	Sanwa Bank	13 Apr. 1991
Korea	Korea Development Bank	29 Dec. 1995
Korea	Hanvit Bank	16 Jun. 1995
Korea	Hana Bank	15 Aug. 2000
Netherlands	ABN AMRO Bank	19 Mar. 1993
Netherlands	ING Bank	15 Nov. 1994
Philippines	Metropolitan Bank and Trust Company	05 Mar. 2001
USA	Citibank N.A.	23 Apr. 1991
USA	Bank of America	20 Jun. 1991
UK	HSBC	11 Jan. 1991
UK	Standard Chartered Bank	15 Jan. 1991
Singapore	Development Bank of Singapore	29 Dec. 1994
Singapore	OCBC Limited	10 Jan. 1991
Singapore	Overseas Union Bank	16 Sep. 1999
Taiwan	First Sino Bank	24 Jan. 1997
Thailand	Chia Tai International Finance Company	30 Mar. 1992
Thailand	Bangkok Bank	07 Jun. 1993

Note: the list does not reflect recent M&A among a few banks.

INSURANCE

The People's Insurance Company of China (PICC) dominated the insurance sector in Shanghai until the mid-1980s. At that time, insurance premiums totaled about RMB460 million per annum. The monopoly of PICC was ended in 1986 when a few new insurance companies were approved. Since then, the industry has developed rapidly. Shanghai was opened to foreign insurance companies in 1992.

Currently, there are 32 insurance companies in Shanghai, of which 3 are wholly state-owned, 15 are state shareholding companies, 8 are foreign-funded and 6 are Sino-foreign joint ventures. These companies work in four business fields: 14 in property insurance, 16 in life insurance, 1 in reinsurance and 4 as insurance agencies.

Shanghai's insurance sector has registered remarkable revenue growth in recent years. In 2001, Shanghai's insurance industry brought in RMB18 billion in premiums, an increase of 42% over 2000. Of the total premiums income in 2001, property insurance accounted for RMB4 billion, or 22%, a 14.5% increase over 2000. Life insurance income increased 52.4% to RMB14.0 billion in 2000, accounting for 78% of the total premium income.

The existing major players in Shanghai's insurance market are PICC, China Pacific Insurance Company and Ping An Insurance Corporation.

Insurance Companies in Shanghai 2001

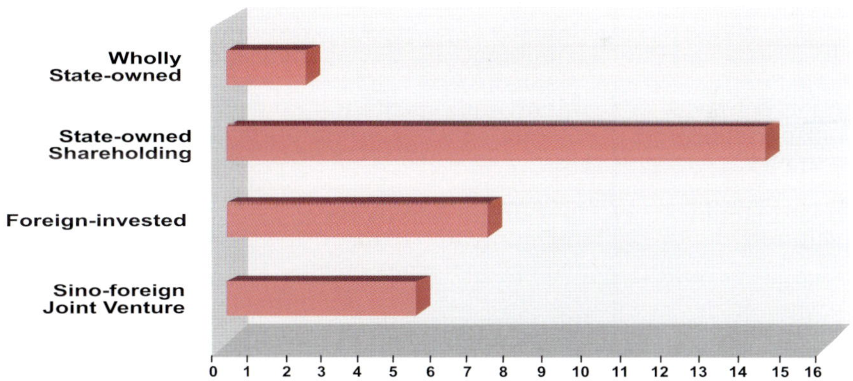

Insurance Premiums of PICC Shanghai Branch

Policy	Content	Rate
Insurance that can be bought by FIEs during the construction period		
Import Cargo Transportation Risk Insurance	For importation of building materials and equipment	0.2 - 0.5%
Constructors' All Risk Insurance	For civil engineering or installation period	Depending on actual circumstances
Liability Insurance for the Third Party of Constructors	Supplementary to the Constructors' All Risk Insurance	Depending on actual circumstances
Vehicle Insurance	All kinds of cars, planes and ships	Decided according to the nature of use and seating capacity etc.
Employers' liability Insurance	Accidental injuries and deaths of the employees during employment	Based on the period insured
Insurance that can be bought by FIEs during the management period		
Import & Export Transportation Risk Insurance	Import equipments and raw materials and export products	According to actual circumstances
Public Liability Insurance	To shift the liability for indemnity due to the damage to the passengers or other third party during the operation period	According to business nature and the number of rooms etc.
Cash Insurance	To insure all the negotiable securities	Depending on actual circumstances
Employees' Fidelity Insurance	To insure against the economic loss caused to the insured by the fraud or dishonesty of his employees (All employers should insure the loyalty of certain employees)	Depending on actual circumstances

Computer Insurance	All kinds of software and hardware	Depending on actual circumstances
Property Insurance	Insured against the loss of properties	Depending on actual circumstances
Property Insurance Plus Theft Insurance	Supplementary to Property Insurance	An extra 0.1 -0.3%
Property All Risk Insurance	Identical with property insurance, only it is more extensive	An extra 0.1 -0.3%
Machine Damage Insurance	In addition to property insurance, this policy insures against the risk of damage due to human error or malfunction of electrical appliances	Depending on actual circumstances
Transportation Vehicle Insurance	Same as in the construction period	Depending on actual circumstances
Employees' Liability Insurance	Accidental injuries and deaths of the employees during employment	Based the period insured

Note: (1) If an insurance policy is taken in a foreign currency, premiums shall also be paid in the same foreign currency. (2) Enterprises can choose the insurance coverage at their own discretion. The details of the insurance coverage are available in the relevant insurance companies.

CAOHEJING HIGH-TECH PARK

Introduction

Caohejing High-tech Park (CHTP) is the only state-level development zone able to offer preferential policies granted by the state government for both economic and technological development zones (ETDZs) and high-tech parks (HTPs). Established in 1986, the 189 ha CHTP was among the first batch of state-level development zones in China.

Located in Xuhui District, southwest of Shanghai, CHTP proves to be an attractive space for investors. It is only 11 km from downtown of Shanghai, four km from Xujiahui – the center of the district, and seven km from Hongqiao International Airport. Among all development zones in Shanghai, it is one of the nearest to the city.

Investment Climate

More than 800 enterprises have already resided in CHTP, among which more than 300 are foreign-invested. More than 20% of the enterprises are recognized as high-tech enterprises by the municipal government.

Major domestic enterprises include Datang Mobilecom, Zhongxin Telecommunication, China Unicom, China Netcom, Fuxin Group and Huaxin Bio-technology, while Taiwanese enterprises include Acer, Inventech, Microtek, Sinowealth Electronics, Kimpo Electronics etc.

Over 40 world-renowned enterprises have invested and set up subsidiaries in the park, such as GE, Lucent, 3M, Intel, Emerson, AMP, Raychem, Dupont, Agilent, Tandem, Lattice and Foxboro from the USA, Air Liquid and Schneider from France, Philips from the Netherlands, Clariant and Mettler-Toledo from Switzerland, Bell from Belgian, Spirax Sarco from Britain, NTT, Toshiba, Mitsui, Epson and Ricoh from Japan, and Nortel from Canada.

The zone is dedicated to the development of advanced technologies in the fields like microelectronics, IT products, software, aerospace technology, telecommunication, laser, bioengineering and new materials.

Caohejing High-tech Park Development Corporation
Tel: (86)(21) 64859900, 64850000
E-mail: contact@caohejing.com
Website: www.caohejing.com

MINHANG ECONOMIC AND TECHNOLOGICAL DEVELOPMENT ZONE

Minhang Economic and Technological Development Zone (MHETDZ), first established in 1983, was among the first 14 state-level ETDZs approved by the State Council in 1986. The total development area is 3.5 sq km.

Located at the southwest part of Shanghai, near the upstream of the Huangpu River, it is 30 km away from the downtown, 27 km away from Hongqiao International Airport, and 15 km away from Longwu Port. By the end of 2000, RMB800 billion had been injected into MHETDZ for infrastructure development.

By the end of 2001, MHETDZ had attracted 154 projects, of which 48 were

Attending trade fairs is a way to promote investment

invested by multinationals, including 28 Fortune 500 companies, such as Bristol-Myers Squibb, Coca Cola, Fuji-Xerox and Ingersoll Rand. Contractual investment had amounted to USD2.2 billion.

Major industries in the zone include mechanical and electronic equipment manufacturing, bioengineering, pharmaceuticals, and food and beverage. A branch of Shanghai Normal University has also been set up within the zone.

Minhang United Development Corpopration
1251 Jiangchuan Road, Minhang,
Shanghai, P.R. China 200245
Tel: (86)(21) 64300888
Fax: (86)(21) 64300789
Email: smudc@online.sh.cn
Website: www.smudc.com

HONGQIAO ECONOMIC AND TECHNOLOGICAL DEVELOPMENT ZONE

Initially established in 1983, Hongqiao Economic and Technological Development Zone (HQETDZ) is a new commercial and business zone in Shanghai that combines office and exhibition facilities, residential area, restaurants and shopping centers. There are even plots of land reserved as consular area for foreign consulates. Japan, the US, Australia, Korea, Singapore and Pakistan have already signed land use or exchange contracts, and general consulates of India, Denmark, Korea, the Netherlands, Switzerland, Argentina, Romania, Israel and Cuba in Shanghai have set up their offices in the zone.

HQETDZ is located in Changning District, west of Shanghai's urban district. It is bounded by four roads of Zhongshan West Road, Gubei Road, Xianxia Road and Hongqiao Road. It extends over an area of 65.2 ha, including 31.09 ha for construction area, 19.54 ha of green land and 14.39 ha for roads. The development zone is only 5.5 km away from Hongqiao International Airport.

The total contractual investments has almost reached USD2.8 billion, with utilized foreign investments totaling USD2.26 billion. Major investors come from Hong Kong, Taiwan, Japan, Singapore and the US. Multinationals who have set up offices in the zone include 3M, GE, Nokia, Ericsson and LG.

Shanghai Hongqiao Economic and Technological Development Zone United Development Co., Ltd.
34-35th Floor, New Town Center
83 Loushanguan Road, Shanghai
P.R. China 200336
Tel: (86)(21) 62756888
Fax: (86)(21) 62194505
Website: www.shudc.com

ZHANGJIANG HIGH-TECH PARK

Introduction

Zhangjiang High-tech Park (ZJHTP) is located in the central part of Pudong New Distrct. It was approved by the State Council in July 1992 and forms one of the four industrial bases of Shanghai. For its prominence and importance in the country's high-tech developments, it is widely known in China that "Zhongguancun in the north, Zhangjiang in the south". "To focus on Zhangjiang" has emerged to be a national strategy to expedite the development in high-tech areas of China.

ZJHTP covers an area of 25 sq km and is surrounded by a picturesque golf course, villas, parks, international exhibition centers and foreign language school. It connects conveniently with the downtown area of Shanghai and the Pudong International Airport by highways. In addition, Metro Line No. 2 ends in the ZJHTP.

Investment Climate

The emphasis of ZJHTP has been put on information technologies, bioengineering, pharmaceuticals as well as real estate. By the end of June 2002, ZJHTP had successfully attracted 457 projects with total contractual investment of USD6.6 billion. It now hosts the State Biotech and Pharmaceutical Base (Shanghai), National Information Technology Industrial Base, National Science and Technology Innovation Base, Pudong Software Development Park, Pudong Java Application Research Center, Motorola, Afataike, LG, SmithKlineBeecham, Roche, Rhodia and United Signals.

Integrated circuit (IC) industry plays a pivot role in the development of information technology. Several world-class IC manufacturers have staged their investment in the park, such as SMIC (USD1.48 billion), Hongli Semiconductor Shanghai and Tailong Semiconductor (USD400 million).

The park is divided into six functional sections, namely, technological innovation, research and education, high-tech pilot and test, residential, commerce and service, and industrial section.

The Administrative Committee of Zhangjiang High-tech Park
200 Longdong Avenue, Pudong New District
Shanghai, P. R. China 201204
Tel: (86) (21) 50801818
Fax: (86) (21) 50800686
Email: zjpark@zjpark.com
Website: www.zjpark.com

JINQIAO EXPORT PROCESSING ZONE

Introduction

Approved by the State Council in 1990, Jinqiao Export Processing Zone (JQEPZ) was among the first batch of Export Processing Zones (EPZs) in China. Separated by Jinqiao Road, the eastern area is a 6 sq km Jinqiao High-tech Park – as approved by the Ministry of Science and Technology in April 1998, and a 1 sq km commercial district; the western part is designated to be a residential area, or the Biyun International Community.

Located in the middle of Pudong New District with a planned area of 20 sq km, JQEPZ adjoins Lujiazui Finance and Trade Zone in the west and Waigaoqiao Free Trade Zone in the north, and it is close to Zhangjiang High-tech Park that sits to its south. The EPZ is 25 km away from Hongqiao

International Airport, 15 km away from Pudong International Airport, and 9 km from Waigaoqiao Port.

Investment Climate

As the total industrial output of JQEPZ stood at RMB29.74 billion for the first half of 2001, up 50% over the same period of the previous year, the zone accounts for nearly one third of industry volume of Pudong. More than 90% of its output comes from high-tech industries.

By the end of June 2001, JQEPZ had attracted 398 projects, most in "industry", with total committed FDI approaching USD9 billion. Investment per project averages as high as USD22.5 million. To date, one in every two multinationals that came to Pudong have taken residence in JQEPZ. Among them are global players like General Motors, Siemens, NEC, Nestle, Hewlett-Packard and Bell. Though a bonded zone initially for export processing, JQEPZ encourages development in electronics, information technology, vehicles and automobile components, electrical household appliances, bioengineering and pharmaceuticals.

In August 2000, JQEPZ was conferred the "ISO14000 State-level Model Zone", the third in China and the first in Shanghai of its kind.

Jinqiao Export Processing Zone Administrative Committee
28 New Jinqiao Road, Pudong,
Shanghai, P.R. China 201206
Tel: (86)(21) 58991818
Fax: (86)(21) 58991812
Website: www.goldenbridge.sh.cn

WAIGAOQIAO FREE TRADE ZONE

Waigaoqiao Free Trade Zone (WFTZ) claims to be China's first and biggest free trade zone. It was approved by the State Council in June 1990 to be set up on an area of 10 sq km. So far, 7.52 sq km has been occupied for international trade, bonded warehousing, commodity display and export processing.

Located in Pudong, WFTZ is at the entrance of the Yangtze River. From there, it takes a 40-minute drive to reach Hongqiao International Airport, 20 minutes to Pudong International Airport, 35 minutes to Shanghai Railway Station and 30 minutes to the city center.

In 2000, the total industrial output of the zone was RMB70.7 billion; total export and import reached USD7.62 billion and USD5.64 billion, respectively. In the same period, Waigaoqiao Port, dedicated to WFTZ, handled 9.64 million tons of cargo and 1.21 million TEUs.

By the end of 2001, 5,022 projects had been set up in the zone with total investment reaching USD6.56 billion. Investors come from 58 countries and regions worldwide. Major MNCs such as GE, Toshiba, IBM, Philips and Intel have invested heavily in the zone. Among others, Waigaoqiao Automobile Exchange Market and a biochemical and medical instruments market are two key projects.

In 2000, 181 new foreign projects were approved and the total investment was USD547 million. Among the 181 projects, 53 are for export processing and 128 for warehousing and logistics.

The Administrative Committee of Waigaoqiao Free Trade Zone
2 Huajing Road, Waigaoqiao Free Trade Zone
Pudong New District, Shanghai
P.R. China 200131
Tel: (86)(21) 50461100
Fax: (86)(21) 50461441
Website: www.waigaoqiao.gov.cn

SONGJIANG EXPORT PROCESSING ZONE

Songjiang Export Processing Zone (SJEPZ) was established by the State Council on 27 April 2000. With a development area of 1.98 sq km, it was founded within the Songjiang Industrial Zone, one of the municipal-level industrial parks of Shanghai.

Key industries encouraged by SJEPZ include IT, biopharmaceuticals, new building materials, fine chemicals and light machinery.

Investors in the zone are able to enjoy special tax incentives. Services and institutions like customs, goods inspection, commercial transactions, taxation, banking, and foreign trade are readily available. Investors can complete all export formalities within the EPZ.

SJEPZ is 20 km away from Hongqiao International Airport, 42 km away from Pudong International Airport, and 47 km from Wusong Port. It is close to the Shanghai-Hangzhou Expressway. A light rail network from Songjiang to the downtown is in the plan.

The Administrative Committee of Songjiang Export Processing Zone
81 Rongle East Road, Songjiang District
Shanghai, P.R. China 201613
Tel: (86)(21) 57741102, 57741859
Fax: (86)(21) 57743188
E-mail: sjiz@public.sta.net.cn
Website: www.sjepz.com

Municipal - level Industrial Parks

SHANGHAI INTERNATIONAL AUTOMOBILE CITY

Introduction

Shanghai International Automobile City (SHIAC) is located in Anting of Jiading District, a junction where the district meets Qingpu District of Shanghai and Kunshan City of Jiangsu. The 68 sq km area hosts Shanghai Volkswagen and Shanghai Auto.

SHIAC consists of an auto manufacturing area, a central business district, an industrial park for spare parts assembly, a quality inspection center, a second-hand automobile market, an F-1 racing field, and the new town of Anting. At the same time, Tongji University will build its Automobile College to accommodate 7,000 postgraduates and 8,000 undergraduates.

SHIAC Spare Parts Assembly Industrial Zone

The Spare Parts Assembly Industrial Zone, occupying an area of 8 sq km, is a municipal level development zone set up in 1998. It is 20 km away from Hongqiao International Airport, 65 km to Pudong International Airport and 35 km to the container terminal at Wusong. Shanghai-Beijing Railway runs through with a station in Anting. Highways and expressways are within easy reach.

Investment Climate

More than 70 enterprises have already invested in SHIAC. Shanghai Volkswagen is the largest and most successful Sino-foreign joint venture in China. Set up in Anting in 1985, it has been taking the lead in China's automobile market and tops the list of all foreign-invested enterprises in China. In 2001, the sales revenue of Shanghai Volkswagen exceeded RMB32 billion.

As automobile industry has become a promising pillar industry for Shanghai's economy, SHIAC is now recognized as one of the four key industrial bases in Shanghai, besides Baosteel Base, Shanghai Chemical Industrial Park and Zhangjiang IC and Microelectronics Base.

With co-efforts from German AS&P GmbH, McKinsey and Debenham Tie Leung, the master plan of SHIAC shows total investment commitment on this area will be RMB50 billion. Allegedly, SHIAC aims to be one of the largest comprehensive automobile industrial bases in Asia Pacific.

FDI is hailed in automobile related industries such as trade, exhibition, education and training, R&D, logistics and other relevant services.

SHIAC Development Corporation was jointly established by Shanghai Automobile Industry Group, Jia'an Group, Shanghai Materials Group and China Automobile Association to look after the development of the whole town.

Shanghai International Automobile City Development Corporation
79 Moyu Road, Anting, Jiading District
Shanghai, P.R. China 201805
Tel: (86)(21) 59562324

Fax: (86)(21) 59563621
SHIAC Spare Parts Assembly Industrial Zone
Email: shdzizd@online.sh.cn
Website: www.shvwip.com

SHANGHAI CHEMICAL INDUSTRIAL PARK

Shanghai Chemical Industrial Park (SCIP) is an RMB150 billion municipal project undertaken jointly by Sinopac Shanghai, Huayi Group, Gaoqiao Petrochemical, Shanghai Industrial Investment Group and Shanghai Jiushi in early 2001. It is one of the four key industrial bases designated by the municipal government to develop petrochemical industries. With registered

SCIP at shows

capital of RMB2.16 billion, SCIP Development Corporation is the sole developer of this mega project, offering one-stop service to all qualified foreign investors.

With total development area of 23.4 sq km and first phase area of 10 sq km, SCIP is mainly located in Jinshan District in the southernmost part of Shanghai, with another part hosted by Fengxian. Perching on the north bank of Hangzhou Bay, it is 60 km away from the downtown and 50 km from both airports in Shanghai.

Major MNCs such as Bayer, BASF and British Petroleum have joined SCIP. The total investment for the Bayer project will be USD3.1 billion, and a joint venture of Sinopac, Sinopac Shanghai Petrochemical and British Petroleum will cost USD2.7 billion. It is expected that by the end of 2005, 12 major projects will start operation.

Shanghai Chemical Industrial Park Development Co. Ltd.
10, Lane 18, Gaoan Road, Shanghai
P. R. China 200030
Tel: (86)(21) 64713298
Fax: (86)(21) 64713301
Email: webmaster@scip-cn.com
Website: www.scip-cn.com

SHANGHAI COMPREHENSIVE INDUSTRIAL DEVELOPMENT ZONE

Originally founded as Shanghai Fengpu Industrial Park in August 1995, Shanghai Comprehensive Industrial Development Zone (SCIDZ) got its existing name after being positioned as one of Shanghai's three key industrial parks in April 2000.

Located in Fengxian District, 30 km south to the city of Shanghai, SCIDZ is a 20.8 sq km area that caters to both MNCs and small and medium enterprises. It is 29 km and 46 km away from Shanghai Hongqiao International Airport and Pudong International Airport, respectively.

According to the Administrative Committee of SCIDZ, major industries encouraged are information technology, new materials, high-tech industries, green products, real estate and services.

Fengpu Complex of SCIDZ

Within the initial 5 sq km area, subsidiary zones have been designed for investors from Europe, Japan and Singapore, as well as a special subzone for SMEs. Major MNCs that have joined SCIDZ include GE, Pioneer Electronics, Matsushita Electric and SGL Carbono. Other foreign investors include Nu Skin, Bagardi, Greek Hitec Plastic, Fuji Electric and so on. Meanwhile, many domestic enterprises have established operations in SCIDZ, for example, Leiyunshang Pharmaceutical Company, Shuangling TCL Air Conditioner, Hangxing Cleaning Equipment, Nanqiao Transformer Group, Zhezhong Electric Equipment and Cixing Bearing Group. Fengxian campus of Shanghai Normal University and other professional schools will provide ample human resources for enterprises in SCIDZ.

The Development Corporation of SCIDZ is in charge of the planning, development and coordination affairs of the zone. Shanghai Industrial Investment Group is an important shareholder of the developer.

Shanghai Comprehensive Industrial Development Zone Development Co. Ltd.

111 Fengpu Avenue, Fengxian District
Shanghai, P. R. China 201400
Tel: (86)(21) 67100345, 67100465
Fax: (86)(21) 67100123

Email: shfpres@public.sta.net.cn
Website: www.fengpu.com

JIADING INDUSTRIAL PARK

With a total development area of 24.8 sq km, Jiading Industrial Zone (JDIZ) was established in 1992 and later conferred municipal-level status in 1994. It is located in northwest Shanghai, bordering Kunshan and Taicang of Jiangsu Province. The park is about 25 km to Hongqiao International Airport and 75 km to Pudong International Airport. The nearest seaport, Zhanghuabang container terminal is just 25 km away.

The state-level Jiading High-tech Park was founded within the zone. Pioneering Park for Returned Overseas Chinese Students in JDIZ has become the hottest one of its kind in China.

Jiading offers rich human resources to foreign investors. Jiading campus of Shanghai University and a few research institutes with more than 6,000 R&D professionals form a ready pool of local talents for investors to tap on.

JDIZ has attracted many companies from Japan, the US, Germany, Hong Kong and Taiwan, as well as domestic firms. Established companies include Koito, Fujitsu General, Aurora Office Equipment, Shanghai Automobile Brake Systems, ZF Shanghai Steering, Shanghai Global Control System, GEM Electronics, Shanghai Morgan Matroc Technical Ceramic, Peggy Food, Shanghai Carrier Transicoid Equipment, Shanghai Tokan Ceramics and Sanei Electric.

To date, 214 foreign-funded projects have been registered in JDIZ and total utilized FDI has amounted to USD1.1 billion.

The Administrative Committee of Jiading Industrial Zone
555 Yecheng Road, Jiading District
Shanghai, P. R. China 201821
Tel: (86)(21) 59162708, 59162331
Fax: (86)(21) 59161486
Email: jdiz@jdiz.com
Website: www.jdiz.com

QINGPU INDUSTRIAL ZONE

With total development area of 16.16 sq km, Qingpu Industrial Zone (QPIZ) was approved by the municipal government in 1995. Located in Qingpu District in the west of Shanghai, QPIZ is 17 km to Hongqiao International Airport and 45 km to Shanghai Port.

The zone is divided into five industrial clusters of IT, biopharmaceuticals, high-tech materials, precision machinery, green food and packaging. One of the two incubation bases for high-tech achievements in Shanghai is hosted by QPIZ, the other one in Zhangjiang of Pudong.

Major companies that have established operation in QPIZ include DuPont and Suzuka International from the US, Hoechst A.G., BASF and CeDo from Germany, Yongji DTF and TLS International from Singapore, UFI Group and Isea Lorenzi from Italy, Fuji Electric, Sunny, Showa and Jentech from Japan, Happy Goal and HCP International from Virgin Islands, and Herganies from Sweden.

The Development Corporation of Qingpu Industrial Zone
5500 Waiqingsong Highway, Qingpu District
Shanghai, P. R. China 201700
Tel: (86)(21) 59724619
Fax: (86)(21) 59722856
Email: sqpiz@sqpiz.com
Website: www.greenin.com.cn

SONGJIANG INDUSTRIAL ZONE

Songjiang Industrial Zone (SJIZ) was established in 1992 as the first municipal-level industrial park in Shanghai suburbs. It is located in Songjiang District in the southwest of Shanghai, about 30 km from downtown area. The total development area is 20.56 sq km. It is about 22 km to Hongqiao International Airport where daily flights are available to many major cities worldwide. Meanwhile, the park is 35 km and 50 km away from Jinshan Container Port and Wusong Port, respectively.

By the end of 2000, around 173 foreign enterprises with total investment of USD1.6 billion had joined the park. Major investors include Hitachi, Fujitsu, Mitsui Toatsu Chemicals, Minolta, Dow Chemical, Weyerhaerser, 3M, ICI, Nestle, ABB, Itochu, Sumitomo, Tomen, Marubeni, Nissho Iwai, Swire, Kenwood, Komatsu, Sunrise and Yeo's. Many small and medium sized enterprises also set up their subsidiaries there.

Most of the enterprises in the park specialize in electronics, machinery, food and beverage, textiles and chemicals. The state-level Songjiang Export Processing Zone is located within its territory.

Songjiang Industrial Zone Administrative Committee
81 East Rongle Road, Songjiang District
Shanghai, P. R. China 201600
Tel: (86)(21) 57741102, 57743493
Fax: (86)(21) 57743188, 57741102
Email: sjiz@public.sta.net.cn
Website: www.sjiz.org

BAOSHAN CITY INDUSTRIAL PARK

Baoshan City Industrial Park (BCIP) was established in November 1995 with an area of 5 sq km in its master planning. Located in the southwest part of Baoshan District, the park is adjacent to the Outer Ring Road of Shanghai of its east and 15 km far from Hongqiao International Airport. Moreover, the northern railway cargo station, Taopu marshalling station, and Shanghai Railway Station for passengers lie 6 km, 3 km, and 10 km away respectively. Wusong Port, Shanghai-Nanjing and Shanghai-Hangzhou Expressway are also located within its convenient reach.

BCIP aims to develop into a high-tech, open, comprehensive and modernized industrial park. The emphasis has been ambitiously put on R&D and entrepreneurial incubation. Led by new materials development, electronic communication, instrument machinery, automobile components manufacturing will together be the industrial mainstay of BCIP.

Industrial land in the park is priced at USD35 per sq m and ready built factory is leased for USD2-3 per sq m per month.

The Administrative Committee of Shanghai Baoshan City Industrial Park
1000, Zhenchen Road, Baoshan District
Shanghai, P. R. China 200436
Tel: 86-21-56136151
Fax: 86-21-56131344

JINSHANZUI INDUSTRIAL ZONE

Shanghai Jinshanzui Industrial Zone (JIZ) is a municipal-level and also a state-level exemplary industrial park for town and village enterprises. Located in southeastern Jinshan District and facing Hangzhou Bay, JIZ covers 22.8 sq km coastal area and consists of Jinshan Industrial Park, Shanyang Industrial Park, Jinshanjui Habor and Jinshanwei Commercial and Residential Area.

As JIZ is next to Shanghai Petrochemical Co. Ltd. and only a few kilometers away from Shanghai Chemical Industrial Park, it has successfully attracted investors like Unilever and China Merchants. So far, FIEs and domestic companies totaled 45 and 236 in the zone, respectively. JIZ owns a 9 km long coastline. With a 10,000-tonnage cargo wharf, a branch railway line and an expressway network under construction within the zone or nearby, JIZ's locational advantage will be further enhanced.

Industries that are emphasized in the zone include chemical product manufacturing, fine chemical engineering, textile, electronics, plastics and new construction materials. It is planned to be an important petrochemical deep processing industrial base in Shanghai's 10th Five-Year (2001-2005) blueprint.

The Administrative Committee of Shanghai Jinshanzui Industrial Zone
1518 Jinshan Avenue, Jinshan District, Shanghai
P. R. China 201508

Tel: 86-21-67241412, 67241000
Fax: 86-21-67241424, 67241617

SHANGHAI CHONGMING INDUSTRIAL ZONE

Shanghai Chongming Industrial Zone (SCIZ) was approved by the municipal government in February 1996 and became the only municipal-level industrial park in county. The 9.97 sq km zone is located in the northwest part of Chengqiao Town, the center of Chongming Island, with less than 1 km distant to Nanmen Port.

As an industrial park on an island, SCIZ enjoys special treatment allocated in land transfer prices and government subsidies. It undertakes the task to attract advanced technologies and to restructure industry of Chongming. Two-square-kilometer kick-off area has been constructed, with infrastructure development amounting to RMB150 million. More than 50 enterprises have already taken residence with total workforce of over 1,500.

SCIZ is determined to be a green industrial park. Non-pollution, high value added, high-tech industries are welcomed. Biopharmaceutical and IT industries are in particular encouraged.

Shanghai Chongming Industrial Zone
588 Ximen Road, Chengqiao, Chongming County
Shanghai, P. R. China 202150
Tel: 86-21-69625800, 69625818
Fax: 86-21-69625830
Website: www.chongming-gyyq.com

Shanghai Office of SCIZ
No. 48, 131 Lane, Nujiang Road, Putuo District
Shanghai, P. R. China 200062
Tel: 86-21-62601046, 62453915
Fax: 86-21-62453917

SHANGHAI PUDONG KANGQIAO INDUSTRIAL PARK

Shanghai Pudong Kangqiao Industrial Park (KIP) was established in May 1992 and approved to be a municipal-level industrial park in August 1994. The total planned area of KIP is 26.88 sq km. Though Kangqiao is a town under the administration of Nanhui District, KIP has its 8 sq km located in the territory of Pudong New District.

The Pudong part of the Outer Ring Road divides KIP into two parts. A few waterways in the park lead to the Huangpu River as well. KIP is only 6 km to Xupu Bridge and 8 km to Nanpu Bridge, two bridges spanning over the Huangpu River. Pudong Airport is located 12 km to its east, with Hongqiao Airport 22 km away to the northwest.

Water supply to KIP will be increased to 120,000 tons per day when the second phase of Dazhi River Water Plant is complete. The maximum daily wastewater discharge of the park is 120,000 tons too. KIP has already built a 220 kV power substation and three 35 kV substations.

In 2000, 119 enterprises registered in KIP, with total registered capital of RMB250 million. Industrial projects numbered 38, with total investment of USD130 million. The annual industrial output was RMB9 billion. Major industries in the park include manufacturing of monitors, transmission shafts, glass, plastics, floorings, storage batteries.

The Administrative Committee of Shanghai Pudong Kangqiao Industrial Park
2502 Hunan Road, Pudong
Shanghai, P. R. China 201315
Tel: 86-21-58121822
Fax: 86-21-58121188

Other Development Zones

LUJIAZUI FINANCE AND TRADE ZONE

Jinmao Tower and China Merchants Tower

Lujiazui Finance and Trade Zone (LFTZ) has snatched the most conspicuous position in the developmental history of Pudong and Shanghai since 1990. It remains the only state-level "finance and trade zone" in China and is set to be the international financial and trading center in the Asia Pacific region by 2015.

The zone occupies a total area of 28 sq km in the mid west part of Pudong New District, right facing the Bund over the Huangpu River. It is within the Inner Ring Road.

So far, more than 83 financial institutions have located or relocated here, including 42 foreign banks, securities firms or their representative offices. Financial trading houses like Shanghai Stock Exchange and Shanghai Futures

Exchange have also moved in. More than 300 famous corporations including Siemens, Alcatel, Tomson and Baosteel have now had their footholds in Lujiazui.

The financial center of the zone was jointly designed by a group of world-renowned urban planners and architects. The world third tallest building – 88-storey Jinmao Tower and the 468-meter Oriental Pearl TV Tower have already become the landmarks of Pudong and Shanghai. Century Avenue, Riverside Avenue, a 10-ha central greenery area, and a sightseeing tunnel connected to the old town are the new attractions for tourists who are constantly curious about the fast-changing urban landscapes in Pudong.

A view from the Oriental Pear TV Tower

Website: www.shld.com

FENGJING INDUSTRIAL PARK

Located on the border of Shanghai and Zhejiang Province, Fengjing of Jinshan District is the southwest gateway to the metropolis. Shanghai-Hangzhou Expressway, Railway and National Highway 320 all run though the town, which makes it an outstanding place for

(From left) China Insurance Building, Shanghai Securities Exchange Building and Pu Fa Building

investors who wish to get into Shanghai but not be confronted with urban congestions and anxiety. It takes approximately 40 minutes to reach the city of Shanghai and 35 minutes to arrive at Hongqiao International Airport. Being a major satellite township of Shanghai, Fengjing is developed into a unique city even with North American features.

Fengjing Industrial Park (FIP) occupies an area of 3.3 sq km. More than 20,000 sq m ready built factories with varied scale have been constructed for companies to choose from. So far, over 50 enterprises have pooled in investment worth RMB2.5 billion. There is another state-level project – Shanghai International Garment Machinery City – to be activated on a 3 sq km area. It will become China or even world's largest and most influential manufacturing and trading base for garment machinery.

Fengjing Industrial Park
281 Zhufeng Highway, Fengjing
Jinshan District, Shanghai
Tel: 86-21-57351743, 57351289, 57354542
Fax: 86-21-57356481

JINSHAN NO. 2 INDUSTRIAL ZONE

Jinshan No. 2 Industrial Zone (or Jinshanwei Industrial Zone, JWIZ) is located in the northwest part of Jinshanwei Town, Jinshan District. It was named because Shanghai Petrochemical Co. Ltd. is already the No. 1 industrial zone in this area. It was jointly approved by three commissions of Shanghai municipal government in May 1990 to deepen the development in fine petrochemical engineering and pharmaceuticals. The total planned area of the zone is 7.5 sq km, of which 2.5 sq km has already been occupied.

By the end of 2001, 140 enterprises had moved in, including 24 FIEs with total investment of USD270 million. In 2001, total industrial output amounted to RMB2.6 billion and products worth USD41.1 million were exported.

A few national and regional highways, Xinzhuang-Fengxian-Jinshan Expressway and Jinshan branch line of Shanghai-Hangzhou Railway connect the zone to the national transportation network. It takes 50 minutes' drive to reach Pudong International Airport. By 2006 when the Hangzhou Bay Sea-spanning Bridge is in operation, the trip to Ningbo, a port city of Zhejiang will only cost one hour.

The zone has daily industrial water supply of 60,000 tons, with additional 20,000 tons of underground water. Industrial sewage treatment is available as daily wastewater of 100,000 tons can be discharged together with that from the neighboring Shanghai Petrochemical. JWIZ is connected to East China power grid with ample supply of electricity. 25,000 optical fiber programmed telephones are already in use.

Up to date, overseas investors and domestic companies from Wenzhou (Zhejiang) and Xiamen (Fujian) have joined JWIZ, such as Henkel of Germany, Phoenix of Japan, Rohm & Haas and Nash of US, AKD of Canada. In addition, a comprehensive market for trading of textile, household commodities and agricultural products is booming in Jinshanwei Town, too.

Shanghai Jinshanwei Industrial Zone Enterprise Development Co. Ltd.
Jinshanwei, Jinshan District, Shanghai
P. R. China 201512
Tel: 86-21-57260742, 57262211, 57260303
Fax: 86-21-57260377, 57260749

SHANGHAI HONGQIAO AIRPORT INDUSTRIAL PARK

Located in Changning District where the state-level Hongqiao Economic and Technological Zone is also situated, Shanghai Hongqiao Airport Industrial Park (HAIP) was invested by the district government to tap on the advantage of proximity to the Hongqiao International Airport that lies only two kilometers away.

HAIP is a comprehensive industrial park hailing both high-tech industries and so-called metropolitan type of industry. Close to the Outer Ring Road, Shanghai-Jiading Expressway and National Highway No. 318, the park has a planned area of 2.8 sq km with additional 2 sq km to be developed –

considerably big for an urban district. The planned extension of Metro Line 2, which is to be operational in 2005, will run through the park and leave a station there. The second phase of Pearl Light Rail will also add a station on the east side of HAIP. It only takes a 20 minutes' drive to the city's center via viaducts.

More than 800 enterprises have joined HAIP, with registered capital totaling RMB1.8 billion. Since 2000, investors have shown added interest in making their presence in the park, 80% of which were referred there by existing tenants. The enterprises in HAIP now represent a wide array of industries, including electrical appliances, software development, garments, sanitary ware and optical fiber coating.

Shanghai Hongqiao Airport Industrial Park Service Center
789 Tianshan West Road
Changning District, Shanghai
P. R. China 200335
Tel: 86-21-62399702, 52180156, 52188446, 52189580
Fax: 86-21-62393625
Website: cnq.sh.gov.cn/zfjg/lkyq

XINZHUANG INDUSTRIAL PARK

Xinzhuang, a town of Minhang District, is located at the geographic center of the municipality of Shanghai. Within its convenient reaches are three state-level development zones: Caohejing High-tech Park, Minhang and Hongqiao ETDZs.

Xinzhuang Industrial Park (XIP) boasts great accessibility as Shanghai-Hangzhou Railway, Shanghai-Nanjing Railway and Expressway all run through Minhang. Shanghai Metro Line 1 has also extended to Xinzhuang. The Inner Ring Road and Hongqiao International Airport both lie 8 km away to the north of XIP.

XIP has a high standard in planning and designing. Nearly 15% of the total area will be greened to build it into a garden-type industrial park. As a result, those industries with high-tech application, high value added and no pollution are preferred. Industrial development will focus on electronic and communication equipment, new materials, fine chemical engineering and biopharmaceuticals.

By now, 115 enterprises have taken their residence in XIP, with contractual FDI of USD400 million. Major investors include C. P. Pokphand from Thailand, Rhone-Poulenc from France, and Daikin from Japan.

Xinzhuang Industrial Park
8 Shenbei Road, Minhang District
Shanghai, P. R. China 201108
Tel: 86-21-64894712, 64890467
Fax: 86-21-64895589
Website: www.minhang-window.com/busi/pk-xzhgyq

SHANGHAI NANOMETER TECHNOLOGY INDUSTRIAL BASE

Shanghai Nanometer Technology Industrial Base (SNTIB) was jointly established by three commissions of the municipal government: Economic Commission, Science and Technology Commission, and Education Commission. The purpose of its establishment is to leverage on the resources and in talent in Shanghai to transfer, hatch, commercialize and industrialize the achievements in the field of nanometer technology. SNTIB aims to be an influential high-tech industrial base in China with market-oriented management and operations.

The base is located in the southwest part of Xuhui District, with an incubation center and an industrial park. The former is adjacent to East China University of Science and Technology (ECUST) and only 2 km away from Shanghai South Railway Station and Metro Station. The total floor area of the center is about 6,860 sq m, which is specifically dedicated to the hatching and fostering high-tech enterprises in nanometer material development and application. The industrial park is located in Xuhui Huajing Industrial Estate, with phase I planned area of 7.7 ha. Basic infrastructures and surrounding amenities are ready.

Shanghai Nanometer Technology Industrial Base Office
Huajing Industrial Estate, Huajing Road
Tel: 86-21-64554222
Fax: 86-21-54283420

462, Shangzhong Road
Tel: 86-21-64105186, 64766680
Fax: 86-21-64763878

SHANGHAI SOFTWARE DEVELOPMENT PARK

Officiated in 1999, Shanghai Software Development Park (SHSDP) consists of three parts, Pudong Software Park (located in Zhangjiang High-tech Park), Fudan Software Development Center, and SJTU (Shanghai Jiaotong Univeristy) Caohejing Software Park. With strong backing from the municipal government, fund for development has reached RMB3.7 billion.

Over 748 enterprises have registered in those parks and 49 of them have started operation, with foreign capital of USD224 million. Some prestigious companies in the park include Shanghai Wonders Information, Shanghai Fudan Guanghua Information Industries, Shanghai VSC, SJTU Withub Information Industries, Shanghai Pudong Software Park Development Co., Shanghai Baud Data Communications, Shanghai Fudan Net-Info, Kingstar Group, Shanghai Integra Info Tech, Microsoft and HP.

The establishment of SHSDP is to boost up Shanghai's capacity in software development. It is estimated that by 2005, the turnover of the industry in Shanghai will be at least RMB50 billion and export will reach USD400 million. The population of software professionals in Shanghai will then increase from 32,000 to 100,000.

Shanghai Pudong Software Development Park Co. Ltd.
Zhangjiang High-tech Park
Pudong New District, Shanghai
P. R. China 201203
Tel: (86)(21) 38954510

Email: spsp@public.sta.net.cn
Website: www.spsp.com.cn

SHANGHAI JIAOTONG UNIVERSITY SCIENCE PARK

Shanghai Jiaotong University Science Park (SJTUSP) was set up in 1999 and was subsequently awarded the status of National University Science Park in May 2001. SJTUSP mainly consists of four subsidiary zones: Withub, Zhangjiang Zone in Pudong, Mingu and Xinhua. Withub is located at the main campus of Shanghai Jiaotong University (SJTU), engaged in development of information technology, new materials, new energy and biotechnologies.

Enterprises in SJTUSP are able to tap on the resources and opportunities offered by SJTU which is composed of four campuses, 17 colleges and one graduate school. It hosts 16 State Key Programs, nine of State Key Laboratories, and two State Engineering Research Center. Among the 1,900 strong university faculty, there are eight CAS (Chinese Academy of Science) fellows, nine CAE (Chinese Academy of Engineering) fellows, 460 professors and around 700 associate professors. The number of students is 22,000, with 4,900 and 1,900 postgraduates pursuing their master and doctoral degrees respectively. SJTU enjoys high reputation in the fields of engineering, IT, management and biological studies, and has established alliances with more than 30 major MNCs and other enterprises to commercialize the academic achievements. Among those projects that have brought attractive returns are high-definition digital TV, MCFC fuel battery, micro motors, piston production line for Volkswagen, 6,000-meter deepwater daggling observation system etc.

There are 24 university-affiliated enterprises running in the park, such as Nanyang Group, Only Group, Shanghai Withub Information Industries and Shanghai GoFly Group. In particular, SJTU Only Group has grown from a small company to become a top player in China's healthcare market with hundreds of millions turnover now.

Shanghai Jiaotong University Scientific

Development and Cooperation Office
Haoran Scientific Building, Shanghai Jiaotong University
1954 Huashan Road, Xuhui District
Shanghai, P. R. China 200030
Tel: (86)(21) 62932047, 62932048
Fax (86)(21) 62932451
Website: www.kejichu.sjtu.edu.cn
E-mail: kaifa@mail.sjtu.edu.cn

FUDAN UNIVERSITY SCIENCE PARK

Similar to SJTUSP, Fudan University Science Park (FDUSP) was inaugurated in April 2000 to leverage on Fudan University's R&D capabilities. It consists of Fudan Software Development Center, Shanghai Yangpu Venture Incubation Center, Fudan-SK Entrepreneurial Center, Guoquan Zone, Fenglin Zone and a few other professional incubation bases.

Founded in 1905, Fudan University has developed into one of the top universities in China. After merging with former Shanghai Medical University, the university now has 17 colleges and 43 departments, and hosts 45 State Key Programs, 5 State Key Laboratories, 57 research institutes and 80 multidisciplinary research centers. The academic fields cover humanities, science, social sciences, economics, journalism, international relations, business administration, law, life science, pharmaceutics, IT and software development. Among its 2,400 staffs, there are 19 CAS and CAE fellows, 1,300 professors and associate professors.

Currently, Fudan University owns 99 affiliate enterprises with total sales revenue reached RMB1.16 billion in 2000. The industries cover IT, biopharmaceuticals, new materials, environmental protection, chemical engineering, communications, medical instruments and investment fund. With registered capital of RMB100 million, Fudan University Science Park Development Corporation is the developer of the science park. Major shareholders include Fudan University, Shanghai Wujiaochang Square High-tech United Corporation, Shanghai Shangke Investment Corporation, Shanghai Science & Technology Entrepreneur Center, Shanghai Lujiazui

Finance & Trade Zone Holdings and Shanghai Yangpu Development Corporation.

Fudan University Science Park Investment Service Center
139 Handan Road, Shanghai
P. R. China 200437
Tel: 86-21-65311017
Fax: (86)(21) 65448060
Email: xcqian@fudan.edu.cn
Website: 202.120.224.90/xiaochan/web/kejiyuan.htm

CHINA-SINGAPORE SUZHOU INDUSTRIAL PARK (CS-SIP)

China-Singapore Suzhou Industrial Park (SIP) is a high-level bilateral cooperative project between the Chinese and Singapore governments. On 26 February 1994, Chinese Vice Premier Mr Li Lanqing and Singapore Senior Minister Lee Kuan Yew signed the Agreement on the Joint Development of Suzhou Industrial Park in Beijing.

Located in Suzhou of Jiangsu Province, the 70 sq km SIP project is carried out in three phases. As the first phase was been fully occupied, the second and third phase have already kicked off since early 2001.

Belonging to the Greater Shanghai area, which covers Shanghai and part of the two adjacent provinces of Jiangsu and Zhejiang, SIP is only an hour's ride to airports in Shanghai and two hours' drive to Nanjing, the provincial capital, via well-developed expressway.

In 2001, SIP's GDP, fiscal revenue and total volume of international trade stood at RMB18 billion, RMB2.4 billion and USD3.7 billion, respectively.

Investment Climate

SIP boasts world-class infrastructures. CSSD (China-Singapore Suzhou Industrial Park Development Co. Ltd.), now a 65:35 joint venture between a Chinese (14 members) and a Singapore consortium (24 members), is in overall charge of the development and even foreign investment promotion.

Join Our Success
Beautiful Environment
Quality Service
Fine Talent
用明天的科技 培训今天的学员
SINGAPORE SUZHOU
Suzhou Industrial Park
857 Foreign Invested Enterprises
US$14.2 billion contractual investment
US$4.9 billion utilized investment
26 projects with total investment exceeding US$100 million
Over one third of the companies have increased their total investments
Data source: SIPAC, June 2002

By the end of 2001, total infrastructure development had cost RMB8.9 billion and laid down superior conditions for investment to the highest standards in China.

Foreign Enterprises

According to CSSD, as at 31 October 2002, SIP had attracted 935 projects with contractual FDI accumulated at USD15.44 billion. Many MNCs, including 40 over enlisted in Fortune Global 500, have already taken their residence in the park, such as AMD, Delphi, Black & Decker, Emerson Electric, Honeywell, Nabisco, Solectron, Littelfuse, Technic Semiconductor, Alcatel, Maybeline, Schneider, Grundfos Pumps, Adidas, Bosch, MTU, Wincor Nixdorf, Nokia, Eisai, Hitachi, Fujitsu, Mitsui, Pokka, Fuji, Towa, Yamaha, TDK, Sumitomo, Samsung, Singapore Technologies, JTC, Wing Tai, GlaxoSmithKline, Schindler etc.

The foreign invested enterprises in SIP have formed a few industrial clusters including electric and electronics, pharmaceuticals and chemicals, precision engineering and new materials. Semiconductor is increasingly becoming an important industry in the park.

Singapore Expertise

The success of SIP can be largely attributable to the initial "software transfer" from Singapore side. This covers Singapore's rich experience in economic development, an extensive international network of investment promotion, and an efficient way in public administration and estate management. In fact, the master urban planning, Central Provident Fund (CPF) and civil servant recruitment are modeled or adapted from Singapore. Since 1 January 2001, Chinese consortium increased its share from 35% to 65% in CSSD and assumed management.

After eight years of construction, SIP has become one of the youngest yet most developed industrial parks China. When fully developed, it will accommodate 600,000 people and generate 360,000 jobs. SIP is undoubtedly among the most competitive industrial parks in the Greater Shanghai area.

中国农业银行苏州分行

AGRICULTURAL BANK OF CHINA SUZHOU BRANCH

Agricultural Bank of China (ABC) is one of the largest state-owned banks in China authorized to do foreign transactions. In year 2000, ABC was ranked among the Fortune 500 companies and the 20th in the 1000 big banks in terms of tier 1 capital by the UK's Bankers magazine.

Agricultural Bank of China, Suzhou Branch (ABC Suzhou), with its largest capacity of deposits and loans, highest level of business ratings, and widest service scope in the local area, has become the most influential state-owned bank in Suzhou. Ten years after its founding, growing with times and meeting the requirements for the first class commercial bank, ABC Suzhou has made progress in almost every aspect. By October 2002, the balance of deposits totaled RMB55.7 billion, of which RMB50 billion are in renminbi deposits; outstanding loans reached RMB40 billion. In the first three quarters of 2002, the bank achieved a profit of RMB494 million. Its international settlement volume and market share have led all local counterparts. By the end of October 2002, international settlement, bankcards and outstanding consumer loans handled by the bank had reached USD9.13 billion, 2.6 million and RMB2.4 billion, respectively.

Focusing on customer services, ABC Suzhou is strongly committed to product innovations resulted in the introduction of new services, such as the one-step financial supermarket, e-banking fund transfers between savings accounts and stock transaction accounts, and Western Union Money Transfer. It has most self-service equipments in Suzhou and makes advancement in the application of the "New Generation" – ABIS, which offers sophisticated, safe and speedy fund clearing service. The bank has established long-term close relationship with a lot of distinguished clients including many renowned companies, institutions and state-level development zones such as 48 of the 81 Fortune 500 enterprises' establishments in Suzhou, and Suzhou Industrial Park.

With China's entry into the World Trade Organization, ABC Suzhou will grow in tandem with the expanding world economy. Facing new challenges, the bank will constantly pursue the spirit of "Self-pressed, High-aimed" in deepening reform and responding to changes in a positive and strategic way. The bank will continue to innovate products, services and functions to create more value for partners by leveraging on its strong financial resources and an integrated global network.

Agricultural Bank of China Suzhou Branch
21-23 Shishan Road, Suzhou New District,
Suzhou, Jiangsu Province
P. R. China 215011
Tel: 86-512-67775580, 68242294
Fax: 86-512-67775800, 68240501

China-Singapore Suzhou Industrial Park Development Co. Ltd. (CSSD)
International Building, No. 2 Suhua Road
Suzhou Industrial Park, Jiangsu Province
P. R. China 215021
Tel: 86-512-6288 2828
Fax: 86-512-6288 1297
Website: www.cssd.com.sg

Economy Overview

China's robust economic growth and recent accession to the WTO have strengthened Shanghai's position as a regional trade and financial center. The modern, cosmopolitan city is home to China's largest and busiest port, a thriving stock exchange and Pudong New District. More and more multinational corporations are relocating their regional headquarters to Shanghai, lured by the city's excellent investment climate, skilled labor force, and huge and sophisticated consumer base.

SHANGHAI ECONOMIC DEVELOPMENT

Shanghai as a commercial center dates back to the Opium War of 1840, when Great Britain forced the Qing Dynasty to open the port and grant territorial concessions. As the foreign presence grew and trade expanded, Shanghai became known as the "Paris of the Orient" for its thriving culture and entertainment industries. The legacies of more than 100 years of foreign investment are still apparent throughout the city, from the charming colonial architecture of the Bund and the French Concession to the pragmatic entrepreneurship on street corners and in the board rooms of Pudong's new high-rise office buildings.

During the Korean War in the early 1950s, many Shanghai-based factories were moved to the interior to protect themselves from the possible attacks. The foreigners flocked away and the factories and businesses were gradually nationalized.

Despite the lack of fuel and raw materials, Shanghai is the largest industrial base of China. In the 1970s and 1980s, Shanghai's economy was restructured to include more light industries in order to reduce pollution. There was much renovation and expansion; new factories emerged around the outskirts of the city, and the northwest section was developed as an industrial district.

In the 1990s, the late Chinese leader Deng Xiaoping redefined the city as the "dragon head" of the Chinese economy. One in five of the world's high-lift cranes were at work in the streets of Shanghai, raising tower after tower. Shanghai became the largest construction site ever conceived. A new and more vital Shanghai has emerged.

Shanghai's infrastructure has been planned and built with careful coordination. The city's beauty can best be appreciated by walking along the Bund or down the streets behind it. Shanghai is a city looking towards the future, but strengthened by its very rich past.

Shanghai's fast development has markedly increased the city's comprehensive economic strength. In 2001, the city's GDP reached RMB495.1 billion, up 65.3 times that of 1952 in constant prices. Since 1992, Shanghai has been registering a double-digit annual GDP growth rate for ten consecutive years. The average annual growth rate hits 11.3%. The city's GDP per capita also increased steadily. In 1952, Shanghai's GDP per capita was only RMB430; in 1978, it stood at RMB2,498; the figure surpassed RMB10,000 in 1990 and jumped to RMB37,305 (USD4,500) in 2001. The figure, comparable to a middle level developed economy in the world, was the highest among provincial level administrative regions in the mainland.

Shanghai has and will continue to lead China's entry into the global economy. In September 1999, the world's top business leaders convened in Shanghai for the Global Fortune 500 conference, and in October 2001 regional leaders gathered for the annual APEC Summit. The city has also been selected amongst five contestant in bid for hosting the World Expo 2010. By then, the city would definately have become a global trade, financial, and technological center.

ECONOMIC STRUCTURE

Shanghai is the major commercial and financial powerhouse in China. With a population of only 1% and land area of 0.06% of the nation's total, Shanghai contributes one twelfth of the nation's total industrial output value, one sixth of the country's port cargo handling volume, one tenth of the country's total exports, and one tenth of the country's total utilized FDI in 2001.

Shanghai GDP Growth Curve

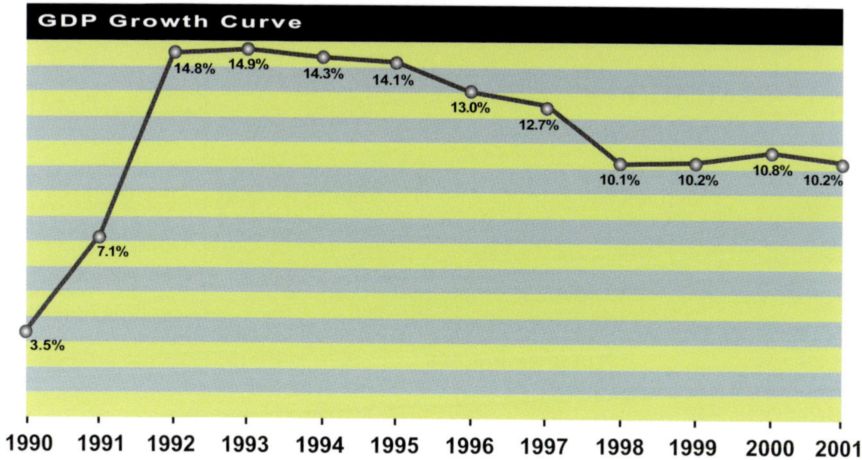

Major Economic Indicators of Shanghai, 2001

Indicator	Value	Over year 2000
GDP	RMB495 billion	10.2%
– Primary Industry	RMB8.5 billion	3%
– Secondary Industry	RMB235.6 billion	12%
– Tertiary Industry	RMB251.0 billion	8.7%
Fiscal Revenue	RMB199.6 billion	13.9%
Fixed Assets Investment	RMB198.4 billion	6.1%
Total Industrial Output	RMB765.7 billion	17.1%
Industrial Added Value	RMB212.8 billion	12.4%
Foreign Trade	USD60.9 billion	11.3%
– import	USD33.3 billion	13.3%
– export	USD27.6 billion	9%
Contractual FDI	USD7.37 billion	15.4%
Utilized FDI	USD4.39 billion	39%
Average Disposable Income Of Urbal Residents	RMB12,883	9.9%
Rural Net Income Of Rural Residents	RMB5,850	5.1%
Urban Unemployment Rate	4.3%	6.9%

Urban Household Expenditure in Shanghai (per capita)

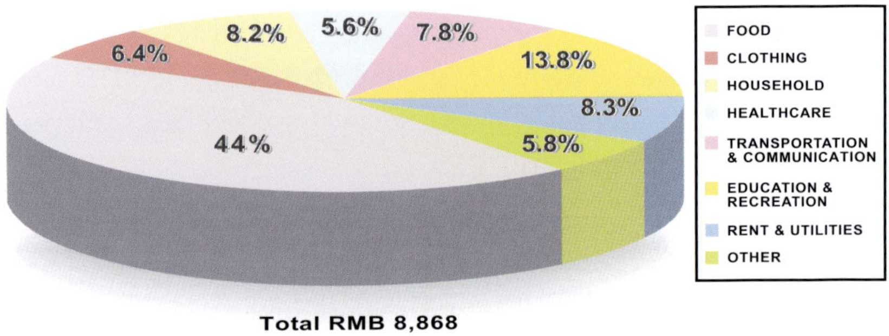

Per Capita GDP, Average Net Income of Rural Residents and Disposable Income of Urban Residents, 1991-2001

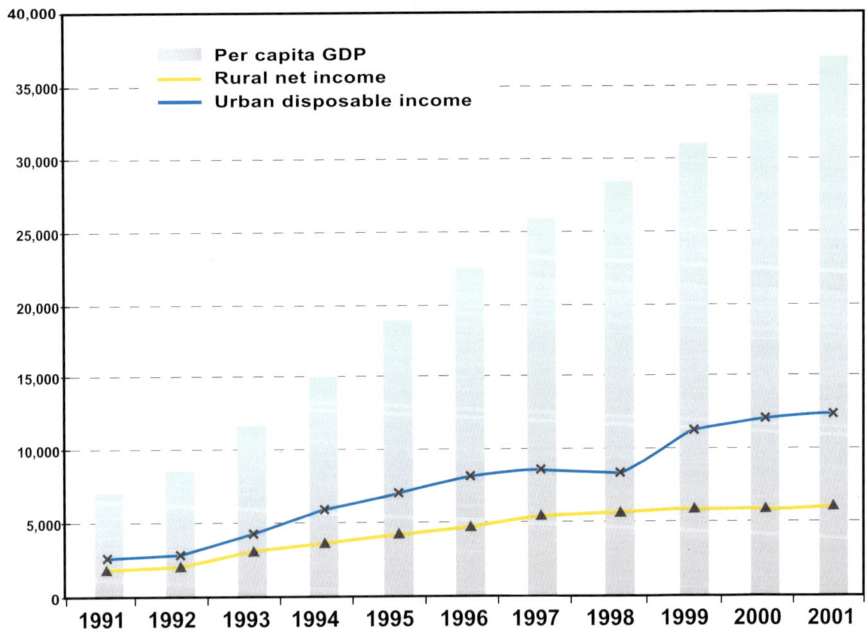

Along with the progress of the economic reform, Shanghai is actively adjusting its industrial structure, giving first priority to the development of the tertiary sector focusing on finance, trade and information technology. As a result, the city's industrial structure has been further optimized. In 2001, the added value of the city's tertiary industry reached RMB251 billion, accounting for 50.7% of the GDP. During the Ninth Five-Year Plan period (1995-2000), the tertiary industry grew at an average speed of 15.1% annually. The ratio of the city's primary, secondary industry and tertiary sector was readjusted from 2.5:57.3:40.2 in 1995 to 1.7:47.6:50.7 in 2001.

The continuing improvement in ownership structure contributes to the city's GDP growth as well. In 2001, the proportion of the state-owned sector in the city's GDP dropped from 82% in 1995 to 74%, accompanying the rise in the non-state-owned sector. While the importance of the debt-ridden state-owned enterprises (SOEs) declined, the contribution of non-SOEs to the GDP quickly increased to 28.6% in 2001 by generating added value of RMB141.6 billion, up 19.6%. Traditionally, non-SOEs refer to economic entities that are of collective, private or individual ownership. With an increasing number of collective enterprises being privatized, the term is now largely equivalent to a private economy and foreign invested enterprises. By the end of 2000, the number of private enterprises had reached 138,000 with a work force of

Performance of Pillar Industries 2001 (RMB Billion)

Pillar Industries	Value Added	Increase	% in GDP
Industry	212.8	12.4%	42.9%
- IT Industry	40.2	20.2%	8.1%
Finance & Insurance	68.5	2.1%	13.8%
Real Estate Industry	30.9	17.8%	6.2%
Construction	22.7	7.5%	4.6%
Commerce	34.0	10.2%	6.9%
Telecommunication, Post & Transportation	34.3	8.3%	6.9%
Tourism	27.3	14.2%	5.5%

nearly 360,000 people. The non-SOEs' share in the city's total fixed assets investment also grew from 46.9% to 52.1%, outstripping the state investment for the first time in 50 years.

Primary Industries

Shanghai's agricultural industry has sustained high growths for the past years. In 2001, the value added of agricultural sector reached RMB22.7 billion, a 4.9% increase over 2000. Of this total, forestry contributed RMB9.47 billion, animal husbandry RMB8.86 billion, and fishery RMB4.10 billion. Besides, the total agricultural exports in 2001 reached RMB825 million, an increase of 4.7% over 2000. Export of new varieties of vegetable, high-quality flowers and special fruits increased remarkably.

Shanghai's rural economy has completed its transition from grain, oil and cotton production to a comprehensive suburban economy that is more diversified, integrated and industrialized. By the end of 2000, the basic development of the city's first four modern agriculture parks had been completed, launching a group of projects for production and processing of vegetables, flowers and edible mushrooms. The city had set up more than 300 key or overseas-funded enterprises undertaking the production, processing and marketing of agricultural products. For example, a total of 234 large modern greenhouses were built for vegetable production.

Secondary Industries

Shanghai now has nearly 40,000 industrial enterprises, with about four million employees and over 400 industrial segments. In recent years, Shanghai's industrial system underwent an overall restructuring with the aim of strengthening the core industries, nurturing high-tech and reforming traditional ones.

Shanghai plays a leading role in the country's heavy industries. Its total industrial output reached RMB765.7 billion in 2001. Shanghai is also at the heart of China's light industrial sector, home to leading brands in food, cosmetics and textile industries.

In the 1990s, Shanghai's industrial development focused on automobile, communications and information equipment, petrochemical and fine chemical, household electric appliances, steel and iron industries etc. In future, it will expedite the development of three major high-tech industries: integrated circuit and computer science, modern biology and pharmaceuticals and new materials.

The six pillar industries of Shanghai, namely, automobile, electronic and telecommunications equipment, iron and steel, petrochemical and fine chemical processing, set equipment manufacturing, and biopharmaceuticals, have further consolidated their dominance by innovation and improvement in technology and product. Their total output value hit RMB396 billion in 2001, up 22.6% from the previous year and a share of 51.7% in the city's total industrial output value. The value added of the six pillar industries amounted to RMB128.3 billion, making up 60.3% of the city's total.

Meanwhile, Shanghai's high and new technology industries have also achieved sound progress. In 2001, the output value by these industries totaled RMB166.9 billion, up 30.3% over 2000. The figure accounted for 21.8% of the city's total industrial output.

Tertiary Industries

In the last few years, both the central and municipal governments adopted a series of measures to stimulate the city's tertiary industry. As a result, the proportion of the tertiary sector in GDP constantly increased from only 18% at the beginning of the economic reforms to over half of the total GDP – it had a share of 50.7% in 2001, surpassing secondary sector's 47.6%. Specifically, several industries have gradually become the pillars over the past ten years, such as finance and insurance, commerce, transportation, post and telecommunications, real estate and information technology. In 2001, these five industries made up nearly 41.9% of the city's GDP. Finance and insurance sector remains the single largest tertiary industry, sharing 13.8% in the city's GDP.

Today, Shanghai has become the capital of China's burgeoning service industry. Banking, retail, finance, trade, insurance, and real estate development contribute half the city's GDP.

Noticeably, the information industry has achieved remarkable advancement. The prime part of the Info Port project, featuring broadband, high speed and multi-functions, has already been completed. In addition, a number of key projects, such as integrated information pipelines, the broadband IP urban network, data network, cable television-Internet transformation, and the broadband information exchange center, have all been completed.

DEVELOPMENT OF PUDONG NEW DISTRICT

With an area of 533 sq km and a population (permanent residents) of 1.63 million, Pudong is separated from downtown Shanghai by the Huangpu River. Prior to 1990, its economy lagged far behind the city's overall level. That, however, began to change when the central government made an official announcement in 1990 to open up Pudong in order to boost the economic development of the entire Yangtze River Delta. This has since transformed Shanghai into an international economic, financial and trading power.

In 1990, Pudong's industrial added value was only RMB6 billion, but the figure soared to RMB108.2 billion in 2001, representing an annual increase of over 20%, 8% higher than the city's average. In 2001, the output value of its secondary sector reached RMB57.1 billion, up 17.6%, and that of its tertiary industry amounted to RMB50.5 billion, up 14.7%. A total of 880 new foreign investment projects were signed, involving USD2 billion of foreign capital, or 27.1% of the city's total.

Given Pudong's ultra-modern facilities and infrastructure and its convenient geographic location, it is not surprising that it has attracted investment from all over the world. To date, one third of fixed asset investment in Pudong is from overseas sources, totaling RMB100 billion (USD12 billion). A total of 146 of the Fortune Global 500 multinationals have

invested in Pudong. Renowned companies include GM, Intel, Bell, Kodak, Sony, Sharp and Siemens.

Within a decade, Pudong has adopted a super-modern look, with eye-catching and glittering highrises of amazing architectural variety. Many visitors, including top leaders of foreign countries, stroll away shaking their heads in disbelief that such a sparkling city could have sprung up in such a short time span.

ENCOURAGED INVESTMENT SECTORS

In the coming five years, Shanghai will make great efforts to attract foreign capital into six major industries and to open the service market to overseas funds on a larger scale. These six new major industries include IT, financial services, commerce, automobile, set equipment manufacturing and real estate. Compared with the city's old six key industries, the new ones are apparently related to the high-tech industry and service trades.

In the near future, the city will give full play to its advantages in the tertiary sector, to boost the opening up of services like commerce, foreign trade, transportation, accountancy and law firms.

Besides directing the introduction of foreign capital, Shanghai has also adopted new policies to promote private enterprises, especially in high-tech area, to utilize foreign capital and encourage foreign enterprises' merger and acquisition.

ECONOMIC OUTLOOK

The 10th Five-Year (2001-2005) Plan of Shanghai clearly demonstrates the city's nearly 360,000 people. The non-SOEs' share in the city's total fixed assets investment also grew from 46.9% to 52.1%, outstripping the state investment for the first time in 50 years. determination to continue and deepen its economic reforms. The municipal government identifies the aforesaid six new pillar industries as the most important engines to power the city's economic growth. In particular, high-tech industry largely represented by IT is considered as the priority task. For example, by 2005, telecommunications, computer and software development are expected to make up 13% of the city's GDP. Meanwhile, the city will give further support to four new industries – biopharmaceuticals, environment protection, new materials and logistics – in the hope that they will turn into new pillars in the future. As for the ownership structure, the city calls for a more flexible "oval" pattern that economic entities with pure state or pure private capital will only constitute a minor part. Instead, those with mixed ownership will dominate. According to the city's economic blueprint, non-state-owned economy's contribution to the GDP will be lifted to about 40% by 2005. Making room for market-oriented capitalization, state investment will gradually draw out from the traditional industries like food, drink, plastics, metal products, and switch to the high-tech and the pillar industries, such as fine steel, petrochemicals, automobile, electronics and information technology.

Agriculture

INTRODUCTION

Surrounding the city of Shanghai, the suburbs offer over 300,000 hectares of fertile soil for arable farming and agricultural purpose. These agricultural products and harvested crops are mainly rice, wheat, cotton, vegetables and subtropical fruits. As far as the yield per unit for these crops is concerned, Shanghai ranks as one of the highest in China. Animal husbandry in the suburbs has developed rapidly with the main output of pork, poultry and milk. Local produce such as mushroom, garlic, frozen livestock and vegetables are popular in the international markets.

In 2001, Shanghai's agricultural sector reported an added value of RMB8.55 billion, up 3% from 2000. The total agricultural output value reached RMB22.69 billion in 2001, growth of 4.9% over the previous year. However, agricultural sector still takes a proportion of less than 1.7% in the economy.

Shanghai Agricultural Output (RMB million)

	Agriculture	Plantation	Forestry	Animal	Fishery
1995	18,247	7,771	45	8,148	2,283
1996	20,095	8,764	67	8,546	2,718
1997	20,441	8,520	47	8,837	3,037
1998	20,675	8,910	84	8,727	2,954
1999	20,690	8,786	98	8,635	3,171
2000	21,650	8,982	141	8,735	3,792
2001	22,685	9,469	264	8,855	4,097

SHANGHAI TO REVITALIZE AGRICULTURE

Shanghai, China's leading industrial and financial hub, is also aiming to be an important trading center of agricultural products. It had worked out a series of strategies in achieving this goal:

- Agricultural production: to allocate one third of the agricultural land for the growing of vegetables and fruits.
- Establishment of agricultural parks: which include the state-level Pudong Sunqiao Modern Agricultural Park, Qingpu Green Project Base, Chongming Green Food Park and other 12 municipal-level parks;
- Improvement in marketing strategies, to establish an agricultural trading platform for those import and export products;
- IT application: to launch a "Shanghai Agricultural Website" to providefirms with online information, enquiry, technical assistance and trading services.
- Education: the merger of the Shanghai Agricultural College and Shanghai Jiaotong University will promote synergy and enhance the competitive advantages in injecting new forces towards the agricultural modernization.
- Agricultural sector in Shanghai has attracted increased attention from foreign investors in the past several years. They found opportunities in Shanghai's agricultural sector because of the huge market with 13 million residents and the conducive business environment.

Statistics reveal that foreign investors have established a total of more than 600 agricultural ventures in this metropolis. The foreign businesses are mainly engaged in farm produce processing, animal husbandry, horticulture, vegetables and fruit plantation.

Current Situation

In the 1990s, agricultural sector in Shanghai had gone through the conversion from traditional to modern in tandem with the pace of the city's prosperity and development, thus forming the "suburban pattern" characteristic of Shanghai agriculture. In 1995, the CPC Shanghai Committee and the municipal government put forward the development strategy to emphasize the so-called "vegetable basket" and "rice bag" projects to construct a suitable municipal agriculture.

In 2001, total cultivated land was 29,090 hectares, including 16,000 hectares of grain plantation. The land area yield remains stable even in case of drought or water logging. The total grain output of suburban Shanghai was 1.51 million tons. Marketable volume of fresh vegetables was 1.85 million. The ratio between grain crops output and economic crops output is 43:57.

The stress of grain production stabilization is to ensure that total grain output of Shanghai will be maintained at about two million tons. Special attention will be paid to reasonable utilization of natural resources, input of science and technology, and constructions of modern agricultural bases, in order to encourage ecology, sightseeing, tourism and foreign exchange earning in many aspects.

Further Advancement of Agriculture

Agriculture is one of the most vulnerable sectors after China's WTO entry. Foreseeing the development tendency and up-coming competition, the Shanghai municipal government has been upgrading its agricultural sector.

Since 1999, the municipality started the construction of 12 modern agriculture parks, launching a group of projects for production and processing of vegetables, fruits and aquatic products. A total of more than 200 large modern greenhouses were built. With the assistance of modern science and technology, and with more than 30 colleges and R&D institutes residing in those parks, a modern agriculture is taking shape.

12 Municipal Agricultural Parks in Suburban Shanghai	
Total planned area:	228 sq km
Total capital input:	RMB1.65 billion
Agricultural support:	RMB550 million
Investment attracted:	RMB1.1 billion
Investment projects:	197
Domestic:	166
Foreign funded:	31

The Shanghai Science & Technology Commission has doubled its funding for agricultural projects to RMB20 million in 2000 and an additional of RMB90 million will be contributed by research institutions and enterprises. Their work includes improvements in seeds, greenhouses, eco-agriculture and biotechnology.

MAJOR AGRICULTURAL INDUSTRIES

There are positive changes done to the agricultural production structure. In the 1995 – 2001 period, the proportion of plantation in the total agricultural output value decreased from 42.6% to 41.7% and that of animal husbandry dropped from 44.7% to 39.0%, while fisheries rose from 12.5% to 18.1%. The output value of vegetable, fruit, poultry and special breeding also reported tremendous increase during the period.

Farming

The total vegetable farming area of Shanghai was 13.3 thousand hectares and the total output 2.7 million tons in 2001. The sales turnover of vegetable was RMB2.6 billion. Together with the large quantity of demand, there is strong additional consumer needs in terms of different types, varieties and quality of vegetable. The area of Shanghai, Zhejiang, Jiangsu and other bordering provinces have a total population of more than 300 million. This particular region forms the Yangtze River Delta and is the most developed region in China. Shanghai's exports of farm products were supported by modern sciences and high technologies, and its agricultural sector has been actively exploring the overseas markets.

In 2001, farming products worth USD244 million were exported, an increase of 68.0% over the previous year. The total volume of vegetables for export doubled in 2001, reaching 80,000 tons. Export of new varieties of vegetables, high-quality flowers and special fruits also increased remarkably. In particular, annual export of flowers from Shanghai, 450 million stalks in 2001, account for one third of the national total.

Animal Husbandry

Since the 1950s, Shanghai's animal husbandry industry has been developed steadily. After the Shanghai municipal government implemented "vegetable basket" project in 1988, animal husbandry industry has been intensively enhanced.

Total output value of animal husbandry of the municipality had reached RMB8.56 billion. There are a few important companies including Dajiang (poultry processing), Songjiang Broad and Dairy Cattle Farm (processing of dairy product), Qingpu Daying (processing of duck) and Chongming (processing of mutton).

Fishery

There is a huge consumption of aquatic products in Shanghai. Not surprisingly, the production of fishery in Shanghai has always been in a state of steady growth. The pattern of fishery production promoting fish harvesting and fish farming simultaneously has been formed.

From 1996 to 2001, the fishery production of Shanghai was kept at a low development speed as fish harvesting was dropping. However, sericulture and prawn production are now on the rise.

Shanghai Fishery 2001		
Total fishery output	RMB4.013 billion	+5.8%
Total aquatic products	297,658 tons	+3.10%
captured from sea	102,296 tons	-14.90%
farming in sea	2,635 tons	+24.76%
captured from fresh water	5,583 tons	+1.16%
farming in fresh water	184,429 tons	+15.99%

Frozen Product And Fresh Food Storage

Shanghai has a cold storage capacity of 330,000 tons, of which 260,000 tons for frozen food and 70,000 tons for fresh food. Its cold storage warehouse is among the largest in China. Among others, there are a few prominent companies such as Wujing Cold Storage Company, the 21st Century Cold Storage Transport Co. Ltd., Waigaoqiao International Freight and Transport, Zhonghong Cold Storage Company and Jiangwan Storage and Transport. Besides, there are other companies that have specialized warehouse for storage of vegetables and fruits. All these have contributed to the development of Shanghai's agriculture and had enhanced the distribution network of agricultural products in Shanghai and other parts of China.

Banking & Finance

China's WTO agreements with the United States and European Union for the first time opened a door to many possibilities and imaginations for foreign investors who ever wanted to make a foothold in China's financial areas. Under the WTO accession agreement, China will completely open its financial market for foreign competition in five year's time. It will thus be a hot contest arena in the world of finance in the next few years. The world-class challenge requires a world-class solution, and certainly deserves the attention of top-notch international financial institutions and professionals. As the de facto financial capital of the country, Shanghai will be at the frontier of all these developments.

WTO COMMITMENT IN BANKING AND FINANCIAL SERVICES

Since the acquisition of WTO membership in December 2001, China has issued a number of new regulations and detailed measures that translate its WTO commitments into specific rules governing foreign participation in the financial market. For foreign financial services companies eager to gain access to the China market, it is crucial to understand these regulatory changes.

Banking Industries

Currently, foreign banks' major business remains in foreign currency business dealing with foreign-funded enterprises and a limited number of Chinese enterprises. According to the WTO agreement, China will gradually lift restriction imposed on foreign banks in handling Renminbi business by regions / cities:

- Shanghai, Shenzhen, Dalian and Tianjin upon China's accession to the WTO;

- Guangzhou, Zhuhai, Qingdao, Nanjing and Wuhan by 11 December 2002;
- Jinan, Fuzhou, Chengdu and Chongqing by 11 December 2003;
- Kunming, Beijing, and Xiamen by 11 December 2004;
- Shantou, Ningbo, Shenyang and Xi'an by 11 December 2005;
- By 11 December 2006, all geographic restrictions will be removed.

In addition, China will also gradually abolish client restrictions on foreign banks in Renminbi business.

- By 11 December 2003, China will allow foreign banks to handle Renminbi business for Chinese enterprises;
- By 11 December 2006, China will permit foreign banks to provide services for all Chinese clients. It will also allow them to set up business outlets in the same region. The requirements of examination and approval are the same with domestic banks.
- By December 11 of 2006, China will abolish all existing restrictions imposed on foreign banks in their ownership, forms of operation and establishment, including their branches, representative offices and the issuance of licenses.

Insurance

The main commitments of the Chinese government in opening the insurance business are as follows.

In terms of the business form:

- Immediately upon China's entry to the WTO, foreign non-lifeinsurance companies are allowed to set up branches or joint ventures in China. Foreign firms will be allowed to hold as much as 51% of the stake in the joint ventures.
- Immediately upon the entry, foreign life insurance companies are allowed to set up joint ventures in China, and hold no more than 50% stake in the joint ventures. They will also be allowed to choose their partners independently.
- Immediately upon China's WTO accession, the foreign stake in Sino-foreign joint venture insurance brokerage companies may reach 50%,

and the proportion may not exceed 51% within three years after the accession.

- Two years after the entry, foreign non-life insurance firms will be allowed to set up wholly owned branches in China, i.e. there will be no restriction regarding the form of enterprise establishment.
- Five years after the WTO entry, foreign insurance brokerage companies will be permitted to set up wholly owned sub-firms. With gradual cancellation of geographical limitations, foreign insurance companies will, after approval, be permitted to set up branches. The qualification conditions for initial establishment do not apply to the establishment of internal branches.

Winterthur Insurance's branch in Shanghai

In terms of geographical restriction:

- Immediately upon WTO entry, foreign life and non-life insurance firms are allowed to offer services in Shanghai, Guangzhou, Dalian, Shenzhen and Foshan.
- Two years after entry, foreign insurance companies' business can be extended to Beijing, Chengdu, Chongqing, Fuzhou, Suzhou, Xiamen, Ningbo, Shenyang, Wuhan and Tianjin. All geographical restrictions will be lifted three years after entry.

In terms of business scope:

- Immediately upon the entry, foreign non-life insurance companies from abroad are permitted to engage in general insurance and large-scale commercial insurance without any geographical limitation, and offer non-life services to overseas enterprises, property insurance to foreign-funded enterprises in China, and related liability insurance and credit insurance services.

- Immediately upon the entry, foreign life insurance companies are permitted to provide individual (non-group) life insurance services to foreign citizens and Chinese citizens.
- Immediately upon the entry, foreign reinsurance companies are permitted to provide life and non-life reinsurance services in the form of branch company, joint venture company or wholly owned sub-firm. There are no geographical restrictions or quantity limits in license granting.
- Two years after the entry, non-life insurance companies from abroad will be able to offer all kinds of non-life insurance services to Chinese and foreign customers.
- Two years after the entry, they will be permitted to provide health insurance, group insurance, pension insurance and annual pay insurance services to Chinese and foreign citizens.

In terms of business license issuance, immediately upon the WTO entry, China is committed to abolishing the restrictions on the number of licenses issued to foreign insurance companies. Foreign insurance companies must satisfy the following conditions before applying for licenses in China: a business history of more than 30 years in a WTO member country, operating a representative office in China for two consecutive years and holding no less than USD5 billion in total assets by the end of the year prior to the application.

In terms of legal insurance scope, China has committed that the regulation of 20% proportion provided by Sino-foreign direct insurance companies to Chinese reinsurance companies will not be changed immediately upon the WTO entry, and will be lowered to 15% one year after the entry, 10% two years after the entry, 5% three years after the entry. Eventually all rates will be cancelled four years after the entry. However, foreign insurance companies will not be permitted to engage in third-party liability insurance of motor vehicles, liability insurance for public transport vehicles, commercial vehicle drivers and carriers, and other legal insurance services.

In terms of general insurance policy brokerage service, national treatment will be granted. However, the geographical scope for opening to foreign insurance brokerage companies will follow that of foreign insurance companies, i.e., they will be allowed to do business in Shanghai, Guangzhou, Dalian, Shenzhen and Foshan immediately upon the WTO entry, in ten more cities two years after the entry, and in all cities three years after the entry.

In terms of insurance brokerage qualification, aside from the conditions of a 30-year operating history and running representative office for two consecutive years, there are also conditions in the aspect of asset scale, that is, in excess of USD500 million at the time of entry, in excess of USD400 million one year after the entry, in excess of RMB300 million two years after the entry, and in excess of RMB200 million four years after the entry.

Besides, the Chinese government has, in accordance with the General Agreement on Service Trade, made commitments with regard to the trans-territory delivery, for example, in international marine shipping, aviation and freight transport insurance and reinsurance and large-scale commercial insurance and reinsurance brokerage services.

Securities

At the end of 2001, the China Securities Regulatory Commission (CSRC) announced the contents of opening securities market after China's WTO entry:

- Within three years after accession, foreign securities firms will be permitted to establish joint ventures, with foreign minority ownership not lower than 25% but not exceeding 33%.
- Securities JVs may engage in underwriting A-shares; underwriting and trading of B and H shares; and underwriting and trading of government and corporate debts.
- More competent domestic enterprises are encouraged to list overseas. While still encouraging them to list in Hong Kong market, global securities markets are to be tapped in such as New York, London, Tokyo, Singapore and Australia.

- Qualified foreign-funded enterprises are to be gradually permitted to issue stocks and get listed in China when conditions are mature.

Fund Management

Upon accession to WTO, foreign investors are allowed to either invest in an existing fund management company or jointly establish a new enterprise. Initially, their share can be more than 25% while less than 33%; in three years that percentage of ownership may grow to 49%.

Other Financial Services

Ater entry to WTO, foreign non-bank financial institutions are allowed to set up wholly foreign-owned or joint venture automobile financing service companies. Within five years after WTO entry, China foreign-funded banks can provide automobile credit service for individual Chinese residents. Foreign-funded financial leasing companies are allowed to provide financial leasing service within the same period of time as that of Chinese firms.

ENTRY REQUIREMENTS ON FINANCIAL SERVICE PROVIDERS

Currently, foreign financial institutions should meet asset and experience requirement before applying for establishing wholly-owned foreign enterprises or joint ventures. They also have to meet minimum registered capitalization and set for prescribed business scope before starting their operations.

Banking Services

The State Council approved the Regulations of the People's Republic of China on Administration of Foreign-Invested Financial Institutions on 12 December 2001. They were promulgated on 20 December 2001 and came into effect on 1 February 2002.

The Regulations cover wholly owned foreign banks, branches of foreign banks, JV banks, wholly owned foreign financial companies and JV financial companies in China. The minimum registered capital (in a freely convertible currency) for wholly owned foreign banks and JV banks is equivalent to RMB300 million. For wholly owned foreign financial companies and JV financial companies, (in a freely convertible currency) it is equivalent to RMB200 million. In both cases, the actual paid up capital shall be 50% of the minimum registered capital. In addition, parent companies should allocate at least (freely convertible currency) the equivalent of RMB100 million to their branches in China as operating funds.

The total assets of a party applying to establish a wholly owned foreign bank or wholly-owned foreign non-bank finance company must not be less than USD10 billion at the end of the year preceding the application. The total assets of a party that applies to establish a foreign bank branch must be at least USD20 billion at the end of the year preceding the application. The total assets of a foreign joint venture partner applying to establish a joint venture bank or joint venture finance company must be USD10 billion at the end of the year preceding the application.

The Regulations provide that a foreign-invested financial institution must meet the following requirements in order to carry out Chinese currency business:

It must have carried on business in China at least three years before the application.

- It must have made a profit in the two successive years preceding the application.
- It must meet other prudential requirements stipulated by the People's Bank of China.

Wholly foreign-owned banks, branches of foreign banks and JV banks may:

- Issue short-term, medium-term and long-term loans;
- Bill acceptance and discount;
- Purchase and sell government and financial bonds and securities in foreign currencies other than shares;
- Engage in credit and guarantee services;
- Handle domestic and foreign account settlements;
- Purchase and sell foreign exchange;

- Engage in foreign currency conversion;
- Execute inter-bank call loans;
- Engage in bankcard services;
- Handle safe keeping services;
- Offer credit investigation and consulting services; or
- Other operations approved by People's Bank of China (PBC).

Insurance Services

The qualifications for establishing a foreign funded insurance company in China are as follows:

- a proven track of operating insurance business for more than 30 years;
- a representative office in China for more than two years;
- total asset of no less than USD5 billion at the year end immediately prior to the submission of the application.

For insurance brokers, the asset requirement is USD500 million, within two years it is reduced to USD300 million, and further reduced to USD200 million within three years after China's accession to WTO.

The minimum registered capital for a joint venture insurance company or a wholly owned insurance company should be not less than RMB200 million or equivalent foreign exchange. The registered capital shall be actually paid up.

A branch is not deemed as a separate legal entity in China. Therefore, the concept of limited liability does not apply. The parent company is required to allocate a minimum of RMB200 million or equivalent foreign exchange as the branch's operating capital.

A foreign-funded insurance company, in accordance with its business scope verified by China Insurance Regulatory Commission (CIRC), is permitted to carry out either of the following categories of business, but not both:

- Property insurance, including property loss insurance, liability insurance, credit insurance and other insurance; and
- Personal insurance including life insurance, health insurance, accident insurance and so on.

Securities

According to the major piece of legislation on Sino-Foreign joint venture securities companies ("Securities JV Rule"), the conditions on a securities JV are as follows:

- it must have registered capital of not less than RMB500 million;
- the Chinese and foreign parties as well as the proportion and methods of their capital contributions must comply with the provisions of the "Securities JV Rule";
- it must have no less than 50 practitioners with professional qualifications for securities business, as well as the necessary accounting, legal and IT professionals;
- it must have a sound international management and risk control system and a standardized system for the separate management of personnel, finance and information for underwriting, brokerage and proprietary trading businesses, and have an appropriate technical system for internal control;
- it must have the required business premises and proper trading facilities; and
- other conditions specified by China Securities Regulatory Commission (CSRC).

Conditions to be satisfied by a foreign party to set up a Securities JV:

- it must be located in a country with sound securities laws and regulatory systems, and the relevant securities regulatory authority must have concluded a memorandum of understanding on securities regulatory cooperation with CSRC;
- it must possess the legal qualification to conduct securities business in its home country, operated financial business for more than 10 years, and received no material punishment from the securities regulatory authority or judicial bodies in the last three years;
- every risk monitoring ration in the past three years must be in compliance with the provisions of laws and the requirements of the securities regulatory authority of its home country;
- it must have a sound internal control system; and

- it must have a satisfactory reputation and performance in the international securities market.

OPPORTUNITIES & CHALLENGES

Shanghai gives high priority to the financial industry in line with the support from the central government. In early 1990s, the late paramount leader Deng Xiaoping made the call for re-establishing Shanghai as a financial center, which he stressed could help China integrate into the world economy. The blueprint of building Shanghai into a financial center was designed on the basis of the prosperous areas along the banks of the Huangpu River. Among the 160 financial institutions located on both sides of the river, there are the People's Bank of China Shanghai Branch, the Industrial and Commercial Bank of China, China Construction Bank, Agricultural Bank of China, China Bank of Communications, Shanghai Stock Exchange (SSE), Shanghai Futures Exchange, Citibank, Bank of America, Bank of Tokyo-Mitsubishi, Mizuho Bank and Bank of Bangkok etc. The area witnesses a cash flow of several trillion U.S. dollars every year.

Since 1990, Shanghai's financial sector has recorded a rapid growth. In 2001, the financial sector accounted for 13.8% of the city's GDP, compared with 10% in 1995. By the end of June 2002, local banks had total assets of RMB1.23 trillion (USD140 billion). The outstanding deposits and loans of these banks stood at RMB920 billion (USD110 billion) and RMB680 billion (USD80 billion) respectively.

Today, Shanghai has become the national center of fund allocation, and leads the formation of a healthy national capital market, including the inter-bank loans market, the bond market, and the foreign exchange market. Many Chinese banks, securities companies and fund management companies have set up their headquarters in Shanghai. Chinese-funded banks in Shanghai make up 6% of the country's total in terms of deposits, loans and assets, while overseas-funded banks in the city account for over 50% of the foreign banks' total deposits, loans and assets in China. This is a clear sign that foreign banks are more concentrated in Shanghai than any other Chinese city.

Shanghai Futures Tower

Due to restrictions on market entry and business scope, foreign financial institutions as a whole have achieved only a small share of Shanghai's banking, insurance, securities and fund management businesses. It is fair to say that, until recently, the potentially lucrative China market was beyond the reach of most foreign financial institutions and that domestic players were enjoying a virtual monopoly.

Responding to China's substantial market opening commitments to joining WTO, financial institutions from all over the world have in the past two to three years begun to take more determined and concrete steps to explore or expand in China.

By the end of May 2002, there are a total of 37 foreign banks in Shanghai having received the license to conduct Renminbi (RMB) business. Foreign currency deposits and loans with the banks totaled USD1.63 billion and USD9.71 billion respectively.

Shanghai is keen to leverage on foreign capital and expertise in order to bring greater sophistication to its financial market. Domestic financial institutions are to be put under more stringent prudential supervision, while at the same time facing foreign competition. The actual pace of the market's opening may therefore go beyond what China has committed.

At present, the partially open mainland financial market may bring greater opportunities to global giants than smaller-scale financial institutions. In particular, the asset/capital requirement stipulated for the foreign partner in a joint venture in many financial businesses virtually block the entry of smaller players. A lowering of the thresholds would therefore facilitate market access for many small foreign financial institutions.

Shanghai's Financial Market 2001	
Total Balance of Deposit	RMB958 billion (USD116 billion)
Total Balance of Loan	RMB719 billion (USD87 billion)
Cash-in Value	RMB1, 010 billion (USD122 billion)
Cash-out Value	RMB1, 031 billion (USD125 billion)
Proportion of Financial Sector in GDP	13.84%
Increased value of Insurance sector	RMB68.5 billion (USD8.3 billion)
Companies listed on SSE	690
Total money raised in SSE	RMB53.4 billion (USD6.5 billion)
Total Transaction Value	RMB4.41 trillion (USD534.5 billion)
- Stock	RMB2.27 trillion (USD275.2 billion)
- Bond	RMB1.98 trillion (USD240 billion)
Total Premium Revenue	RMB18 billion (USD2.2 billion)
- Property Insurance	RMB4 billion (USD0.5 billion)
- Personal Insurance	RMB14 billion (USD1.7 billion)
Total Insurance Compensation	RMB3.9 billion (USD0.5 billion)
Premium per capita	RMB1,355 (USD164)
Operational Foreign Institutions	69
Foreign Banks	53
- With right to do RMB business	24
Total Assets of Foreign Institutions	USD23.6 billion
- Deposit Balance	USD3.3 billion
- Loan Balance	USD9.7 billion

Banking Services

China's banking services are in fact dominated by the big-four state commercial banks – Construction Bank, Industrial and Commercial Bank, Bank of China and Agricultural Bank – that control 80% of the market. However, all of them suffer from problems like huge non-performing loans, lack of modern banking products, uncreditworthy customers (most are state owned enterprises), and overstaffing and over-branching.

The government is using asset management companies to purchase the banks' bad loans at apparently full book value by converting to bonds guaranteed by the State. Despite of their advantages of very large deposit bases, branch networks and government support, these problem-ridden banks remain unattractive for any large international institution to consider a serious tie-up.

As a result, most of the foreign banks that wish to enter China market are eyeing on small and medium-sized banks. As these Chinese banks have a big share in niche markets, they offer convenient vehicles for foreign banks to obtain related market demand information. For the Chinese banks, it would be a viable channel to quickly expand their capital and strengthen their capacity by allying with big foreign players.

Chinese rule now permits foreign banks to take minority stakes in, or form joint venture with, domestic banks. Many of the second tier Chinese banks have been seeking investments from major international banks. For example, in December 2001, Hong Kong and Shanghai Banking Corp (HSBC) bought 8% shares in the Bank of Shanghai, becoming the first overseas bank to take a stake in a mainland bank. Almost at the same time, the International Finance Corpor-ation (IFC) signed an agreement in Beijing on mak-ing an equity investment in the Nanjing City Commercial Bank. According to the agreement, the International Finance Corporation would spend USD27 million to buy over 180 million shares of the Nanjing City Commercial Bank or 15% of its share capital after expansion. This made IFC the largest foreign shareholder in the Chinese banking industry till the end of 2001.

Billboard of HSBC

Since August 2002, Citibank has also been negotiating with Shanghai Jinqiao Export Processing Zone Development Co. and Shanghai State Asset Management Co Ltd. to buy over 1.66% and 8.26% shares, respectively, of Pudong Development Bank. If successful, this will make Citibank the single largest shareholder in the local bank, which has a market value of RMB46.4 billion and 261 branches.

A key distinction here is whether the operating bank will be a "foreign-invested enterprise" (FIE) or a domestic bank under Chinese law. During the WTO transition period FIEs are still subject to many of the prior limitations on foreign banking activities, to be gradually lifted over five years. In contrast, a foreign investment in a Chinese bank with less than 25% stake means the Chinese bank in practice is not treated as an FIE, so that it can continue to do full local currency and other business permitted to domestic banks. However, the lack of control associated with this structure will be unappealing to many international banks.

Compared to mainland banks, foreign banks may be more interested in corporate and investment banking. Foreign banks are thus in an advantageous position to capture a significant share of the market once it opens. Limited by their branch network, foreign banks may have difficulties competing with mainland banks in the mass market. However, they may be more successful in providing customized services to higher income customers.

So far, Citibank Shanghai maintains the first ranking among all foreign banks in China as measured by the PBC Shanghai in terms of total assets, local currency deposits, total deposits and local currency loans. Originally established in 1902, Citibank Shanghai was among the first batch of foreign banks to receive RMB licenses in 1997 and also the first foreign bank in China granted all-around foreign currency services licenses to Chinese customers in March 2002. Other prominent international banks include Standard Chartered Bank. It set up its first branch in Shanghai 150 years ago and just recently opened another branch in Puxi, which claims to be the biggest among all foreign banking branches in Shanghai.

Insurance Services

The great potential and liberalization of the China's insurance market made insurance industry a new focal area for foreign investment. Compared with 11% in Japan and 8% in the United States, the insurance industry only represents less than 2% of China's GDP. By 2005, the total value of insurance premiums in China is expected to reach USD33.82 billion, constituting 2.3% of the total GDP; the average premium per person will be USD27.78, still at a considerably low level. With 16 million people and GDP per capita over USD4,500, Shanghai holds great attractions to foreign players such as AIG, AXA and Allianz. Currently, Shanghai takes up 13.6% of foreign insurance companies' market share in China.

A few state-owned companies, in particular the People's Insurance Company of China (PICC), monopolized the insurance services till the late 1986. Shanghai was opened to foreign insurance companies in 1992.

Shanghai Insurance Market

Non-life Insurance Company	Market Share (%)
Ping An	43
China Life	29
AIA	13
CPIC	10
Manulife-Zhonghong	2
CPIC-Aetna	1
Allianz-Dazhong	0.3
AXA-Minmetals	0.3
Taikang	0.5
China Life–CMG	0.1

Non-life Insurance Company	Market Share (%)
PICC	51
CPIC	15
Ping An	10
Dazhong	8
Tian'An	5
AIG	3.7
Huatai	2.5
Winterthur	2.6
Tokyo Fire & Marine	1.5
Royal & Sun Alliance	0.75

Compared with overseas rivals, China's insurance industry is obviously less competitive. According to a report released by Beijing office of the China Insurance Regulatory Commission (CIRC), the results of a recent survey of 5,000 residents on the Beijing insurance market show that among the residents having bought life insurance, only 17% are satisfied with the after-sale services. Besides, the insurees know little about their entitled rights: only 25.7% say they are very clear about the insurance clauses; 19.2% say

Total number of listed companies as at year-end (1990-2002)

Year	1990	1991	1992	1993	1994	1995	1996	1997	1998	1999	2000	2001	2002 (Till 15 /08)
Total	10	14	53	183	291	323	530	745	851	949	1088	1160	1192
Shanghai	8	8	29	106	171	188	293	383	438	484	572	646	686
Shenzhen	2	6	24	77	120	135	237	362	413	465	516	508	504

Number of newly listed companies (1990-2002)

Year	1990	1991	1992	1993	1994	1995	1996	1997	1998	1999	2000	2001	2002 (Till 15 / 08)
Total	10	14	39	130	108	32	207	215	106	98	139	68	38
Shanghai	8	0	21	77	65	17	105	90	55	46	88	74	42
Shenzhen	2	4	18	53	43	15	102	125	51	52	51	- 6	- 4

Sources: CSRC (www.csrc.gov.cn), Shanghai Stock Exchange (www.sse.com.cn), Shenzhen Stock Exchange (www.sse.org.cn); figures may contain discrepancies.

they have not even read the clauses; 47.7% say they have read but do not fully understand the clauses; and 7.9% say they have tried to read but can not understand. Meanwhile, a survey of 1,600 residents who have not bought insurance shows the respondents are reluctant to buy insurance on the grounds that "it is easy to buy insurance but difficult to claim for indemnity", "insurance is unnecessary for the moment" and "no suitable insurance products have been found". Poor service quality has become an important reason restraining the development of the insurance market in China.

So far, there are 8 foreign-controlled and 6 Sino-foreign JV insurance companies operating in Shanghai. Several foreign insurance companies have already taken minority stakes in Chinese domestic insurance companies, pursuant to an insurance regulation specifically authorizing foreign minority investments of less than 25%. Similar to the banking area, such a structure preserves the domestic character of the insurer and exempts it from restrictions on foreign insurance companies. Alternatively, establishing an FIE insurance company with a 25% or greater foreign interest is also possible, but the scope of business will be limited to that permitted to foreign insurance companies, bearing in mind this scope expands during the course of the following three years.

The predecessor of AIA was originally founded in Shanghai in 1919. In September 1992, the returned AIA Shanghai became the first foreign insurer that obtained a license to provide life insurance for Chinese nationals.

Having brought over its founding site at No. 17, the Bund, AIA has come back to be the leading life insurer in China.

Shanghai Stock Exchange

STOCK EXCHANGE

Securities

After more than a decade of development, securities market in Shanghai, the first in China, has reached a considerable scale. Shanghai Stock Exchange (SSE) had listed 688 companies as in the mid of August 2002. The capitalization of Shanghai's stock market has risen to RMB2.949 trillion (USD357 billion), against RMB3 billion (USD375 million) when it established in 1990. SSE now ranks 13th among over 200 bourses around the world in terms of capitalization, following the stock exchanges of Tokyo and Hong Kong in Asia.

From the beginning, SSE possesses its own distinctive personalities from Shenzhen Stock Exchange. In Shanghai, the listed companies are mainly large state-owned enterprises; the Shanghai market's performance is therefore sometimes seen as an indicator of China's domestic economy. Manufacturing and export companies doing business with nearby Hong Kong dominate the Shenzhen Stock Exchange, so is sometimes a barometer of that sector.

Seven Types of Shares in China

State Shares - Shares owned by the state;

Legal Person Shares - Shares owned by companies or institutions;

A-shares – Owned only by Chinese individuals;

B-shares – Transacted in foreign currency, used to be purchased by overseas residents, opened to Chinese nationals since February 2001;

H-shares – Shares in Chinese companies that are traded on the Stock Exchange of Hong Kong, or Hang Seng China Enterprise Shares;

Red Chips – Shares in Hong Kong companies that are traded in Hong Kong but derive most of their profit from business in Mainland China, or Hang Seng China-Affiliated Shares;

N-shares – American Depositary Receipts (ADR's), issued by Chinese companies and traded on the New York Stock Exchange.

Of this group, the first two, with huge volume held by government or SOEs, remain largely non-circulating, though occasionally the central government intends to sell into the open stock. Due to strong market resistance, in June 2002 the State Council decided to suspend its previous plan on reducing state-owned shares by trading in the stock market, which was interpreted as a positive signal in both stock markets of Shanghai and Shenzhen. For foreign portfolio investment, last four are the major ways to invest in Chinese stocks. To date, no foreign-funded companies have been approved to be listed on SSE and no foreign stock brokers have been allowed to buy seats in the exchange yet.

Construction

Shanghai has been one of the world's fastest growing economies since the last decade. It has undergone continuous development in urban construction and infrastructure. The city's landscape is constantly changing. Infrastructure development has been an important growth engine for Shanghai's economy. With over RMB360 billion being injected into such projects. The annual average growth stands as high as 30.7%. Major functional and hub infrastructure projects include the Inner Ring Road, Metro Line 1, the North-South Viaduct, Yan'an Road Viaduct, Metro Lines 2 and 3, and the Pudong International Airport.

Construction sites are visible everywhere in Shanghai

Up to now, a three-dimensional express transportation network has taken its shape in Shanghai. It is formed by the Inner and Outer Ring roads, viaducts, Humin Elevated Road, Yanggao Road, highways to Jiading, Xinzhuang and Songjiang, Shanghai-Nanjing and Shanghai-Hangzhou expressways, Huqingping Expressway, Metro lines, the Longhua-Jiangwan light railroad, Phase I Project of Pudong International Airport (already in operation) and suburban ring roads (presently under active construction). Apart from Songpu Bridge built in 1970s, four grander bridges spanning the Huangpu River have been built since the Pudong development in early 1990s, namely, Nanpu, Yangpu, Fengpu and Xupu Bridges.

WTO COMMITMENTS ON CONSTRUCTION

Contract Construction

Within three years after WTO accession, wholly-owned foreign enterprises (WOFEs) are allowed, though still restricted to undertake the following contract construction projects:

- Projects solely funded by foreign investment or foreign donation;
- Projects financed by international financial institutions' loan through international tendering;
- Joint projects undertaken by Chinese and foreign enterprises with the latter's share over 50%;
- Joint venture projects and special domestic projects that are technically difficult for a domestic enterprise to undertake by itself; relevant government bodies have agreed for them to seek foreign contractors.

At the moment, a joint venture contractor, which has the status of a Chinese legal person, is theoretically capable of undertaking all construction projects in China.

Within three years after WTO accession, Sino-foreign joint venture can enjoy national treatment. Within five years after WTO accession, WOFEs are allowed without projects restriction.

Survey and Consulting

- Equity joint venture or cooperative joint venture are allowed to establish;

- Architects, engineers or enterprises who wish to undertake survey or consulting businesses in China must be licensed architects, engineers, or enterprises in their home country;
- Within five years after WTO accession, WOFEs are allowed to establish in this area.

Real Estate

- WOFEs are allowed to undertake real estate development projects except for the high-grade projects (star hotels, condominiums, golf courts etc);
- Sino-foreign joint ventures are allowed in real estate agency services (real estate valuation and management etc.);
- Within five years after WTO accession, WOFEs are allowed.

Urban Planning

- Sino-foreign joint ventures are allowed in urban planning and design except the master urban planning;
- Foreign individuals or enterprises who undertake businesses in this area must be licensed planners or enterprises in their home country.

OPPORTUNITIES AND CHALLENGES

In 2001, the total value added of Shanghai's construction industry was RMB22.7 billion (USD2.75 billion), up 7.5% over the previous year. In the urban infrastructure construction, RMB46.1 billion was invested and 28 major infrastructure projects were completed, such as Shanghai Science Museum, International News Center and Shanghai New International Exhibition Center. The total number of major infrastructure projects under construction (expressway, railway transportation system, cross-river bridge) surpassed the sum of previous 10 years.

Construction Projects

In the housing construction market, the city's total investment was RMB48.6 billion (USD5.87 billion) that was up 14% from the previous year and accounted for 11% of China's total. The figure also contributed 6.2% to the city's GDP. Housing area under construction in 2001 reached 47.48 million square meters (up 5.4%), of which 19.17 million square meters (up 48%) was newly started, and 15.68 million square meters (up 7.5%) was completed.

As for home decoration, the amount that Shanghai's residents spent in 2001 reached RMB67, 000 (USD8,095) per house on average.

In 2002, Shanghai municipal government announced a mega plan to spend a record RMB50 billion (USD6 billion) on major construction projects. These include another elevated road, an underground tunnel across the Huangpu River, a light railroad, a 98-kilometre ring road and three expressways. Phase 1 of Metro Line 2, a 16.3 km line runs from Zhongshan Park in Puxi to Longdong Road in Pudong, may be completed ahead of schedule.

In the first half of 2002, over RMB5.56 billion had already been invested in the city's construction projects, which stood for 60% of Shanghai's total fixed assets investment in the same period. A total of 22 major construction projects were launched, among which the most remarkable include the first phase of the Yangshan Deepwater Port, Shanghai Railway South Station and the public transportation interchange at People's Square.

Another 23 major projects including the Gonghexin Viaduct will be completed in the second half of 2002. Nine projects including the extension of Metro line No.2 will be launched by the end of year 2002. The first phase of the Suzhou Creek dredging project will be completed soon and bring up the city's greenery coverage to over 25%, or 6.5 square meters per capita.

Shanghai's Construction Scale 2001

Project	Value
Total investment for major projects	RMB46 billion (USD5.58 billion)
- Percentage increase over 2000	84%

- Of total fixed asset investment	23%
Number of major projects completed	28
Number of major newly–started projects	26
Expressway	
- Planned	650 km
- Under Construction	160 km
- In Operation	111 km
Subway	
- Routes under construction	5
- Total Length	100 km

Shanghai is one of the fastest growing construction markets in the world with great potential of growth over the coming years. According to the 10th Five Year Plan (2001-2005), investments in residential housing in Shanghai will be RMB250 billion (USD30.2 billion), which accounts for 8-9% of the city's GDP and about 25% of the total fixed assets; the total housing floor area to be built will reach 75-80 million square meters, after 750,000 new home units are built; per capital residential space will be lifted to 19 square meters; and green land coverage will be increased to 2,200 hectares. New houses are to be distributed as follow:

Distribution of New Houses (2001-2005)

Area	million sq m
Within the Inner Ring:	19.5-20.8
Between the Inner and Outer Ring:	32.2-34.4
Beyond the Outer Ring:	23.3-34.8

Major Infrastructure Projects in Shanghai 2001

Project	Planned Investment (RMB100 million)	Realized Investment (RMB100 million
Port Construction		
- Phase 3 of Waigaoqiao Port	14.82	5.12
- Phase 4 of Waigaoqiao Port	28.50	6.78
Expressway Construction		
- Outer Ring Project Puxi Section	35.01	7.2
- Outer Ring Project Pudong Section	33.50	13.0
- Phase 2 of Jialiu First Grade Highway	3.83	1.33
- Tongjiang Sanya State Highway Shanghai Section	44.75	10.0
- Xin Feng Jin Expressway	22.38	5.5
- Hu Qing Ping Expressway	16.68	6.0
Railway Construction		
- Airport Magnetic Levitating Train Line	89.47	37.0
- Phase 2 of Pearl Project (22 km from Baoshan Road to Hongqiao Road)	132.08	18.01
- Gongehexin Road Comprehensive Project	45.0	8.0
- Urban Elevated Line (17 km from Xinzhuang to Minhang)	38.34	70.67
- Phase 1 of Yangpu Line	110.7	5.0

(22.6 km from Zhongyuan to Zhongshan South Road) - Westward Extension of Metro Line 2	 50.0	 30.0
Cross-river Projects - Outer Ring Lower Reach Huangpu Tunnel - Lupu Bridge - Fuxin East Road Cross River Project - Dalian Road Cross River Project	 17.48 22.15 14.0 15.0	 4.7 7.5 1.5 2.0
Urban Gas Transmission Network (Phase 1)	18.0	1.5
Suzhou Creek Comprehensive Treatment (Phase 1)	66.97	16.85
Information Infrastructure Construction	14.33	12.33

Construction Companies

Currently, in Shanghai's construction market, most of the large players are state-owned and medium-sized ones are often collectively owned. Private or quasi-private enterprises also exist but of less influence.

Top 50 Construction Companies in Shanghai, 2001

Rank	Construction Company
1	Shanghai Baoshan Iron & Steel Metallurgy Construction Co.
2	Shanghai Tunnel Engineering Co. Ltd
3	Shanghai No.3 Construction Co. Ltd
4	Shanghai No.7 Construction Co. Ltd

5	Shanghai No.1 Construction Co. Ltd
6	Shanghai No.4 Construction Co. Ltd
7	Shanghai No.13 Metallurgy Construction Co. Ltd
8	Shanghai No.8 Construction Co. Ltd
9	Shanghai No.5 Metallurgy Construction Co. Ltd
10	China No.20 Metallurgy Construction Co. (Shanghai)
11	Shanghai No.5 Construction Co. Ltd
12	Shanghai Installation Engineering Co. Ltd
13	Shanghai No.2 Construction Co. Ltd
14	Shanghai Kaitian Construction (Group) Co. Ltd
15	Shanghai Railway Construction (Group) Co. Ltd
16	Shanghai No.1 Municipal Engineering Construction Co. Ltd
17	Shanghai No.2 Municipal Engineering Construction Co. Ltd
18	Shanghai Urban Construction (Group) Co.
19	Shanghai Port Construction Co.
20	Shanghai Infrastructure Construction Co.
21	Shanghai Pudong New District Construction (Group) Co. Ltd
22	Shanghai Baoshan Iron & Steel Construction Co. Ltd
23	Shanghai Zhuan Construction Development Co. Ltd
24	Shanghai Zhuzong (Group) Co.
25	No.3 Airport Bureau No.2 Engineering Co.
26	Shanghai Guangsha (Group) Co. Ltd
27	Shanghai Construction Decoration (Group) Co. Ltd
28	Shanghai Petrochemical Installation & Maintenance Co.
29	Shanghai Highway & Bridge Construction Co. Ltd
30	Shanghai Fareast International Bridge Construction Co. Ltd
31	Nanhui Construction Co.
32	Shanghai Telecommunication Engineering Co.
33	Shanghai Construction & Decoration Engineering Co. Ltd
34	Shanghai Machinery & Construction Co.
35	Shanghai Airport Highway Construction Engineering Co. Ltd
36	Shanghai Genggeng Municipal Engineering Co. Ltd
37	Shanghai Power Transmission & Transformation Engineering Co.

38	Shanghai Pengxin Construction & Installation Co. Ltd
39	Shanghai Dongya Construction Industrial Co. Ltd
40	Shanghai Zhule Construction Development Co.
41	Jinshan Petrochemical Construction CO.
42	Shanghai Power Construction Engineering Co.
43	Shanghai Shanyang Construction (Group) Co.
44	Pudong Highway & Bridge Construction Co. Ltd
45	Shanghai Congming Construction (Group) Co. Ltd
46	Shanghai Kangye Construction Decoration Engineering Co. Ltd
47	Shanghai Yangzi River Construction Installation Engineering Co. Ltd
48	Shanghai Haizhi Construction Engineering Co.
49	Shanghai Pudong Beicai Municipal Construction Engineering Co.
50	China Railway Communication Signal Engineering Co. (Shanghai)

As China joined the WTO, opportunities for foreign construction companies arise. First, the WTO accession is expected to create a more open, regulated, and transparent market for foreign players. meanwhile, reduction in import duties will lower the market threshold and improve market access.

Entry Requirements for Foreign Construction Company

Foreign-invested construction enterprises shall be established in accordance to the 'Law on Sino-foreign Equity Joint Ventures of PRC', the 'Law on Sino-Foreign Cooperative Enterprises of PRC', and the 'Regulation on the Control of the Qualifications of Construction Enterprises' and other related laws, decrees and regulations.

In addition, the establishment of a foreign-funded construction enterprise shall meet the following conditions:

- The Chinese partner to a foreign-funded construction enterprise shall be a construction enterprise holding at least a second-grade qualification certificate; the foreign partner shall be a construction enterprise with the status of a legal person that possesses advanced technology, efficient management and a good reputation.

- Foreign construction enterprises, the applicants, can import advanced technology and equipments for construction from overseas and can train Chinese staff in engineering and management.
- The minimum registered capital of a foreign applicant is USD10 million for first-grade construction engineering enterprises, USD5 million for second-grade construction engineering enterprises, and USD1.6 million for third-grade construction engineering enterprises.
- The minimum registered capital is USD2 million for first-grade construction decoration and fitting enterprises, USD1.5 million for second-grade decoration and fitting enterprises, and USD600,000 for third-grade decoration and fittings enterprises.

RELEVANT RULES AND REGULATIONS

According to the Regulations of Shanghai Municipality on the Administration of Construction Market, Shanghai Municipal Construction Commission (SMCC) is the major government authority responsible for the municipality's construction market. The district/county construction bureaus or committees, within its scope of authority, are responsible for relevant affairs in their areas.

Individuals or organizations have to register at local industrial and commercial administration and obtain the certificates of professional qualifications issued by the government authorities before they can undertake the following:

- survey, design and construction for construction projects;
- contracting-out agency, supervision and cost consultation for construction projects. For individuals or organizations from Hong Kong, Macau, Taiwan or other countries to engage in construction activities, they have to obtain the business contracting permit approved by both Shanghai Municipal Foreign Economic Relations and Trade Commission (SMERT) and SMCC, and register at Shanghai

Industrial and Commercial Administration (SICA) before they are allowed to commence operations in Shanghai.

The project proposal and feasibility study for establishing foreign-funded construction enterprises shall be examined and approved by the relevant authorities. The examination and approval will be carried out at different levels based on the capacity of the business. Applications for first-grade construction enterprises will be examined and determined by the Ministry of Construction (MOC) and approved by the Ministry of Foreign Trade and Economic Cooperation (MOFTEC); applications for second-grade and lower level foreign-funded construction enterprises will be examined and determined by SMCC and approved by SMERT.

If the Chinese partners are enterprises directly affiliated to State Council departments, the applications shall be examined by MOC and approved by MOFTEC.

The application for establishing a foreign-funded construction JV will go through the following procedures:

- The Chinese partner shall submit the project proposal and feasibility study report and related documents of the proposed foreign-funded construction enterprises to the government authorities. If all the requirements are met, a 'Recommendation for the Examination of Foreign-Funded Construction Enterprises' shall be issued.
- The Chinese partner shall, on the effect of the 'Recommendation for the Examination of Foreign-Funded Construction Enterprises', submit the contract and articles of association and related documents for examination and approval by SMERT. If all the requirements are met, a 'Certificate of Approval for the Establishment of Foreign-Funded Enterprises' shall be issued.
- The Chinese partner shall go through the legal person registration procedures with SICA upon the effect of the 'Recommendation for the Examination of Foreign-Funded Construction Enterprises', the

'Certificate of Approval for the Establishment of Foreign-Funded Enterprises' and other related documents.

- After obtaining the business license, the foreign-funded construction enterprise shall go through the qualification examination and approval procedures with the construction authorities.

In applying for a foreign-funded construction enterprise, the Chinese partner shall submit the following documents:

- Application letter for the establishment of foreign-funded construction enterprises;
- Qualification certificates of the Chinese partner;
- Document of examination by departments in charge of the Chinese partner (except those that do not have senior administrative bodies);
- Project proposal for establishing foreign-funded construction enterprises;
- Feasibility study jointly compiled by all partners of the joint venture;
- Certificates of all partners for the registration with SICA; and
- Credit rating certificates of all partners and other relevant documents.

Information Technology & Communication

The information technology and communication industry in Shanghai is one of the current six pillar industries in Shanghai – the other five include automobile, petrochemicals, iron and steel, set equipment manufacturing and pharmaceutical. The development and industrialization of advanced technologies in microelectronics, computer, communication, biopharmaceuticals, new materials and laser technology have been actively promoted. Amongst them, communication, IT and modern biopharmaceutical science have shown their initial strength.

The wave of "information superhighway" swept across the world in 1997 and simultaneously, Shanghai was determined to explore the new horizon by building an "information harbor" with five fundamental projects outlined. In the next few years, Shanghai will keep abreast with Hong Kong and Singapore in terms of IT application and infrastructure. It is set to become the most important communications hub in the Asia Pacific region.

In 2001, the total value added of Shanghai's IT and communication industry was RMB40.3 billion, a growth of 20.2% over 2000. The value added of manufacturing, retailing and service industries was RMB23.83 billion, RMB1.49 billion and RMB14.92 billion, respectively. The manufacturing of communications equipment focuses on developing large-scale broadband, multimedia and other types of communications equipments.

Shanghai IT Industry

	2000	2001
Total Output (RMB bn)	143.55	167.14
Share in Shanghai's Total	20.6%	21.8%
Value Added (RMB bn)	37.85	44.13
Share in Shanghai's Total	21.0%	21.4%

A large variety of mobile phones are available in Shanghai

In 2001, the subscribers of Internet, fixed telephone line and mobile phone reached 3.10 million, 6.16 million and 6.26 million respectively – for the first time the number of mobile phone users has surpassed that of fixed line subscribers. In the same year, the commercialization of technology in Shanghai hit a new high – with a total number of 18,863 contracts signed in technology transfer and the amount of all transactions reaching RMB2.88 billion. The government also encourages cooperation and alliance among enterprises, universities and research institutes.

HIGH-TECH COMMUNICATION

Large-scale investment and localization have boosted up the high-tech communication sector. The output value of the high-tech communication sector was RMB91.41 billion in 2001, an increase of 24.77% over the previous year.

Shanghai has established several major high-tech communication networks over the past four years, including a foreign trade data network, a social security network and a community service network. The municipality had also set up 20 key IT systems in areas such as urban planning, finance, employment and industrial and commercial administration.

Shanghai has put priority on the development of high-tech communication sectors. Over the past few years, it has formed a base for manufacturing top quality integrated circuits, computers, mobile telecommunication facilities and other high-tech products. At present, Shanghai produces one-fifth of China's integrated circuits, one-third of telecommunication equipments and one third of IC cards.

New digital communication and multimedia market have enjoyed vehement advancement. The ISDN network and the ATM technology facilitate high speed and obstruction-free data exchange.

SOFTWARE

Shanghai has declared favorable policies to promote its software and integrated circuit (IC) sector to propel development. Shanghai Informatization Office (SIO), together with other related departments of Shanghai Municipal Government, announced the favorable conditions offered to software and IC companies ten months after the central government announced policies of encouraging the development of software and IC industries. Shanghai plans to build 10 to 20 IC production lines by 2005, making the city China's largest IC production base. The city has allocated funding of RMB500 million to the industries, of which RMB300 million is to be used in aiding projects that meet the qualification standard required by SIO and the rest to be used as venture capital. SIO will set up a special channel for the export of software products under the supervision of the Shanghai Customs, which simplifies exports procedure.

NEW TECHNOLOGIES

Focusing on modern telecommunications, modern biology and pharmaceuticals, and new materials, Shanghai's new technology development has achieved sound progress. In 2001, the output value of new technology sector totaled RMB142.72 billion, an increase of 28.3% over 2000. The figure is 20.6% of the city's total industrial output. In 2001, the value added of information and telecommunication sector was RMB20.8 billion, an increase of 42.6% over the last year. This single sector generated a total industrial output value of RMB79.64 billion and profits of RMB8.25 billion, up 39.1% and 75.2% respectively over 2000. The industrial output value and profits generated by the modern biology and pharmaceutical sector jumped 19.5% and 48.3% respectively, reaching RMB17.56 billion and RMB755 million respectively.

A good example is the new airport departure controlling system installed at Shanghai Pudong International Airport.

This system adopts IBM hardware and services plus SITA's CUTE (common use terminal equipment) system expertise to handle and manage the passenger departure process, from assignment of seats through to boarding.

Another new technological symbol is the establishment of a new data sub-center in Shanghai. The sub-center integrates import and export business information, capital flow data and cargo distribution information, which is a new breakthrough in the electronic port regulation system. The data center allows different departments, different industries and different regions to share information online. It also offers companies comprehensive online services related to customs clearance.

The third accomplishment is the opening of the Cadence High-Speed Technology Center in Shanghai by Cadence Design Systems, Inc. – the world's leading supplier of electronic design products and services. It is the first of its kind in Asia Pacific and will serve a growing customer base in the region with training, education programs, and methodology and consultancy services. The objective is to increase the productivity of high-speed printed circuit board (PCB) companies and develop the skills of designers and engineers by providing education as well as customized design solutions. The center will use the Cadence Specctra Quest Design and Analysis Environment as a standard platform to develop customized design flows and methodologies that will enhance productivity in customer-oriented industrial applications. Initially, the Technology Center will serve 3 markets: wireless communication, wired communication and computing applications. The scope of service will expand to the advanced packaging design and digital consumer applications over the next two years.

The fourth sample of new technology advancement is the manufacturing of DWDM super narrowband optical filters. Shanghai New Industry Photoelectric Technology Co. Ltd is officially opened at Zhangjiang High-Tech Park. It is a joint venture between Changchun New Industry Photoelectric Technology, Zhangjiang Investment, Zhangjiang High-Tech

Output Value of Technological Sectors

	1999		2000		2001	
	RMB million	%	RMB million	%	RMB million	%
High-tech Communication	57,502	65.733	73,261	70.525	91,411	73.377
Biomedical Technology	15,296	17.486	13,960	13.439	15,212	12.211
Optical-mechatronics	13,709	15.671	15,667	15.082	16,487	13.234
Environmental Protection	222	0.254	301	0.290	451	0.362
Aeronautics & Astronautics	684	0.782	589	0.567	871	0.699
Physics Geography Engineering	61	0.070	97	0.093	142	0.114
Nuclear Applied Technology	4	0.005	4	0.004	4	0.003
	87,478	100	103,879	100	124,578	100

Value Added of Technological Sectors

	1999		2000		2001	
	RMB million	%	RMB million	%	RMB million	%
High Technology Communication	14,988	65.333	16,542	63.864	20,659	67.031
Biomedical Technology	4,284	18.674	4,339	16.752	4,731	15.350
Optical-mechatronics	3,415	14.886	4,695	18.126	4,946	16.048
Environmental Protection	76	0.331	95	0.367	143	0.464
Aeronautics & Astronautics	140	0.610	190	0.734	282	0.915
Physics Geography Engineering	36	0.157	39	0.151	57	0.185
Nuclear Applied Technology	2	0.009	2	0.008	2	0.006
	22,941	100	25,902	100	30,820	100

Output Value of Technological Sectors (RMB million)

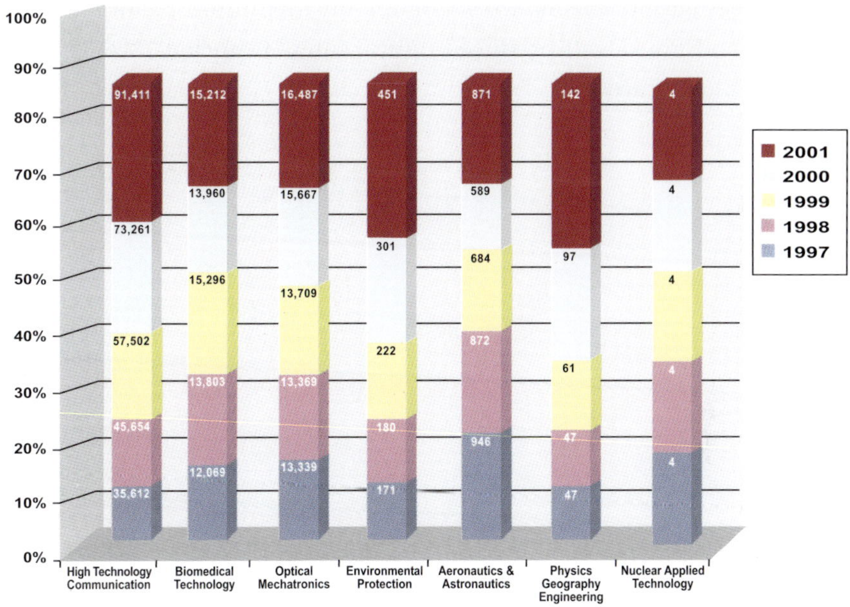

Value Added of Technological Sectors (RMB million)

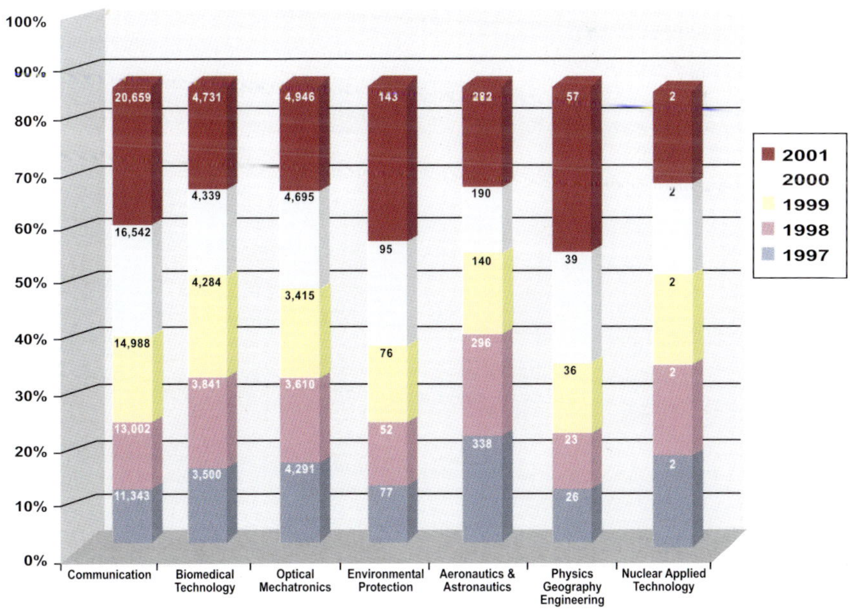

Park Development Co. Ltd and Pudong Technology Investment. It received technological support from CAS Changchun Institute of Optics, Fine Mechanics and Physics. It produced optical filters featuring 200GHz and 100GHz channel space.

Logistics

According to official statistics, China's logistics industry will be worth USD144.8 billion by 2010, of which Shanghai will contribute about USD21.7 billion, or 15% of the total. It is predicted that logistics industry in Shanghai will grow at an annual rate between 15%-20% over the next five years and holds huge potential for foreign investment.

INTRODUCTION

Technically, logistics was not a well-defined industry in China previously. For a long time, different government bodies regulate different sub-sectors in logistics services. For example, the Civil Aviation Administration of China (CAAC) controls airlines, Ministry of Communications (MOC) looks after road and water transport, Ministry of Railway (MOR) takes care of rail transport, and State Economic and Trade Commission (SETC) is responsible for commodity distribution.

Logistics business in China is largely under state control. While only 45% of China's products are contributed by state owned enterprises (SOEs) – the rest evenly shared by collectively owned enterprises and private sector, 90% of transport and warehousing remains in the hands of SOEs.

Shanghai's logistics industry has developed rapidly since the start of the economic reform. It has established its integrated transportation system, including railway, land, waterway, aviation and pipeline transportation.

In recent years, third-party logistic firms have emerged, distribution centers have been popping up and the application of modern logistic technology continues to be strengthened. However, China's logistic industry is still at its burgeoning stage. Each element of logistic process is still separate and supply chain management remains premature. Therefore, generally, circulation or distribution cost accounts for a great proportion of a company's total expenses.

The export of Shanghai in the first quarter of 2002 totaled USD17.2 billion, 13% higher over the same period in 2001. Imports totaled USD11.7 billion, which is a slight increase of 0.3% over the same period in 2001. The rapidly growing foreign trade of Shanghai puts a strong demand on a more flexible and comprehensive logistic system.

As a prominent distribution center for the prosperous East China as well as for the rest of China, Shanghai clearly needs to develop its strength in logistics-related areas. In April 2002, the municipal government announced a plan to set up three logistics parks at Waigaoqiao, Pudong International Airport and northwest Shanghai to attract and host more international logistical firms.

SHANGHAI LOGISTICS CENTER

In May 2002, Shanghai Logistics Center (SLC) started its first phase of operation in Waigaoqiao, the country's first and largest free trade zone, providing services for both resident or non-resident companies.

According to the Administrative Committee of Waigaoqiao Free Trade Zone (WFTZ), more than 70 Fortune 500 multinationals, 3,000 trading companies and 500 logistics specialists have made their presence in the zone, with import and export volumes reaching USD9.0 billion in 2001, an increase of 18.1% over 2000. The volume of containers handled by Waigaoqiao Port reached 1,430,000 TEUs, an increase of 18.3% over 2000. Free trade zone is the only kind of development zones allocated by Chinese government to accommodate foreign trading companies and has three functions: international trade, bonded warehousing and export-processing. Being the only one of its kind in Shanghai, WFTZ will exert significant power in the development of Shanghai's logistics industry.

With registered capital of USD15.7 million, Shanghai Logistics Center is a 50:50 joint venture between WFTZ United Development Corporation and Hong Kong-based Shanghai Industrial Holdings. More than RMB10 billion (USD1.23 billion) will be invested over the next five to 10 years in the Waigaoqiao Logistics Park. Aimed at attracting multinationals, the park will mainly offer services such as container storage, bonded warehousing, freight forwarding and distribution.

It is estimated that by 2010, the cargo flows at WFTZ will amount to 20 million tons, annual foreign trade will hit USD40 billion, and the value added of the logistics industry will account for 50% of WFTZ's total. By then, Waigaoqiao will be built into a procurement, distribution and transshipment center in the Asia-Pacific region.

In addition, Pudong International Airport Logistics Park will provide cargo transshipment and warehousing, multi-mode transportation, intermediary services as well as online trading. Some RMB7 billion will be invested in the second phase development of Pudong International Airport.

WTO COMMITMENT

Under the rules of the World Trade Organization (WTO), China is expected to open its service sector and logistics market within three years. By December 2004, foreign companies will be able to operate wholly-owned logistic units in China to provide a wide range of services ranging from inventory management, sorting and grading, to light assembly.

In most logistics sub-sectors, foreign-majority owned joint ventures are allowed within one to two years after China's WTO accession, and so are WOFEs in three to six years.

Foreign-invested freight forwarders are no longer restricted in international freight forwarding; domestic freight forwarding and other logistics services are open to foreign participation after WTO accession.

On the whole, new opportunities for foreign logistics service providers arise not only because of the relaxation of regulatory constraints, but also in the face of fast growing domestic and global demands.

Freight Forwarding

- Foreign majority ownership in JVs allowed one year after accession;
- Wholly owned subsidiaries allowed four years after accession;

- JVs not confined in international freight forwarding business only. Storage & Warehousing
- Foreign service suppliers allowed to establish as minority-owned JVupon accession and allowed to hold a majority equity share within one year;
- Restrictions to be phased out within three years.

Courier Services

- Commitments cover land-based international courier services and all services related to an international shipment handled by an express carrier;
- Foreign majority ownership in JVs allowed within one year. Wholly owned subsidiary allowed four years after accession.

Land Transportation

- For road transport, foreign service suppliers will be able to establish JV upon accession, hold a majority equity share within one year, and be free of ownership restrictions within three years;
- For railroad transport, foreign service suppliers will be able to establish JV upon accession, hold a majority equity share within two years, and be free of ownership restrictions within six years.

LOGISTIC INFRASTRUCTURE IN SHANGHAI

Estimated by the American Chamber of Commerce in Shanghai, logistic costs account for more than 16% of total product costs in China, compared with less than 4% in many developed economies.

With 1.3 billion potential customers, there is tremendous momentum for multinationals to invest and do business in China. However, the country's current supply chain largely remains underdeveloped and fragmented with major bottlenecks in transportation, distribution, logistics, warehousing, cargo handling, port facilities and information technology systems.

Shanghai enjoys the highest level of logistics infrastructure in China. Located at the midpoint of China's coastline and the start of Yangtze River waterway, Shanghai has easy access to many inland provinces and coastal cities. It has been developed into the largest port in China. Shanghai Port is expected to become the world's second largest port after Singapore with its annual freight topping 250 million tons by the end of 2002. In the first six months of 2002, it handled a record 125 million tons of cargo, up 17.2% on a year-on-year basis. The number of containers handled by Shanghai Port totaled 6.3 million TEUs in 2001, ranked the fifth in the world; and 3.84 million in the first half of the year, rising 30.9%, catching up with the world's fourth largest container port – Kaohsiung. It is expected to handle 10 million TEUs annually by the year 2005.

Container Throughput of Shanghai Port (1997-2002)

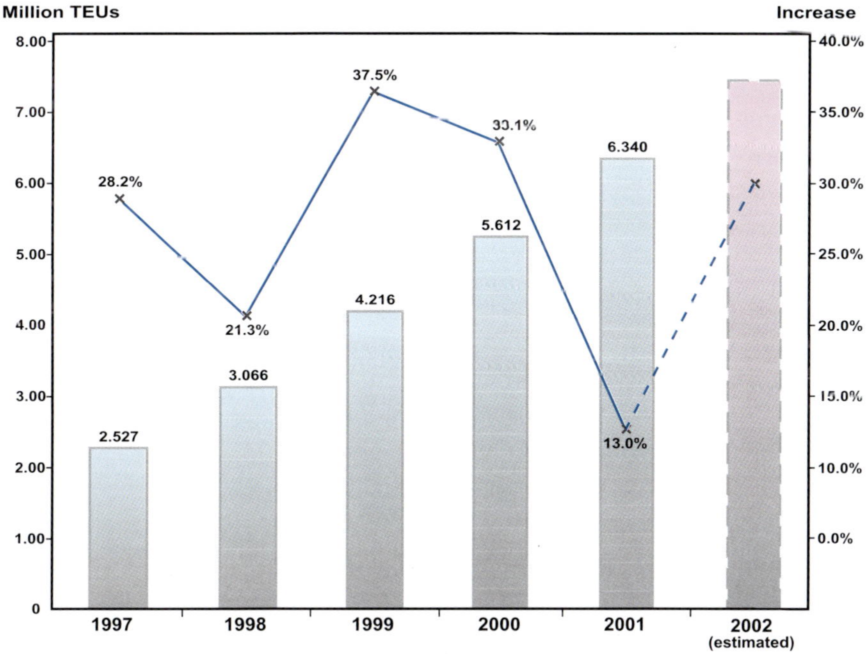

The major constraint of Shanghai Port is its depth of water channel at only 8.5 m. Even after dredging, it still has difficulties in accommodating ships loaded with more than 6000 TEUs. Currently, Ningbo's Beilun Port supplements Shanghai in catering for the large container liners. In this regard, Shanghai is developing three deepwater container berths at Waigaoqiao and a new port off its southeast coast at Yangshan Islands.

Beijing-Shanghai and Shanghai-Hangzhou railways links Shanghai to the national railway network. The highways network radiates out in all directions to provinces nearby. And a number of new grand bridges are in the plan to connect to cities over sea.

Shanghai also contains two of the busiest airports in the world. Hongqiao Airport and the newly built Pudong Airport are both under the management of Shanghai Airport Co. Ltd.

Performance of Two Airports in Shanghai 2001

	Hongqiao Airport	Pudong Airport	Total	Increase
Flights	116,495	77,575	194,070	20.89%
Passengers (million)	13.76	6.90	20.66	16.83%
Cargos (ton)	584,000	416,000	1,000,000	13.78%

LOGISTIC MARKET IN SHANGHAI

UPS aims to expand its market in China

Although the logistics industry has been enjoying quick development in recent years, still few domestic logistic players are capable of efficiently competing with foreign counterparts. Foreign companies have been actively setting up logistics business in China to serve their MNC clients. Three big multinationals, including Maersk Logistics, APL Logistics and TNT, were all recently allowed to operate nationwide as wholly foreign-owned logistic companies.

The Danish shipping giant A.P. Moller Maersk Group has set up a national distribution center in the western suburb of Shanghai to provide logistic services ranging from procurement and warehousing to transportation. Singapore-based APL Logistics, one of the world's leading companies in logistic sector, has joined hands with two Chinese partners to tap the logistics market in China. It has already set up branches in other six large cities across China, including Dalian, Tianjin, Qingdao, Xiamen, Shenzhen and Nanjing, with other five to be opened in the coming two years. Another Singapore shipping company, PIL, has just inaugurated its Shanghai office in September 2002. With constantly increasing import and export volume and cargo transportation needs after China's entry into WTO, more foreign logistics providers are flooding into the country making Shanghai a highly popular outpost to for businesses.

Domestically, after restructuring and consolidation, a few big transporters and freight forwarders are likely to become major competitors in logistic services. These include Sinotrans, COSCO and China Post. In fact, COSCO International Freight, China Ocean Shipping Agency, Sinotrans Road Transport, Sinotrans International Multi-mode Transportation and China Goods and Materials Storage Corporation have already taken the lead in developing logistics services.

Besides these large transportation companies, there are a number of emerging logistic companies which have been growing fast over the past two years, such as PG Logistics Group, Annto Logistics and EAS International Transportation Co. Ltd. In addition, a few large manufacturers are also integrating logistics into their business dimension. For instance, Haier Group, a top Chinese leader in home electronics production, has transformed its in-house distribution unit into an independent logistics service company and formed an alliance with China Post. The alliance gave Haier Group access to the vast network and assets of China Post.

The strengths of the domestic logistics companies lie in their familiarity with the local market and provision of low-cost inland transportation, distribution and warehousing. However, they are intrinsically less able to cope properly with the supply chain management, especially in the areas of global multi-mode network, high-tech warehousing, process integration services (i.e. JIT and processing trade), sophisticated information and communication technology, and logistics consultancy. Although the number of distribution centers in Shanghai is shooting up, only five are able to distribute more than 1,000 tons of goods per month. Amid the expectation of fierce market competition driven by the WTO entry and globalization, there is growing demand from local companies for strategic partnerships offering total solution in supply chain management.

Manufacturing Industry

CHINA – THE WORLD'S FACTORY

China has for decades exported mostly low-end products like textiles and toys to the world, but the country is now starting to sell more sophisticated goods to western consumers, like computers and DVDs. As China emerges as the world's manufacturing powerhouse, it is, claimed by many economists, becoming an increasingly powerful global deflationary force. Its manufacturing prowess is pushing down prices on a growing range of products that it sells around the world. In today's bearish world economy, especially after September 11 attacks, the surge of Chinese manufactures come into sight of foreign businessmen more prominently and attractively. In May 2002, exports from China to the US surpassed that from Japan; and in June 2002, the electronic exports to the US market hit USD1.2 billion, a further 12.3% from May. And China's high-tech exports jumped even more sharply, up 47% in the period of January-July 2002 over the same period a year earlier.

Although the fourth largest manufacturer, after the US, Japan and Germany, China is constantly marching up to be the top producer of white goods and consumer electronics. Today, apart from apparels, toys and canned food, half of the world's cameras, one third of the world's air-conditioners and televisions, a quarter of all washing machines and almost one fifth 20% of all refrigerators are being produced in the world's factory - China.

SEMICONDUCTOR

Based on a recent McKinsey report, China has great potential to be the global semiconductor powerhouse by year 2010. And according the Ministry of Information Industry, the size of semiconductor market in China will expand from USD13 billion to USD40 billion. It will be the second largest market in the world by year 2010. As the largest industrial city in China, Shanghai is ambitiously making maneuvers to become a world-class production center of microelectronic chips, widely used in digital telecommunication, computers and other electronic applications.

At present, the market demand for chips in China only accounts for 6% of the world's total, ranking the 4th largest after US, Japan, and Taiwan. As more semiconductor manufacturers hastily expand or shift their fabs into China, chip fabrication in the country will increase by 42% annually, much faster than the world's average of 10%. Like Taiwan, three factors will support the rise of semiconductor industry in the mainland: domestic demand for semiconductors as fueled by more electronic products produced or assembled in China, intensive supply of talent and capital, and government's preferential policies.

In 2000, China announced absolute tax breaks for semiconductor manufacturers, eliminating taxes altogether in many cases. For example, import duties on semiconductor materials were cut to zero from rates of 6% to 30%. Income taxes on chip design companies are exempted for the first five profit-earning years and 7.5% for the following five years. Even the full rate of 15% is much lower than the current tax rate of 20% in Taiwan. Among others, the top two customized chipmakers – TSMC, UMC from Taiwan, Intel, Motorola, Amkor, Applied Materials and AOS from the US, and Sony, Toshiba, Fujitsu, Hitachi, Sanyo and NEC from Japan have all expressed their deepest interest in building chipmaking plants or design houses in China, following a bad year of 2001 when global semiconductor industry dropped 33% in sales. Conspicuously, Shanghai, Beijing and Shenzhen are the three most competitive cities in leading the new trend.

As Shanghai is home to some of China's best microelectronics institutes with over 4,000 professionals churned out every year, and never short of foreign investment, it will play a pivot al role in enhancing the nation's overall manufacturing capability.

Contrary to the world's worst decline in semiconductor industry, year 2001 saw a surge of foreign investment in Shanghai's chip manufacturing industry. About USD4 billion equivalent of domestic and foreign investment has been injected into 72 microelectronic projects and related enterprises. Semiconductor Manufacturing International Corporation (SMIC) has invested USD1.47 billion to establish 3 production lines at Zhangjiang High-tech Park and will produce around 37,000 chips per month by the end of 2002. Another chip giant, Grace Semiconductor Manufacturing Corporation (GSMC), is also building its chip production base with total investment of USD1.63 billion. It is expected to start production at the end of 2002 and will maintain close collaboration with Amkor for assembly and testing. The two chip giants, both of which are of Taiwan origin, will become the flagship IC projects in Shanghai.

Shanghai Belling, the first listed company in China's microelectronics industry, started on July 2001 to build a chip production base at Zhangjiang High-tech Park. The production base, with total investment of RMB1.3 billion (USD157 million), is scheduled to start operation in 2003. It is reportedly under discussion of the possibility of collaborating with UMC since Taiwanese authority lifted the ban on the "go-west" of eight-inch wafer.

Currently, Shanghai with the surrounding Yangtze Delta is home to more than 6 large-scale semiconductor fabrication plants. Local demand for chips is soaring as more and more Taiwanese PC makers have shifted their production to the Great Shanghai region. According to the development blueprint of Shanghai municipal government, by 2005, a number of encapsulation and testing lines and 250 chip-design companies will be set up to create a complete microelectronic production chain in the city.

AUTOMOTIVE INDUSTRY

The automotive industry is one of the pillar industries in Shanghai. With about 50 plants, Shanghai Automotive Industry Corporation (SAIC) is one of China's largest automotive firms. SAIC makes passenger cars, tractors, motorcycles, trucks, buses, and spare parts. In 2001, the sales volume of SAIC hit 302,000 units, an increase of 20.5% over 2000. The corporation generated RMB97.9 billion in sales with profits reaching RMB7.22 billion. SAIC owns 43.3% of the existing domestic car market. In 2001, the corporation attracted total foreign investment of USD314 million. Currently, its major foreign partners are Volkswagen and General Motors, both of which have established successful manufacturing joint ventures in Shanghai. The former has topped the list of the most successful foreign-invested enterprises in China for many years. Among the 40,000 taxis on the road, you can hardly find one of other than Volkswagen brands.

Private cars will be a growth engine for Shanghai

The Shanghai Volkswagen Co. Ltd. is established at Anting of Jiading District, which is located in northwest Shanghai, in 1985 and its major models include Santana, Santana 2000 series, Passat series and Polo. Located in Pudong New District, the Shanghai General Motors is the largest Sino-American JV project with total investment of USD1.57 billion. The major brands produced include Buick series and Saio.

In the coming five years, Shanghai will invest RMB35 billion in car production and the output value of the sector is set to reach RMB150 billion by 2005, or 14% of the city's total industrial output then.

Still an infant industry throughout the 1990s, China's car manufacturing is expected to receive protection for a limited time span even after China's entry to WTO. However, in the long run, China's entry to WTO will definitely present new opportunities to foreign investors, leding to more competition in the automobile industry.

The first and most remarkable change happens in trade barriers. For a long time, China's car industry has been protected by high tariffs and other non-tariff barriers (NTB) such as quota and licensing. Before 1986, import duty for car was a formidable 220%; it dropped to 150% in 1994, 100% in 1996 and 80% in 1997. The average tariff rate for motor vehicles is 38.8%. For spare parts, the highest tariff rate stands at 50%. For other auto-related imports, such as machinery, iron and steel, rubber and electronics, import duty ranges between 10-20%. As a result, the effective protection rate for the automobile industry is as high as 219%. As to NTBs, China adopts a quota and license system for import of automobile products, which accounts for about 60% in the catalogue of quota products. However, price gaps between domestically-made motor vehicles and imported foreign ones are narrowing. According to its WTO commitment, China will cancel NTBs from 1 January 2005. Starting from 1 July 2006, the tariff rate for cars will be reduced to 25% and that for parts and accessories will go down to 10%. Since 1 January 2002, China had already cut the import duty on automobiles of up to 3,000 cc from 70% to 43.8%, and on higher-powered cars from 80% to 50.7%.

China's WTO entry will also bring changes to the automobile distribution. Currently, car manufacturers must use Chinese distributors to sell their vehicles. Within three years after WTO accession, distribution rights for foreign firms will be phased in. And foreign firms will be allowed to provide car finance by 2005.

Chinese car buyers have already benefited from the WTO membership. Domestic producers begun to cut prices to expand market share in anticipation of a surge of cheaper cars in response to the tariff reductions. According to the China Association of Automobile Manufacturers (CAAM), sales of passenger cars during the first five months of 2002 increased rapidly to reach 375,500 units, an increase of 33.14% from the same period in 2001. At the supply side, the auto manufacturing companies in China produced 1.29 million units from January to May of 2002, an increase of 30.37% from a year earlier.

With the support of the Chinese government, multinational carmakers like GM, Volkswagen, Chrysler, Honda, Citroen and Ford are joyfully assembling cars in the mainland, while leading auto parts manufacturers such as Delphi, Eaton, TRW and United Technologies have also made their presence more prominent. Recently, Toyota Motors signed a joint venture agreement with China First Auto Group to actively expand their base in the China market, with Tianjin as the foothold.

More production plants need to be established in order to boost car sales in China. For the time being, imported cars help meet growing demand from the swelling group of middle-class consumers. A recent survey reveals that 20% of Chinese households, totaling 26 million people, have a strong desire in buying cars.

Car Prices in China, June 2002

Brand/Model	Average Purchase Price
Bora 1.6LAT	RMB193,800
Polo CLi	RMB127,500
Peugeot 607	RMB495,000
New Beetle	RMB355,000
SAAB 9-5	RMB500,000
Buick G	RMB258,000
Audi A8-2.8	RMB820,000
Volvo S80-2.9	RMB768,000
Benz S600	RMB1,610,000
BMW 735i	RMB1,100,000
SAIO SLX	RMB103,800
Geely HQ6360	RMB 39,900
Passat 2.8V6	RMB355,000

Passat 1.8T	RMB244,100
Santana 2000GSi	RMB179,500
Charade 7131UL	RMB76, 400
Jetta GIX	RMB129,000

Professional Services

INTRODUCTION

China's service industries, especially professional services, are among the most heavily regulated and protected sector of the national economy. However, for sustainable economic growth, China needs to adopt effective and efficient measures to open its service sector to foreign competition. A strong service sector will help improve economic productivity along the value chain of all industries, be it Chinese or foreign-dominant.

China has made WTO commitments to gradually phase out most restrictions in a broad range of services, including accounting and auditing, legal and advisory, advertising, management consulting, IT and engineering consulting services. Shanghai, being a pioneer in the modernization of China, has once again caught global attention with the opening of these service sectors following the country's accession to the WTO.

WTO COMMITMENT ON PROFESSIONAL SERVICES

China's WTO accession agreements explicitly exclude accounting, taxation, management consultancy, and legal services from the general restriction that representative offices (ROs) are not allowed to engage in profit-making activities. However, in the past, ROs of legal firm were excluded from profit-making activities. China's entry into the WTO allows existing operations to continue under current arrangements, and at the same time broadens possibilities for new participation by foreign nationals and foreign equity. In short, grandfather clauses protect existing joint ventures, member firms, consulting firms and other offices from future regulatory changes that might interfere with operations.

Accounting Services

China will give market access and national treatment for accounting, auditing and bookkeeping.

- Foreign accounting firms can affiliate with Chinese firms and enter into contractual agreements with their affiliated firms in other WTO member countries;
- Foreign accounting firms must be represented by Certified Public Accountants (CPA) licensed by Chinese authorities, but existing accounting firms are exempted from this requirement;
- Foreigners who have passed the CPA examination will receive national treatment (i.e. they can form partnerships or incorporated accounting firms);
- CPA certifications are issued on a national treatment basis. Applicants will be informed of results in writing no later than thirty days after submission of their application;
- Accounting firms can provide taxation and management consulting services that are subject to JV restriction;
- There is no mandatory localization requirement.

Legal Services

China's commitment related to foreign law firms are as follows:

- Foreign law firms can provide legal services in the form of profit-making ROs;
- Within one year of China's accession in to the WTO (i.e. by 11 December 2002), all geographic and quantitative restrictions will be phased out, which means that foreign firms can open more than one office anywhere in China.

As of 1 January 2002, the "Regulations on the Administration of Foreign Law Firms' Representative Offices in China", which rules the representative offices of foreign law firms in China, came into force. Under the regulations, the ROs of foreign law firms may be set up, if they meet the following requirements:

- Such a representative office must be affiliated with a foreign law firm that has been legally registered in its home country;
- The representative thereof must be a legally registered attorney, having been qualified as a member of the bar association in the country where his/her license is issued, and exercising his/her license for no less than two years outside China. All representatives must reside in China no less than six months each year;
- The chief representative is required to have been practicing as a registered attorney for no less than three years outside China, being a partner of the firm or holding an equivalent position.

Any representative offices of foreign law firms, legally established in China, cannot be involved in any Chinese legal business, but they can:

- provide the clients with legal consultation with regards to the laws and regulations of the country, where its attorneys have been licensed to practice legal business and consultation on any relevant international conventions and treaties or common practice;
- handle the legal affairs in the country, where its attorneys have been licensed to practice legal business, as entrusted by the relevant parties or Chinese law firms;
- entrust Chinese attorneys to handle Chinese legal affairs, on behalf of foreign clients;
- maintain long-term cooperative relationship with Chinese law firms by entering into contracts;
- provide information of Chinese legal environment.

Such an RO of a foreign law firm should be named as "Representative Office in (city name in Chinese) of the (Chinese translation of its foreign name) Law Firm". Foreign law firms or organizations of any kind are not allowed to be involved in legal services in China in the name of a consulting company or others.

The RO of a foreign law firm in China may not employ any Chinese attorney, and the assistants hired are not allowed to provide legal services to the clients. All of the service charges must be settled in China.

To set up such an RO, a foreign law firm shall file an application to the local judicial department at the relevant provincial level.

Law firms in Hong Kong, Macau and Taiwan shall refer to other rules and obey the major principles of the Regulations for setting up ROs in Mainland China.

While the foreign firm cannot employ Chinese nationals as lawyers for the practice of Chinese law, it can enter into long-term "entrustment" contracts providing for close working relationships, including the right to provide instructions with firms practicing Chinese law.

OPPORTUNITIES

Accounting Services

China started to open up its accounting market to foreign investors in 1992, following its determination to revamp the state-owned enterprises and restructure the central-planned economy into a market-oriented one. Since then, many of the world's top international accounting firms have established their presence in the Chinese mainland. The mainland market was further liberalized in September 1994 when the establishment requirements for joint-venture firms became much less restrictive. Foreigners were since allowed to sit for the Chinese National Accounting Examination. A number of overseas candidates have passed the examination and qualified as non-practicing members Certified Public Accountants (CPAs) in China, most of them were overseas Chinese, including those from Hong Kong.

In China, the accounting market is growing at an average of 20-30% annually and the revenue for the sector exceeded RMB7 billion (USD848 million) in 2001, of which joint venture firms took up about one seventh. The growth of foreign accounting firms in China is remarkable.

Traditionally, foreign accounting firms only provided services for their multinational clients operating in China and projects of World Bank and other international organizations. However, the growing ambition of China's leading companies to make initial public offerings (IPOs) abroad helps to expand the business activities of foreign accounting firms because hardly any Chinese accounting firm is internationally recognized. Domestic firms, such as Unicom and Sinopec, have no choice but to hire foreign accounting firms if they plan IPO in New York and other major international stock exchanges. Reportedly, over 95% of Chinese companies that have sold shares to foreign investors use international accounting firms with operations in China. In addition, China's determination to integrate its economy into the global system provides a bright, albeit medium-term, future for foreign accounting companies.

Recent developments in Shanghai's accounting sector demonstrate that the growing demand for quality accounting services is growing. First, as part of a broader program to separate business from government, accounting firms become independent from government-related entities. The fundamental economic restructuring that aims to separate ownership from management will create opportunities for international accounting firms.

Second, China's accounting industry "clean-up" and revision of its Accountancy Law paved the way for the development of China's capital market to which the growth of the accounting sector is largely tied. International accounting firms may benefit in two ways. On one hand, the expanding market and demand for quality services require the expertise and intelligence that domestic accounting firms do not yet possess. On the other hand, international firms are expected to play a role in the process of regulation drafting.

Finally, with China's entry to WTO, more areas are to be liberalized, restrictions to be loosened, national treatment to be applied, and procedures to be followed with more transparency. These will work together to the advantage of foreign accounting firms in developing their capacities and delivering quality services in China.

It can be surely expected that accounting professionals who are proficient in international accounting and auditing standards will be much needed in the post-WTO China. According to a survey conducted by British's ACCA, China's market would soon demand over 300,000 accounting professionals, especially those with eight or more years of working experience in multinational companies. However, the Chinese Institute of Certified Public

Accountants, the largest accounting professional association in China, currently has only 130,000 members, and most of them are non-practicing. In Shanghai, there are a total of 84 accounting professional firms with 2,504 CPA practitioners and 6,090 non-practicing members. By the end of 2001, Shanghai saw 34,888 people who attended national CPA examination with a pass rate of 10.59%.

Eyeing the great market potential, major international accounting firms, namely, Deloitte Touche Tohmatsu, Ernst & Young, KPMG, PricewaterhouseCoopers (PWC) and the former Arthur Andersen, all have had branches and reaped considerable profits in China.

At the end of 2000, China Securities Regulatory Commission (CSRC) announced a rule requiring "supplementary auditing" for A-share companies accounting firms. According to the rule, when a company issues IPO or raises funds through a secondary offering, it must have a domestic accounting firm to audit its books and then have an international accounting firm to perform an additional audit.

Only the large international accounting firms were licensed to do the "supplementary audit". CSRC regards the policy as a way to prevent listed companies from faking profits. Experts estimated that the requirement would have led to increased revenue of RMB300 million for the large accounting firms. Seven domestic firms were later added into the list of firms for the special audit checking, which was a change resulted from the recent corporate scandals like Enron and Arthur Andersen's involvement in the questionable accounting practices. However, China's recognition of the need for international accounting standards and practices remains unchanged.

In the past years, the large firms have expanded their market share from 2% to over 20% in China. The sector for providing auditing services for B- and H-share companies occupies at least one seventh of the total auditing market, and this sector is almost dominated by international renowned accounting firms. In 2001, Shanghai's total revenue of accounting professionals reached RMB1.2 billion, while PWC, Deloitte Touche Tohmatsu and the former Arthur Andersen together enjoyed a share of over 30%. It is estimated that international accounting firms are likely to occupy more than half of the market within the next five years.

Some of the ways to access China's accounting market are as follows:

- International accounting firms can establish membership association. So far, foreign accounting firms have set up over 12 membership associations;
- International accounting firms can incorporate joint ventures with domestic partners. To date, there are over eight JV accounting firms in China. Ernest & Young Da Hua was the first one established in Shanghai;
- International accounting firms can establish representative offices. More than 10 international accounting firms have set up their branches in China;
- Foreign accounting practitioners can undertake auditing business in China if certain criteria are met;
- Foreigners can attend the national CPA examination;
- Foreigners who have passed the CPA examination can register as a member of the Chinese Institute of Certified Public Accountant (CICPA). They will receive national treatment in partnerships or incorporated accounting firms. To date, there are over 300 foreign non-practicing members.

At for the time being, cooperation with local firms is necessary for foreign firms to set up business in China. Foreign firms intending to build a presence in Shanghai are advised to choose local partners with similar objectives and to work with Shanghai Municipal Finance Administration and the Shanghai branch of CICPA to be better informed of rules and regulations.

Currently, domestic accounting firms are still very small in size; their operations are usually confined to a particular region and their clients are mainly small and medium sized Chinese enterprises that are cost-sensitive. Some of the leading domestic accounting firms in Shanghai include Da Hua, Shu Lun Pan, Gong Xin Zhong Nan, Wen Hui, Jiahua Dacheng, Jiuzhou and Ruihua Certified Public Accountants etc.

Legal Services

China has approximately 9,000 law firms and 110,000 lawyers. Of 80,000 active lawyers, only about 5,000 to 6,000 are capable of handling international legal issues, with most of them being located in major coastal cities. In Shanghai alone, there are now over 4,700 lawyers (0.036% of the local population) and 477 law firms. Due to the growing business in the legal sector, some firms have undergone mergers and restructuring to form large-scale ones – usually with over one hundred employees.

In recent years, many law firms in big cities, such as Beijing, Shanghai and Guangzhou, have adopted the form of partnership. China allows three types of law firms: state-invested, cooperative and partnership. A law firm established with the assistance of government capital shall be independent in its practice and shall undertake liability for its debts with its total assets. Lawyers can also establish cooperative law firms, which are also liable for their debts within their total assets. For a partnership law firm, all partners shall undertake unlimited and joint liability for all debts. The only difference between a cooperative and a partnership law firm in China is the scope of liability.

China's accession to WTO has brought changes to its law service industry. All state-invested law firms and cooperative law firms are being transformed into partnership law firms. In Shanghai, almost all law firms are partnership law firms.

Since the restoration of the legal professions, the number of lawyers and quality of legal services rendered have both risen significantly. However, few lawyers in China specialize in dealing with foreign-related issues and litigations and even fewer are able to provide legal services in a foreign language.

The opening of China's legal service sector can be dated back to the early 1980s, when the implementation of reform and open-door policies strengthened China's trade ties and technological cooperation with other countries. Many multinational corporations came to China to conduct business activities. These activities generated tremendous demand for legal services, and some foreign law firms followed their clients into the Chinese market. At that time, the Chinese government did not permit foreign law firms to set up branch offices directly inside China. Considering clients' needs and self-interest, some foreign law firms showed up in China in a different identity – as consulting firms. Foreign law firms such as Coudert Brothers, Baker & McKenzie, Paul Weiss, Grahm & James and Dewey Ballantine set up such firms in cities like Beijing and Shanghai.

In 1992, China started to open its legal service market to foreign law firms. With permission from the State Council, the Ministry of Justice finally started its official experiment in allowing foreign law firms to open offices in China. Up till now, over 130 overseas law firms, including half of world's top 50, have set up offices in the mainland, most having presence in Shanghai. These offices greatly facilitate China's cross-border business transactions and legal exchanges. In particular, the management models and professional practice of these foreign law firms set examples for the growing Chinese legal profession.

With China's accession to the WTO, overseas law firms are now able to set up multiple offices. Its bilateral agreement with the United States and the European Union lift the quantitative and geographical restrictions on the establishment of ROs by foreign law firms within one year after China's accession to WTO. China's agreement with the EU also allows foreign law firm ROs to provide information on the impact of the Chinese legal environment. This provision acknowledges the role of foreign law firms in providing their understandings of the Chinese legal system with respect to foreign investment and trade without disturbing the prohibitions on the issuance of legal opinions on Chinese law or representing clients in Chinese courts.

To date, there are over 20 international law firms have filed their applications to set up multiple ROs in China. The current restriction that their offices can only be established in one of the 15 cities was also lifted. Following WTO entry, the foreseeable rapid economic development and more Chinese companies venturing abroad will fuel greater demand for legal services. As a result, more large foreign law firms armed with financial and human resources will enter to explore the tremendous opportunities and exert great influence on China's legal service market.

However, the WTO accords did not alleviate other fundamental barriers to the operation of foreign law firms in China. Foreign law firms mainly offer legal consultation to clients with investments in China. They are not permitted to interpret the Chinese law, appoint Chinese lawyers or represent their clients in court. They can only act as legal consultants. Legal services relating to litigation, public listing, loans, real estate and intellectual property rights must be offered by mainland Chinese lawyers.

Furthermore, unlike their counterparts in other service industries including accounting, architecture and insurance, foreign law firms are not permitted to establish joint ventures with Chinese law firms. Lesser relationships will be permissible but these are unlikely to be sufficient.

In a certain sense, the WTO accession agreements have actually caused tightening of restrictions on foreign law firms in some areas. China's bilateral agreement with the United States and European Union provide that the chief representative of a foreign law firm representative office must be a partner or equivalent, which is more stringent than under current requirements. All attorneys or representatives under the EU agreement must be members of the bar of a WTO member and also have practiced for no less than two years (which need not be consecutive). These conditions limit the ability of foreign law firms to assign junior attorneys to their offices in China. The experience requirement for representatives also seems unnecessary since the resident partner or equivalent can supervise and train junior attorneys on the job as such is done in the United States.

Top 20 Law Firms in Shanghai 2000

Rank	Name of Law Firms
1	Duan & Duan Law Firm
2	Pan Asia Law Firm
3	United Law Firm
4	Fang Da Law Firm

5	Allbright Law Offices
6	Jin Mao Law Firm
7	Jian Wei Law Firm
8	Tong Li Law Firm
9	Hua Ting Law Firm
10	Shen Da Law Firm
11	Zhong Xin Zheng Yi Law Firm
12	Guo Hao Group Shanghai Branch
13	Zhen Dan Law Firm
14	Jin Du Law Firm
15	Kang Da Law Firm
16	Zhong Jian Law Firm
17	Xin Hua Law Firm
18	Jun He Law Firm Shanghai Branch
19	Hong Qiao Law Firm
20	Bang Xin Yang Law Firm

Real Estate

OVERVIEW

Shanghai is encouraging a healthy and sustainable development of real estate sector. The market saw profound changes in 2001. On 1 July 2001, the municipal government started to implement the Measures on the Transfer of Land Use Rights in Shanghai, which officially defines the authority, scope, procedure and mechanism for bidding the land use rights in Shanghai. This would be a crucial milestone in normalizing land supply for real estate development, to a lesser degree, stabilizing the property market in Shanghai. As an immediate result, year 2001 already saw 433 ha of land transferred through various auctions, although still a small slice of 8.3% in total land transactions in Shanghai.

Since 1 August 2001, the government announced another aggressive move, merging the previous inter-isolated two-tier market – overseas-selling and domestic-selling housing markets – into one. The merger would further institutionalize the market-oriented practices already adopted in Shanghai's residential property market. However, the measure, in a short term, would devalue the land stock held by overseas developers and push down the property prices previously targeted at foreign buyers. In the long run, real estate industry in Shanghai will experience a sustainable development and fair competition.

The Real Estate Sector of Shanghai, 2001

Indicator	Volume	Increase
Total Investment	RMB62 billion	9.6%
Total Value Added	RMB30.8 billion	17.8%
Land Transferred	RMB240 million / 5,228.3 ha	
Through tender	433.4 ha	
New Residential Properties Sold	17.67 million sq m	13.5%

Top Domestic Real Estate Companies in Shanghai, 2001

Ranking	Company Name	Sales Revenue (RMB mil)
1	Shanghai Greenland Group	1,523.5
2	Shanghai China Star Group	1,286.1
3	Dahua Group	1,243.8
4	Shanghai Yanlord Real Estate Co. Ltd	1,039.6
5	Shanghai Hengli Real Estate Co. Ltd	1,038.9
6	COSCO Land Co. Ltd	973
7	Pudong Xinxiang Real Estate Co. Ltd	890.3
8	OOCL Xujiahui Real Estate Co. Ltd	865
9	Fodi Group	680.9
10	Jing'an New Century Enterprise Development Co.	609.7
11	Minhang Real Estate Development Co. Ltd	599.8
12	Shanghai Vanke Xuhui Land Co. Ltd	592.3
13	Tomson Golf (Shanghai) Co. Ltd	517.8
14	Shanghai Jiagang City Real Estate Co. Ltd.	510.4
15	Shanghai Zhonghuan Investment Development Co.	498.2
16	Shanghai Tomson Real Estate Co. Ltd	495.2
17	Shanghai Wantai Land Co. Ltd.	485.3
18	Shanghai Hongyi Real Estate Co. Ltd	478.3
19	Shanghai Hongsheng Land Co. Ltd	470
20	Shanghai New Riverbay City Development Co. Ltd	448
21	China Enterprise Holdings Co. Ltd.	436
22	Shanghai Nongkou Real Estate Group	431.4
23	Shanghai Tianyang Real Estate Co. Ltd	406.9
24	Shanghai Jiatai Real Estate Co. Ltd	399.9
25	Shanghai Southwest Mingyuan Co. Ltd	387.9

The following article is contributed by Colliers International

LAND MARKET IN SHANGHAI

Land Use Rights

In China, all land belongs to the government. Real estate investors are only able to obtain the "land use rights" which, whether in the primary or secondary market, are granted to the user or investor for a certain period of time. Therefore, whenever land purchase is mentioned, it is the land use right, not the ownership per se, that is transferred. The land use tenure is based on the different usage of land:

Land Usage	Tenure
Residential	70 years
Industrial	50 years
Education, Science & Technology, Cultural	50 years
Retail, Tourism, Entertainment	40 years
Mix-used	50 years

Base Land Price System

The base land price system promulgated in Shanghai indicates the minimum prices to be quoted by the government when the land use right is purchased. However, the system is more for reference than for common practices, as the purchase of the land use right will still be assessed on a case-by-case basis and subject to auction or negotiation and government approval.

Land Market

In the second quarter of 2002, 1,935,660 sq m of land was newly purchased in the primary land market, up 884.5% over the same period of the previous year. Since 1 July 2001 when the bidding system was implemented, land market in Shanghai has developed positively. However, as the secondary land market was immature, speculation on land purchase has been much hyped up in Shanghai, especially in the town area. Local developers, domestic developers, and even overseas real estate giants are rushing into the city, pouring money on prime locations.

Reportedly, land for mix-used in Lujiazui area of Pudong is now priced at USD600 per sq m. In 2001, both China Ping An Group and Government Investment Corporation (GIC) of Singapore invested in Lujiazui. In 2002, Sun Hung Kai Properties from Hong Kong acquired a parcel of land from Lujiazui Development Co., with an area of 69,400 sq m and permitted gross floor area capped at 420,000 sq m. According to the initial planning, construction of hotel, office building and serviced apartments will be completed by 2011. Due to the recent controls imposed in Lujiazui Finance and Trade Zone, land transfer shows signs of slowdown in Pudong. On the other hand, land for mix-used is a scarcity in major commercial areas of Puxi, such as Nanjing Road and Huaihai Road, priced at a higher USD750-800 per sq m.

In the past few years, residential property market in Shanghai developed rapidly, which boosted the land price for upmarket housing development. Current development can be mainly seen out along the Huangpu River or in the neighboring CBD. Xintiandi, a new landmark in Puxi, was developed by Shui On Group, a Hong Kong listed company investing aggressively in Shanghai. Housing land prices nearby now have now risen above USD600 per sq m. Anderson Group, another Hong Kong developer, and Singapore CapitaLand are now working on their sites there too. China Overseas Holding Ltd. will also build a housing estate on a 23 ha land at Jianguo East Road behind Xintiandi. CRC, Guangcai Group and Huazhe Group have all purchased land at Dongjiadu with a unit price between USD450-600 per sq m on buildable area.

The successful bidding of World Expo 2010 will have great impact on the development of four key areas as planned in the blueprint of the Huangpu

River Comprehensive Development. A total of 9 million sq m gross floor area is projected for construction.

Yangpu Bridge Area: Occupies an area of 1.99 sq km under the administration of Yangpu District. It aims to embrace a riverside residence with traditional urban dwelling characteristics cum science, education and office area.

Shanghai Shipyard – North Bund Area: Occupies an area of 1.06 sq km. In tandem with the construction of International Passenger Transport Center and reconstruction of Shanghai Shipyard, the area will utilize the conjunction of the Huangpu River and Suzhou Creek to create a new scenic site complementary to the Bund and the modern Lujiazui. Public facilities like a cruise center and top-notch houses will be displayed along the river.

Shiliupu – Dongchang Area: Occupies an area of 0.35 sq km. The area focuses on the reconstruction of Shiliupu and Dongchang ports.

Nanpu Bridge Area: Occupies an area of 3.43 sq km. It will develop into a large-scale comprehensive area with cultural, education and research, sports, living, entertainment and working facilities. The coming Shanghai World Expo 2010 will have the greatest influence on its housing development. A green community with quality environment and high-end priced residences will take shape there. The area is promising for real estate development, and has great potential in property appreciation.

RESIDENTIAL PROPERTY MARKET

Policy Changes

The housing market in Shanghai has undergone a series of changes in accordance with the city's economic reforms since the mid of 1990s:

Year	Policy Changes
1996	Public housing reform (privatization of house ownership); Relaxation of transaction handling charges;
1998	Permission on exchange of un-saleable public houses in the housing market;
1999	Amalgamation of domestic-selling housing market;

2000	Promulgation of Lease Act; Introduction of new standards for pre-marketing residential properties (pre-sale license); Cessation of "housing allocation" policy;
2001	Merger of the local and expatriate (domestic-selling and overseas-selling) housing market; Implementation of land use rights acquisition via auction and bid;
2002	Deed tax increase; Plot ratio control in urban development (not yet formally enacted)

The 1996 reform in public housing activated a secondhand market and has since provided more options for homebuyers in Shanghai.

The introduction of the pre-sale housing standards in 2000 was essentially to support the government to regulate the scale of development and put a deterrent to under-funding. This tighter control placed on the entry of pre-sale property has induced a temporary under-supply, and put up pressure on property prices.

The two-tier market system was abolished in August 2001 in line with the norm of the WTO. Restrictions were lifted for foreign buyers, which in turn explains the reason why overseas purchasers in high-end market brought up price increases rapidly in the overall market.

Luxury Houses

Most of Shanghai's luxury houses are situated at Hongqiao, city center of Puxi and Pudong.

Hongqiao used to be the primary upper-market residential district for foreigners in Shanghai. After more than ten years of development, this area now boasts a wide range of amenities and is becoming a cluster for foreign consulates. As the most mature expatriate living habitat in Shanghai, Hongqiao is rich in high-class villas and condominiums.

Luxury houses in the city center of Puxi are mainly located in four districts of Changning, Xuhui, Luwan and Jing'an. Quiet neighborhoods surrounded by bustling commercial area, convenient transportation and communication, complete living facilities are very attractive to the rich and foreign businessmen. In addition, the collection of Grade A office buildings in the proximity gives further credit to these luxury housing estates.

In terms of luxury villas, Pudong has definitely become the most important host area. Widespread greens, growing facilities, and an ever-increasing number of foreign staff from senior management of MNCs located in modern industrial parks nearby, add up to a robust demand in Pudong's luxury housing market.

By the end of Q3 2002, the total supply of luxury houses in Shanghai was 10,913 units, of which 8,861 were luxury apartments and the rest 2,052 were villas. However, it is anticipated that supply is limited in the coming two years. Major projects include Marriott Hotel Serviced Apartments and the Xintiandi Lakeville.

Foreign investment in Shanghai has been on a rising trend since 2000 with many companies relocating their regional or country headquarters to Shanghai. An expanding foreign community has resulted in a growing demand for luxury houses. The average vacancy rate of Shanghai's luxury apartments was about 16.4% as at Q3 2002, and in many cases, it was as low as 5%. Hot premises like Huashan Royal Pavilion, Shangri-la Apartments and Somerset Grand Serviced Apartments require a waiting period before vacant units become available.

Luxury villas at Hongqiao and Pudong are still highly occupied. The vacancy rate for Q3 2002 was approximately 13.2%. Due to the recent shift of most flights from Hongqiao to Pudong Airport, demand for Pudong villas has been soaring. Premises like Green Villas and Seasons Villas maintained an occupancy rate of above 90%.

Rents for luxury houses have been steadily rising since 2002. Pushed by the launch of Westin apartments, the average monthly rent in Q3 climbed up by 3.8% over the previous quarter, reaching USD20.9 per sq m per month.

In the villa market, the average rent was USD25.5 per sq m per month, an increase of 2.4%.

The luxury house sales market is much more heated. Currently, luxury apartments in Shanghai are sold at USD2,454 per sq m on average. In the city center, prices have reached USD2,586 per sq m. Even in this situation, the market has remained somewhat bullish. The Lakeville, situated at Xintiandi of Luwan District, has most of its 280 units preoccupied before it is ready for sale. Hutchison Whampoa, one of the big four Hong Kong developers, is working on another large project – the Summit – on Wulumuqi Road. Its 395 units are priced at USD2,300 per sq m. Relatively, the villa sales market, on a smaller scale, has average unit price stabilized at about USD2,634 per sq m.

High-end Properties

Housing near old industrial estate

After the merger of the two-tier market, foreign capital poured into Shanghai. Xuhui, Changning and Jing'an are the top three districts supplying

80% high-end housing properties in Shanghai. The future development of such properties will concentrate on Huangpu, Jing'an, Changning and Luwan where urban redevelopments are to be carried out intensively. Areas alongside rivers with splendid views, such as the Huangpu River banks and the north Bund, will see clusters of high-end houses soon.

Since the abolition of the wide gap between domestic- and overseas-selling properties, people from overseas are enthusiastically buying real estate in Shanghai, in particular, overseas Chinese from Hong Kong, Macau and Taiwan. Furthermore, non-local residents from rich neighboring provinces like Jiangsu and Zhejiang have the investment sentiment too. According to a recent survey on high-end house dwellers in Shanghai, 53.6% of the buyers for properties with unit price above RMB7,000 per sq m are locals; 30.9% are citizens from other regions of China; and 22.7% are from overseas. Statistics also show that such sales rose 172.1% in the first half of year 2002.

The average price of houses in Shanghai has been increasing constantly in 2002. Between January and June, 30% of all houses for presale had unit price exceeding RMB5,000. In Q3 2002, the average unit price of upper-market houses was between RMB8,800 and RMB12,000 per sq m, up RMB500~1,000. Many of the latest properties on sale are in Jing'an District

Unit Price of High End Houses in Shanghai

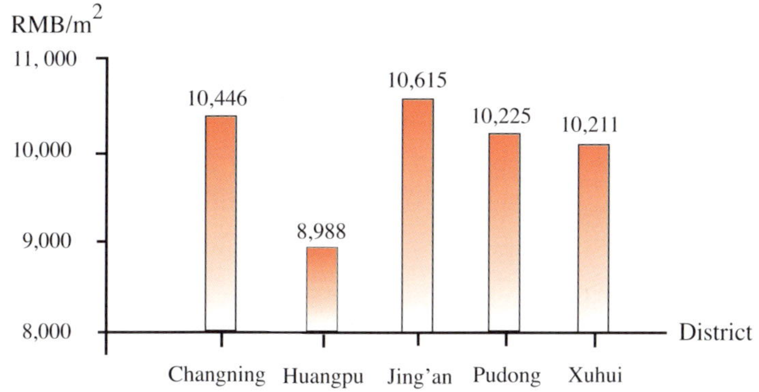

Source: Colliers International

where the average unit price has reached RMB8,373. Newly completed projects like Ladoll City in Jing'an, the second phase of First Block, and One Park Avenue are all selling at RMB10,000 per sq m or more.

Market Outlook

Shanghai's absorption of foreign investment has followed a fast track. In the first ten months of 2002, the city saw such investment soar up 37.3% to USD9.108 billion. More expatriates are coming together with the establishment of more FIEs, creating strong demand for luxury houses and pushing down vacancy rate.

High-end houses will continue to see a dynamic market. Prices have risen rapidly and demand is on an optimistic side. The successful bidding for World Expo 2010 provides additional momentum for a sustainable development in Shanghai's residential property market. The Expo will not only push forward the city's economy as a whole, but also enhance urban dwellers' house-purchasing power and attract more foreigners to invest, work and reside here.

COMMERCIAL PROPERTY MARKET

Introduction

Identified by Colliers International, there are five major office areas in Shanghai.

Nanjing West Road in Jing'an District, Huaihai Middle Road in Luwan District, and Central Finance District in Lujiazui of Pudong are three of the primary and most prosperous office areas, as measured by the convenience in transportation, business environment and a critical mass of quality office buildings mostly developed by Hong Kong or other Southeast Asian developers.

Hongqiao Area in Changning District and Yan'an Road East in Huangpu District are the other two areas – historically the prime choice for office seekers though now of secondary importance. Between 1998 and 2000, a vast migration out from these areas to the three other places was observed. However, since the second half of 2001, there has been a return to the traditional office areas, because higher rents and occupancies of the office buildings in the primary office areas have forced some MNCs to seek alternatives – fair quality office buildings with much lower rents – in these secondary office areas.

Current Market

As at September 2002, total office stock in Shanghai was approximately 7.16 million sq m. Among them, 18% are identified as Premium and Grade A office buildings, which are most favored by MNCs; 34% are Grade B office properties that are still sought by MNCs and other overseas companies; the remaining 48% consist of other grades which are usually built by local developers and mostly patronized by small and medium sized enterprises.

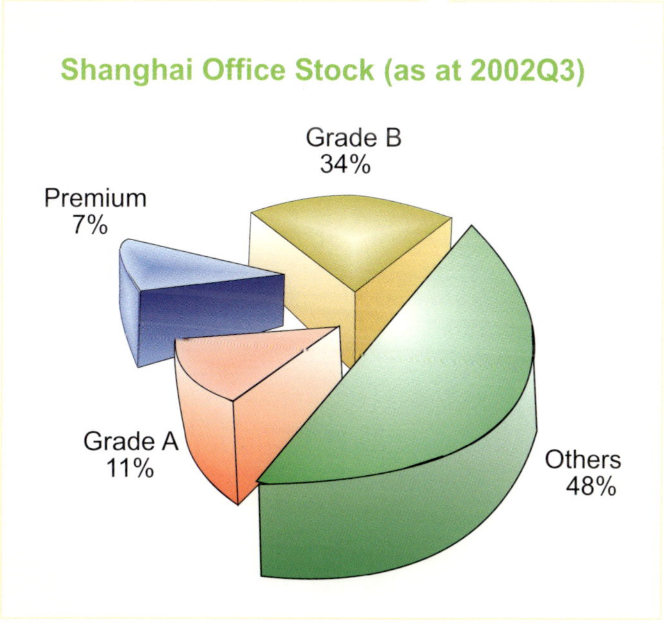

Source: Colliers International

The physical vacancy rate of offices in all categories, as at September 2002, stood at around 19.9% in Puxi and 19.4% in Pudong, and thus an overall vacancy of approximately 19.7% in Shanghai. Premium and Grade A office sector has been performing much better than the overall market. Their vacancies averaged around 12% and 18.9% in Puxi, and 8.2% and 19.4% in Pudong – an overall rate of 15.6% for this sector.

As a booming year for office market, total take-up exceeded 1.2 million sq m in 2000, more than double that a year earlier. In 2001, due to the global economic recession and the September 11th attack, take-up slowed down, particularly in Q2 and Q3, having recorded a total of 720,000 sq m for the whole year.

The negative impact on the market gradually faded in Q1 and Q2 of 2002, thanks to the US economic recovery and China's WTO accession. Due to the stronger-than-expected demand for office space, the overall office market regained momentum from Q3 2002 onwards, leading to both growing rentals and increasing take-ups. Office occupancy within the first nine months of 2002 reached 480,000 sq m and the annual take-up for the whole year is expected to be a total of 580,000 sq m.

New supply in 2003 is forecasted to be moderate, as compared to that in 2001 and 2002, and will average at 398,965 sq m. On the other hand, take-up

Shanghai Office Supply, Take up & Vacancy 1993 - 2004F

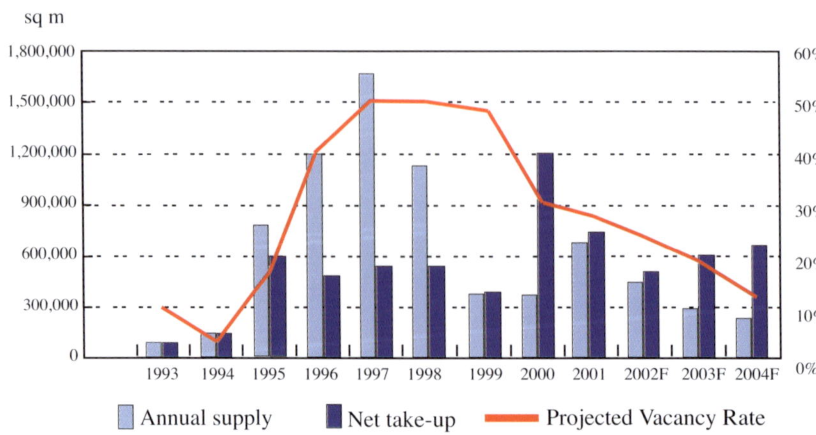

Source: Colliers International

is still expected to continue on its rising trajectory and projected to reach 690,000 sq m. This will bring down the overall office vacancy rate to 18% approximately.

Shanghai Premium & Grade A Offices Supply, Demand & Vacancies 1996 - 2004F

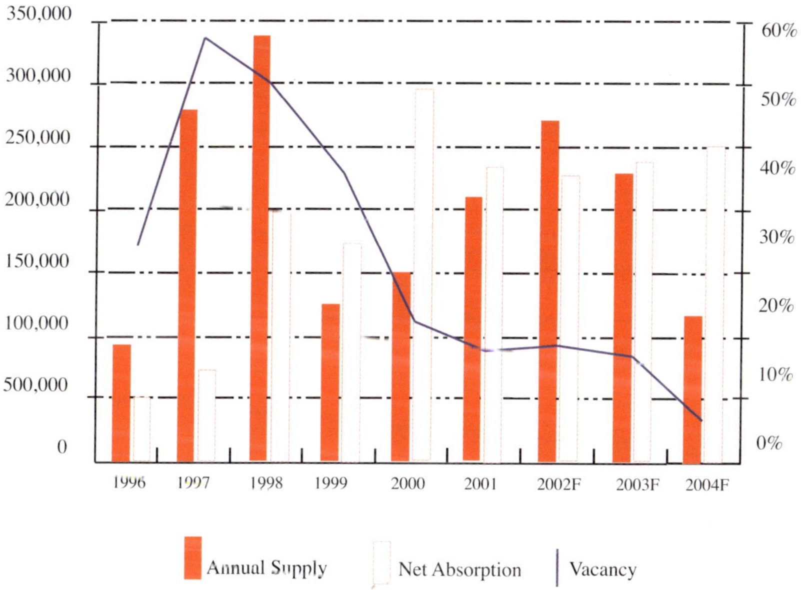

Source: Colliers International

The total take-up of Premium and Grade A offices was about 230,931 sq m in 2001, and will command a continuous and stable growth over 2002 and 2003.

Year 2000 saw a rebound in all office rents, specifically in the Premium and Grade A office sector where rentals went up by almost 40% from its bottom at Q3 1999 to the year end of 2000. The strong recovery of Super Grade A and Grade A office sector has been a support to the market of lower grade offices (Grade B or B-). Rentals improved in Q1 and Q2 and remained stable in Q3 2001. However, the fourth quarter of 2001 recorded a negative

Shanghai Premium & Grade A Offices Average Rents & Capital Values

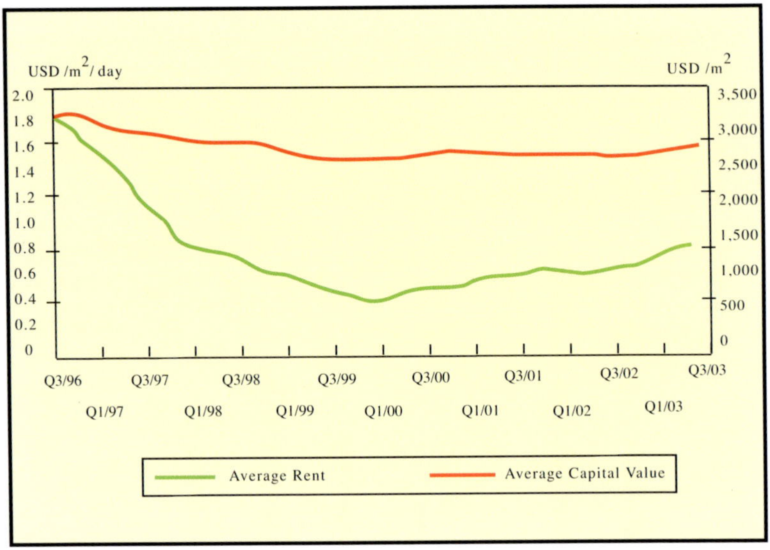

Source: Colliers International

growth of 8.8%. This was largely due to the low-rent strategy for the newly launched projects at year-end which had to cope with the slow-down in the market by sacrificing rentals to secure more leases.

However, expectations of China's economic growth coupled with WTO accession have resulted in stronger-than-expected demand for quality office space. Premium and Grade A office rents have therefore regained the real momentum to increase again since the second quarter of 2002. As at the end of September 2002, average Grade A rents averaged at USD0.68 per sq m per day, up nearly 2% from the previous quarter and already 51% higher over the bottom.

Future Market

Total new Grade A office supply for 2002 and 2003 is limited to 373,233 sq m, which is mostly spread over the districts of Huangpu, Luwan and Pudong. In contrast, there will be no new quality office supply in the other two office areas, i.e. Hongqiao and Nanjing Road West.

Fuelled by the optimistic office rental growth outlook, some developers have either resumed their office building construction or purchased new sites recently. It is projected that there will be another supply wave starting from 2004/5 onwards, including a number of large-scale projects, such as Hutchison Whampoa's Walton Plaza Phase in Xuhui District, Wheelock Center and Cross Ocean's project in Jing'an District, Phase II of Shui On's Xintiandi Office Development in Luwan District, and GIC Building and a World Finance Center in the Central Finance District of Lujiazui, Pudong.

New supply in 2003 is moderate. Total annual supply in 2003 and 2004 is projected to be some 400,000 sq m and 350,000 sq m, respectively. In contrast, take-up is to be as large as 690,000 sq m in 2003 and 770,000 sq m in 2004, which will bring down the overall office vacancy rate to around 12% by 2004. It is forecasted that the annual Premium and Grade A office take-up will grow at a rate of 15% with office absorption likely to reach 220,000 sq m in 2002. The average vacancy rate will increase slightly to 15.9% by the end of 2002, but is likely to drop to 13% in 2003.

MARKET PROSPECTS

The time series data available on the Shanghai market is insufficient to allow a detailed econometric analysis. Despite dramatic market changes in recent years, the Shanghai prime office market remains immature as compared to other major cities in the world. In view of this, any rental projections would be based on the following general assumptions:

- In the wake of WTO entry, a series of measures to remove barriers and streamline the legal systems will attract more foreign investment;
- Shanghai economy will continue to grow at 9% -11% per annum in the coming five years;
- Combining the two above assumptions, demand for prime office space will continue to strengthen;
- Overall quality of office buildings expected to increase with more projects meeting international standards.

Outdoor advertisement selling newhouses

Forecast of Foreign Investment

In the early 1990s, China revised its foreign investment policies and set up Pudong New District to further its economic development. Just over five years ending 1995, Shanghai's FDI experienced a five-fold increase to reach USD 5.36 billion. It continued to remain at USD5 billion level until the Asian

Foreign Direct Investment in Shanghai (Contractual Value)

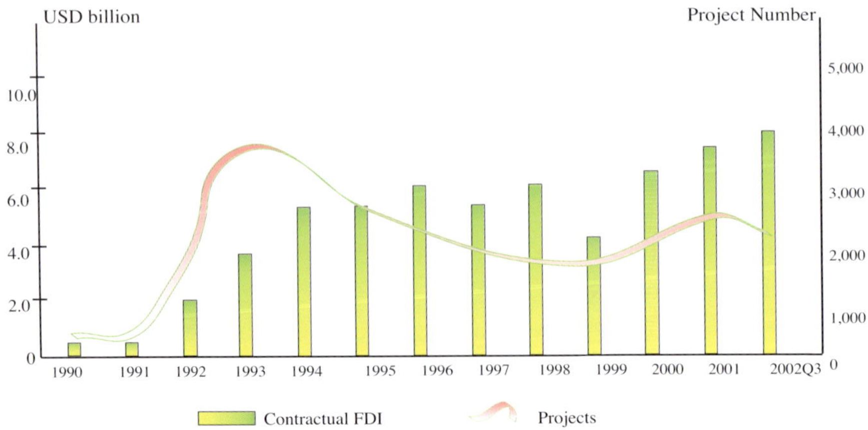

Source: Colliers International

financial crisis, which led investors to withdraw their funds from Asia. As a result, FDI into Shanghai dropped to USD 4.1 billion in 1999.

However, the prospect of Shanghai becoming a major financial center in Asia combined with China's entry into the WTO revived investors' confidence. In 2000, FDI in Shanghai surged to USD6.39 billion, a significant increase of 55.7% over the previous year. In 2001, FDI reached USD7.37 billion, up another 15.3%. Shanghai is likely to attract an even larger proportion out of the total FDI inflow to China as the city's streamlining measures in investment related policies and regulations become clearer in the wake of WTO entry. In the first ten months of 2002, Shanghai attracted a total of USD9.1 billion FDI, 37.3% higher than the same period last year. Year 2002 is expected to see a record-breaking USD10 billion FDI.

FDI in China vs FDI in Shanghai (Contractual Value)

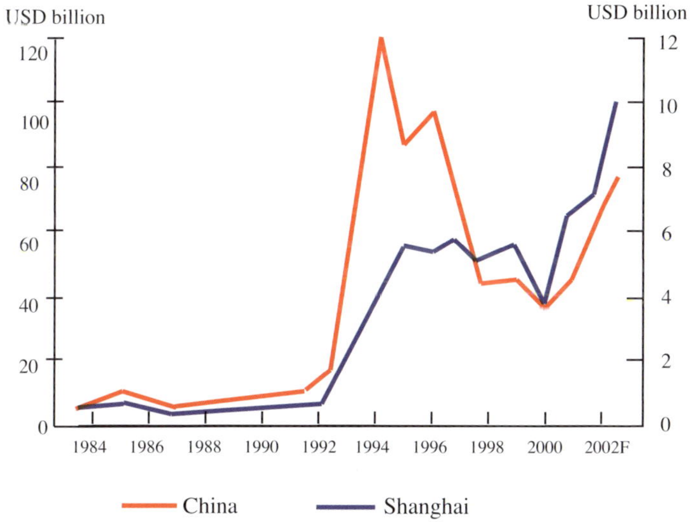

Source: Colliers International

In the first half of 2002, close to 2,000 new FIEs were set up in Shanghai, an increase of 52.74% on a year-on-year basis. This brought the total number of FIEs to 19,681 by the end of Q2 2002. Despite a sluggish global economy and deteriorating international investment environment, the country's fulfillment of its commitments to the WTO, such as lowering tariffs, lifting restrictions on overseas investors and improving the legal framework, is largely attributed to the city's success in attracting overseas investment.

Reportedly, an average of 11 FIEs was approved in Shanghai everyday. If the trend continues, the total number of FIEs is likely to reach 21,800 and 26,000 by the end of 2002 and 2003, respectively.

Strong FDI inflows should bode well for Shanghai's future economic growth and, as a result, demand for office spaces will surge.

FDI Structure

Only 23.6% and 25% of Shanghai's FDI was derived from the tertiary sector in 2000 and 2001, respectively. That was a significant drop compared with year 1995 when the percentage was as high as 62.1% caused by a real estate investment fever then. However, service industries (and therefore office occupiers) are becoming an increasingly important component of foreign investment in 2002. Statistics show that, 1,045 FIEs in the tertiary industry with contractual FDI worth USD2.78 billion were set up in the first nine months of 2002, contributing 34.6% of the total foreign investment. Based on the government's WTO schedule, finance, tourism, logistics, retail, education, healthcare and entertainment will attract more foreign investment in the coming years. Clearly, the tertiary industry has entered a new era.

It is worth noting that setting up WOFEs in China is becoming the norm of foreign investors since 2002, due to China's improving investment environment, immense opportunities and adoption of internationally accepted practices. Nearly 50% of all foreign investment in China between 1992 and 1999 used to take the form of a joint venture (JV). But about 80% of new setups in 2002 preferred WOFEs. In the latest Industrial Catalogue for Foreign Investment effective from April 2002, the central government has relaxed some requirements on shareholding issues, allowing WOFE to set up in certain areas previously for JV only.

Investment Opportunities in Real Estate

Shanghai economy marches on an uprising path. Growth for the period of 2001-2005 is projected at about 10% per annum. By the end of 2005, Shanghai's GDP per capita will reach USD6,500, providing enhanced purchase power and hence a strong support for the real estate market. Currently, per capital residential area of Shanghainese is only 10 per sq m, much lower than a developed country's level. By the end of 2005, it is planned to reach 15 sq m. Given a large population in Shanghai, demand for residential properties is equally huge.

Shanghai's five-year (2001-2005) economic and social development blueprint includes real estate development as one of its six pillar industries. This would further energize the industry and propel the real estate sector to contribute 10% of the local GDP.

In another round of urban construction, Shanghai will be focusing on comprehensive development of the two sides of the Huangpu River, cross-river tunnel and bridge, rail transportation, bus interchange, magnetic levitation rail train and large-scale ecological environment projects, especially after its recent successful bid for World Expo 2010.

Since China's WTO accession, corporate, industrial and economic operations will gradually conform to the internationally acceptable practices. As the economic locomotive for China, Shanghai is, unquestionably, the prime location for foreign investment. The influx of world-renowned organizations and MNCs will greatly increase the demand for premium offices, residential properties and hotels. Meanwhile, relocation and expansion of domestic companies in Shanghai will stabilize high-graded office market, too.

Wholesale & Retail

COMMERCE IN SHANGHAI

Shanghai's rapid economic growth since 1978 has led to dramatic increases in per capita income for urban residents. In 2001, the per capita disposable income of urban residents in Shanghai reached RMB12,883 (USD1,562), up 9.9% over 2000; the disposable income of rural households also grew steadily to reach RMB5,850 (USD790) per capita, up 5.1%. Increases in household consumption fueled the explosive development of the retail sector in Shanghai. Color TV sets, air conditioners and mobile phones, deemed luxurious goods decade ago, are now commonly seen in ordinary families.

Durable Consumer Products Possession in Shanghai (per 100 households)

Items	Urban	Rural
Color TV	154	105
Air Conditioner	100	16
VCD Player	56	29
Mobile Phone	50	35
Home Computer	38	7

The total retail sales volume in 2001 was RMB186.1 billion (USD22.5 billion), an 8.1% increase over the previous year. Of this total, foodstuff accounted for RMB75.7 billion, up 7.9%; apparels took RMB24.7 billion, up 7%; and consumable goods amounted to RMB84.2 billion, up 8.5%. The total value-added of "commerce", based on statistics, climbed up 10.2% to RMB34.0 billion. It is projected that by the end of 2005, the total retail turnover and value added of commerce will reach RMB250 billion and RMB75 billion respectively, a yearly increase of 8%-10%.

Forecast of Shanghai's Commerce 2001- 2005

Items	Value in 2005	Annual Growth
Value added of the whole sector	RMB75 billion	10%
Total Retail Sales	RMB250 billion	8%
Total Wholesale Trade	RMB670 billion	10%
Total Chain Store Sales	RMB100 billion	
Increase in Profit Rate	0.3% ~ 0.5%	

The Spring Festival, or Chinese New Year period, and newly implemented Golden Weeks (one-week long public holidays for May Day and National Day) have benefited city retailers dearly. In the first quarter of 2002, turnover of Shanghai's retail sector reached RMB50.73 billion, an increase of 8.8% on a year-on-year basis. Visitors to exhibitions like the East China Fair and traveler influx have pushed up retail sales, with the sales of food and apparels surging 8.6% and 8.1% respectively.

Buildings with huge billboards at Xujiahui

Domestic retailers, including China's two largest chain supermarket groups – Lianhua and Hualian, still dominate Shanghai's retail sector. Lianhua, Hualian and the third largest group, Nong Gong Shang (literally, Agriculture, industry and commerce) have all enjoyed local preferential treatment, including low-interest bank loans, tax reductions and discounts in rental. Lianhua has also benefited from the experience and know-how of its French joint-venture partner, Carrefour, with which it has already opened five successful hypermarkets in Shanghai.

Top Ten Domestic Retailers in China, 2001

Rank Company	Sales (RMB bn)	Increase	No. of Stores
1. Shanghai Lianhua	14.1	26.24%	1,225
2. Shanghai Hualian	8.5	51.7%	818
3. Beijing Hualian	8.0	60.0%	42
4. Shanghai Nong Gong Shang	7.5	38.4%	315
5. Shandong Sanlian	7.0	32.3%	177
6. Beijing Guomei	6.2	119.8%	74
7. Jiangsu Suguo	5.3	31.4%	663
8. Parkson (China) Investment	5.2	24.0%	635
9. Shanghai Jinjiang Metro	4.9	32.2%	15
10. China Resources Wanjia	4.6	34.9%	344

Development in Chain Stores

Apparently, retail business in Shanghai is leading the trend in China. The gathering popularity in retail chain stores has boosted its retailing strength further. To take advantage of economies of scale and brand name, many retail players have established their retailing network in Shanghai and even ventured into other regions of China. For example, Shanghai Lianhua has built its purchasing networks in Jilin, Henan, Guangdong, Shandong, Sichuan and Xinjiang, having extended its retail business into the east and south of China.

Shanghai's Top Ten Chain Stores

Rank	Company	Sales (RMB bn)
1	Shanghai Lianhua	14.1
2	Shanghai Hualian	8.5
3	Shanghai Nong Gong Shang	7.5

4	Shanghai Jinjiang Metro	4.9
5	Shanghai Ek Chor Lotus	1.9
6	Shanghai Hualian Jimaisheng	1.6
7	Shanghai Jia De Li	0.9
8	Shanghai Da Run Fa	0.8
9	Shanghai Jie Qiang Tobacco, Sugar & Wine	0.8
10	Shanghai Homemart	0.7

Homemart is a construction and decoration material supermarket chain

By year 2001, there were 2,020 chain supermarket outlets and 1,980 convenience stores in Shanghai. The total sales of chain stores reached RMB52 billion (USD6.3 billion), showing a remarkable tide of 26.8% over year 2000.

Chain Stores in Shanghai, 2001

Category	Outlets	Sales (RMB bn)	Increase	% in Total Retail Sales
Supermarket	2,020	28.90	35.03%	15.52%
Convenience store	1,980	2.74	60.88%	1.47%
Hypermarket	53	11.67	16.54%	6.27%
Fast Food	415	1.67	4.5%	0.9%
Others	932	7.03	59.8%	3.78%
Total	5,400	52.0	26.83%	28.0%

Source: *Shanghai Economic Yearbook 2002.*

Commercial Groups and Department Stores

In terms of total trade volume, Hualian as a group still takes the lead in Shanghai, followed by major department stores and shopping centers like Friendship, New World and the No. 1 Department Store.

Shanghai's Top Ten Commercial Groups, 2001

Rank	Company	Sales (RMB bn)
1	Shanghai Hualian (Group)	19.3
2	Shanghai Friendship	17.5
3	Shanghai New World	14.1
4	Shanghai No.1 Department Store	11.8
5	Shanghai Sugar & Wine	10.6
6	Shanghai Yuyuan Group	7.7
7	Shanghai No. 9 Department Store	5.6
8	Shanghai Xujiahui	4.9
9	Shanghai Liang You	4.6
10	Shanghai Xinya	4.4

Based on individual shop sales, the well-known Shanghai No. 1 Department Store was constantly ranked the first, although its sales dropped recently. And its sister company, the No. 1 Yaohan (the Next Age) in Pudong New District, stood at the third place.

Shanghai's Top Ten Shopping Centers, 2001

Rank Company	Retail Turnover (RMB mil)	Increase
1. Shanghai No. 1 Department Store	1,744.3	-20.3%
2. Shanghai New World	1,663.6	0.3%
3. Shanghai No.1 Yaohan	1,402.2	7.7%
4. Shanghai Pacific (Xuhui)	1,087.0	7.0%
5. Shanghai Orient Shopping Center	875.2	13.1%
6. Shanghai Hualian	807.6	2.5%
7. Shanghai Huijin Department Store	663.5	22.8%

8. Shanghai No. 6 Department Store	661.9	1.5%
9. Shanghai Pacific (Huihai)	623.1	10.0%
10. Shanghai Jiuhai Parkson	574.5	5.0%

Shanghai No. 1 Yaohan or the Next Age is the largest department store in Pudong

Challenges Ahead

Retailers in Shanghai have started a new round of competition, as markets now are more open for foreign investors after WTO entry. Relevant regulations on the percentage of shares held by foreign investors, the number of store branches and store scale will all be gradually phased out over the next three years. More and more multinational retail chains are seeking to establish footholds in Shanghai. Presently, RMB140 billion (USD16.91 billion) of the total RMB430 billion (USD51.93 billion) in commercial capital is coming from foreign companies in Shanghai. There are 84 foreign-funded retailers operating in Shanghai, which temporarily hold a collective 10% market share in the municipality's retail sector. Among the large foreign hypermarket and warehouse store operators in Shanghai, there are Carrefour (France), Metro (Germany), Er Chor Lotus (Thailand), and E-Mart (Korea). Carrefour and Metro both have a substantial presence, while the US-based Wal-Mart, which has already strengthened its foothold in south China, is now eyeing Shanghai.

Carrefour currently operates five joint-venture hypermarkets in Shanghai, each with floor space exceeding 10,000 square meters. Apart from its experience in operating hypermarkets, extensive market research, competitive prices, well-chosen store locations and high reputation, Carrefour's success can be largely attributed to its preemptive move into the market. It sources directly from local producers, and caters to specific local demands, especially in the areas of price and product range. Less than 20% of merchandise at Carrefour Shanghai is imported. However, it did not generate any profit in Shanghai until it opened its fourth store.

WTO COMMITMENT

Before its accession to the WTO, China prohibited foreign companies from distributing imported products or providing repair and maintenance services. China is liberalizing its distribution system to delegate full distribution rights for WTO member companies, with a comprehensive set of commitments covering commission-based services, wholesaling, retailing, franchising, sales away from a fixed location, and related services such as inventory management or repair and maintenance. China has also agreed to open up rental and leasing services, air courier services, freight forwarding and packing services. Current restrictions on most distribution-related services will be phased out within three years from the date of accession on 11 December 2001, although the timetable of commitments varies in individual industries.

Commission-based Distribution and Wholesale

- Within one year after accession, foreign investment of up to 50% will be allowed in joint ventures to engage in the commission-based distribution business and wholesale business of all imported and domestically produced products;

- Within two years after accession, foreign investment will be allowed to have controlling shareholdings;
- Within three years after accession, wholly owned foreign enterprises (WOFEs) will be allowed to set up in this area.

Retail Business

In retail business, there are restrictions on both foreign shareholding and product range. With regards to shareholding control, the terms are similar to those in the wholesale sector:

Air-conditioned and hygenic food courts in shopping centre mushroomed in Shanghai

- Within one year after accession, foreign investment of up to 50% will be allowed;
- Within two years after accession, foreign investors will be allowed to have controlling shareholdings;
- Within three years after accession, WOFEs will be allowed;
- Foreign investors are not allowed to have controlling shareholding in the business operations on cars (restrictions will be removed no later than 11 December 2006), books, newspapers, magazines, publications, pharmaceuticals, pesticides, mulching film, chemical fertilizers, processed petroleum products, rice, vegetable oil, sugar, tobacco and cotton, which have more than 30 branch outlets.

As many products are still considered strategic or sensitive for foreign controls, the government has a list of restrictions on products as to what extent foreign companies may deal with. However,

- Within one year after accession, foreign investment will be allowed to deal with books, newspapers, magazines and publications;
- Within three years after accession, foreign investment will be allowed to deal with pharmaceutical products, pesticide, mulching film and processed petroleum products;
- Within three years after accession, foreign investment will be allowed for franchising and wholesale and retail at unfixed points of sale.
- Within five years after accession, foreign investment will be allowed to deal with chemical fertilizer.

Book business remains in the hands of a few Chinese distributors

In addition, the government has cautiously singled out a few locations for experimental implementation of the above schedule. The geographical

Books on sale at the Shanghai Foreign Bookstore

restrictions mixed with quantitative constraints imposed on foreign retailers are as follows:

- Upon accession, foreign service providers are permitted to establish joint ventures in Zhengzhou and Wuhan;
- Within one year after accession, foreign investment will be allowed to establish no more than two joint ventures in the five Special Economic Zones (i.e. Shenzhen, Zhuhai, Shantou, Xiamen and Hainan) and in four cities (i.e. Tianjin, Guangzhou, Dalian and Qingdao). In the case of Beijing and Shanghai, where foreign capital penetration was already seen before China gained the WTO memebership, four joint ventures are permitted. Two of the four joint ventures established in Beijing may set up branches in Beijing;
- Within two years after accession, foreign majority equity shareholding is allowed in joint ventures; and geographic coverage will further include all provincial capitals, plus Chongqing and Ningbo;
- Within three years after accession, there will be no restrictions on foreign shareholding, geographic areas, or the number of business entities.

Will these shops be affected by China's WTO commitment?

However, China still has some reservations in completely opening its distribution, retail and wholesale sector to foreign investments. For example, its WTO commitments did not include wholesaling of salt, and wholesaling and retailing of tobacco; and for joint venture department stores and chain stores, only minority ownership is allowed.

Repair and Maintenance Services

This sector refers to repair and maintenance services rendered for office machinery and equipment including computers. Upon WTO entry, foreign investment engaged in such services must be in the form of joint ventures. Within one year after WTO entry, foreign majority ownership will be permitted. Within three years, foreign suppliers of maintenance and repair services will be permitted to establish WOFEs

Entry Requirement

To establish a commerce-related joint venture in China, the foreign party has to meet the following requirements:

- It must possess strong financial ability, advanced management expertise, extensive sales networks, good reputation and healthy track record;
- It should be capable of helping the export of Chinese products via the proposed joint venture;

- For foreign investors who wish to set up a retail joint venture, its assets in the year immediately prior to the application should exceed USD200 million and its average annual sales in the three years prior to the application should be more than USD2 billion;
- For foreign investors who wish to set up a wholesale joint venture, its assets in the year immediately before making the application are more than USD300 million and its average annual revenue in the three years prior to the application should be more than USD2.5 billion.
- In other words, given those stringent requirements, only giant retailers are welcomed.

On the other hand, the Chinese party of a Sino-foreign joint venture has to meet the following requirements:

- It must possess strong financial and operational ability;
- Its assets in the year immediately prior to making the application must exceed more than RMB50 million (RMB30 million for applicants in central and western regions);
- If the Chinese party is a commercial enterprise, its average annual sales in the three years prior to the application shall be more than RMB300 million (RMB200 million for applicants in central and western regions);
- If the Chinese party is an international trading company, its average annual import and export trade volume (not including those conducted on behalf of others on an agency basis) for three years prior to the application shall be more than USD50 million, with export volume of at least USD30 million.

Based on the prescribed qualifications and regulations, evidently, foreign retailers must find a local partner before they have the chance to explore the China market. The size of their investment, store location and even an exit decision require government approval. In view of the strict market protectionism, it is extremely difficult for small overseas companies to obtain a license to operate a shop in China. Even if the foreign investor does pass the qualification test, they may still face problems in locating a qualified Chinese party to set up a joint venture with, let alone a cooperative one.

Directory

To make phone calls from outside Shanghai, please add country code (86) for China and area code (21) for Shanghai. To make local calls, dial the number directly. For domestic long-distance calls, please dial "0+area code+telephone number. For IDD calls, please dial "00+ country code+area code+telphone number".

USEFUL NUMBERS

Ambulance	☎ 120
Fire	☎ 119
IDD Code (English)	☎ 106
Int'l Operator	☎ 106
Int'l Directory Assistance	☎ 116
Police	☎ 110
Tel Number Enquiry	☎ 114
Time Report	☎ 117
Weather (English)	☎ 121

Airport - Hongqiao (English)
☎ 62688918-2

Airport - Pudong (English)
☎ 38484500-2

Boat/ Ship Information
☎ 63260050 (general inquiries)
☎ 63261261 (schedule & ticket)

Operator-Assisted Yellow Pages
☎ 86000

Police Station (English)
☎ 63576666

Railway Station
☎ 63179090, 56234692

Railway Ticket Delivery Service
☎ 63171880

SOS 24 hour Service
☎ 62950099

Tourist Information (English)
☎ 64398947

ACCOUNTANTS

Deloitte Touche Tohmatsu
☎ 63936292
🖷 63936290

Ernst & Young Hua Ming
☎ 62191219
🖷 62193219

KPMG
☎ 53594666
🖷 62881889

Lehman Brown
☎ 62881635
🖷 62881636

Lee Seng Chan & Co.
☎ 62099258, 62095141
🖷 62093425
Website: www.lsccpa.com.cn

Pan Chen & Zhang Associated Certified Public Accountants
☎ 52896828, 52896650
🖷 52896395

Lee Seng Chan & Co.
A member of UHY International

SINGAPORE
6001 Beach Road
#14-01 Golden Mile Tower
Singapore 199589
Tel: 65-63955100
Fax: 65-62986263
Web: www.lsccpa.com.sg

SHANGHAI
318-322 Xian Xia Road
#21-03 Xin Da Building
Shanghai 200336, China
Tel: 86-21-62099258, 32231022
Fax: 86-21-62093425
Web: www.lsccpa.com.cn

SUZHOU
518 Su Xin Mansion
88 Jinjihu Road, Suzhou Industrial Park
Jiangsu 215021, China
Tel: 86-512-62522545
Fax: 86-512-62522551

TIANJIN
9 Floor, Guotou Building
157 Dagu Road, Heping District
Tianjin 300040, China
Tel: 86-22-23142273
Fax: 86-22-23142290

Pricewaterhouse Coopers
☎ 63863388
🖷 63863300

Roedl & Partner
☎ 58300708
🖷 58201218

Shanghai Gong Xin Zhong Nan Certified Public Accountants
☎ 63785350, 63080296
🖷 63084377

Shanghai Shangshen Certified Public Accountants Co. Ltd.
☎ 63666967, 63663688
🖷 63674211

Shu Lun Pan Certified Public Accountants Co. Ltd.
☎ 63606600
🖷 63501004

Xin Zheng Guang Certified Public Accountants Co. Ltd.
☎ 63514599

ADVERTISING & PUBLIC RELATIONS

Asatsu Advertising
☎ 64674118

Asiaray Advertising
☎ 64031999

B & B (Bauquis & Boyd) Int'l Ltd
☎ 28903121

Bates Shanghai
☎ 63582908

BBDO CNUAC
☎ 64679699

Carat Media Service
☎ 52984280

Creasia Advertising
☎ 63509156

D'arcy Masius Benton & Bowles
☎ 52984333

DDB Shanghai
☎ 63509180

Dentsu Advertising
☎ 63501660

Dentsu Yong & Rubicam Brand Communication
☎ 63867770

Eastern Draftworldwide
☎ 65975180

Euro RSCG Partnership
☎ 53965666

FCB China
☎ 63915252

Field Force Euro RSCG
☎ 63917766

Golden Horse Advertising
☎ 64380260

Grey Worldwide
☎ 63508660

Guangdong YC Press Advertising
☎ 62520515

J. Walter Thompson
☎ 52985598

Leo Burnett Shanghai Advertising
☎ 84049602

Lowe Lintas & Partners Worldwide
☎ 52984428

McCann-Erickson Guangming
☎ 65683300

Medai Partners Int'l
☎ 64401568

Mediacom
☎ 63508660

Megacom Advertising
☎ 63916262

Metro Ads Advertising
☎ 64748058

Mindshare China
☎ 52986388

Mission Advertising
☎ 62772771

Motivator Shanghai
☎ 53965666

Ogilvy & Mather
☎ 62183009

Optimum Media Direction
☎ 63758855

Publicis Ad-Link
☎ 63503678

Saatchi & Saatchi
☎ 62138822

Senses Filmpower
☎ 63278603

Shanghai Hakuhodo Advertising
☎ 64156776

Sino Media Group
☎ 62792541

Starcom Worldwide
☎ 62172284

TBWA Leedavis China
☎ 63906798

The Media Edge
☎ 63867770

Universal McCann
☎ 52100008

Vision & Value
☎ 62162000

Senith Media
☎ 62133232

Zigma Advertising Associates
☎ 62791234

AIRLINES

FOREIGN

Air France (AF)
☎ 63606688
🖷 63606655

Air Macau (NX)
☎ 62481110
🖷 62487870

All Nippon Airlines (NH)
☎ 62797000
🖷 62797002

Ansett Australia
☎ 64155210
🖷 64155209

Asiana Airlines (OZ)
☎ 62194000
🖷 62703167

Austrian Airlines (OS)
☎ 63759051
🖷 63759055

Canadain Airlines Int'l (CP)
☎ 63758899

Charter Jets & helicopter Services
☎ (86)13901623878

Dragon Air
☎ 63756375
🖷 63756700

Japan Airlines
☎ 64723000
✈ 68345008
🖷 62882505

KLM Royal Dutch Airlines
☎ 68355699

Korean Airlines (KE)
☎ 62756000
🖷 62752777

Lufthansa German Airlines (LH)
☎ 58304400
🖷 58300616

Malaysia Airlines (MH)
☎ 62682900
🖷 62798657

Quantas Airways (QF)
☎ 62798660
🖷 62798650

Nepal Royal Airlines
☎ 62708352

Philippines Airlines
☎ 63506311

Singapore Airlines (SQ)
☎ 62891000
🖷 62892000

Swiss Air
☎ 63758212
🖷 63758214

Thai Airways International (TG)
☎ 52985555
🖷 52986066

Turkish Airlines
☎ 32220022
🖷 32220121

United Airlines (UA)
☎ 62798009
🖷 62798853

Virgin Atlantic
☎ 53534605
✈ 53534600
🖷 53534601

DOMESTIC

China Eastern Airlines
☎ 62472255
✈ 62686268

China Northwest Airlines (NW)
☎ 62798088
📠 62798007

China Southern Airlines
☎ 32160876

China Xinjiang Airlines
☎ 62474497

Hainan Airlines
☎ 63270259

Shandong Airlines
☎ 62688899-51122

Shanghai Airlines
☎ 62558888
☎ 800-6208888 (Toll Free)
Website: www.shanghai-air.com

上海航空股份有限公司
SHANGHAI AIRLINES CO.,LTD.

18F, No. 212, Jiangning Road
Shanghai 200041, China
Tel: 86-21-62555000
Toll Free: 800 620 8888
Fax: 86-21-62555333
Website: www.shanghai-air.com

Business Jet Operations Department
Email: charter@shanghai-air.com

BANKS

FOREIGN

ABN AMRO Bank
☎ 63299303

American Express
☎ 62798062

Boston No 1 National Bank
☎ 63203772

ANZ Bank
☎ 68400111

Australia & New Zealand Banking Group
☎ 63509599

Banca Commerciale Italiana
☎ 63200517/8

Banca Di RomaABN AMRO Bank
☎ 63559010

Banca Intesa
☎ 63513204

Banca Monte Deipaschi Di Siena Spa
☎ 63746158

Banca Nazionale del Lavoro
☎ 62490462

Banco Espirito Santo
☎ 58870016

Bangkok Bank
☎ 63233788

Bank Bali
☎ 62494303

Bank Boston
☎ 63299303

ABN AMRO Bank
☎ 62798090

Bank of America NT & SA
☎ 68818686

Bank of East Asia
☎ 63297338

Bank of New York
☎ 62494108

Bank of Tokyo Mitsubishi
☎ 64723166/99

Banque Indosuez
☎ 63292228

BNP Paribas
☎ 64728762

Bayerische Landesbank
☎ 68766600

Chase Manhattan Bank
☎ 62797288

Citibank NA
☎ 58791200

Commerzbank AG
☎ 63747680

Commonwealth Bank of Australia
☎ 63553939

Chase Manhattan Bank
☎ 62797288

Credit Agricole Indosuez
☎ 58795559

Credit Lyonnais
☎ 63550070

Credit Suisse First Boston
☎ 68818418

Czech Savings Bank
☎ 53060749

Daiwa Bank Ltd
☎ 62755198

DG Bank
☎ 63300100

Deutsche Bank
☎ 68410808

Development Bank of Singapore
☎ 58767698

Dresdner Bank AG
☎ 50495588

First Union National Bank
☎ 58795418

Fortis Bank
☎ 68412975

Generale Bank
☎ 62486600

German Bafalia United Bank
☎ 50663208

Hana Bank
☎ 68763938

Hang Seng Bank Ltd
☎ 64728781

Hanil Bank
☎ 62190606

Hong Kong Youlian Bank Co Ltd
☎ 58793628

Hypo-Bank
☎ 62798549

ING Bank N.V.
☎ 68413355

KBC Bank N.V.
☎ 58791599

Kookmin Bank
☎ 62701616

Mees & Pierso N.V.
☎ 62701616

Metroband Shanghai
☎ 62192020

Mizubo Bank
☎ 68410001

National Westminster Bank
☎ 62798804

Natexis Banque
☎ 58875775

National Bank of Canada
☎ 62798102

NatWest Bank
☎ 62798820

Overseas-Chinese Banking Corp
☎ 58200200

Po Sang Bank
☎ 63212377

Rabo Bank
☎ 58889888

Royal Bank of Canada
☎ 63202823

Sanpolo Imi Bank
☎ 62496517

Societe Generale
☎ 62497500

Standard Chartered Bank
☎ 58871230

State Bank of India
☎ 63852770

Sumitomo Mitsui Bank
☎ 68415000

Swiss Bank Corp
☎ 62781868

The Bank of Nagoya
☎ 62754207

The Chiba Bank
☎ 62780482

The Int'l Bank of Paris & Shanghai
☎ 58405500

The Joyo Bank Ltd
☎ 62090258

The Korea Development Bank
☎ 68751234

TM Int'l Bank
☎ 58886688

Unicredito Italiano
☎ 68412555

Union Bank of Switzerland
☎ 63291438

Westdeutsche Landesbank
☎ 68413399

DOMESTIC

Agricultural Bank of China,
Shanghai Branch
☎ 63153315

Agricultural Bank of China,
Suzhou Branch
☎ 512-67775580, 68242294
℻ 512-67775800, 68240501

Bank of China, Shanghai Branch
☎ 63867697

Bank of Communications,
Shanghai Branch
☎ 63213400

Bank of Shanghai,
Shanghai Headquarter
☎ 63370888

China Construction Bank, Shanghai Branch
☎ 63265388

China Export & Import Bank, Shanghai Branch
☎ 38804588

China Merchants Bank, Shanghai Branch
☎ 58790443

China Mingsheng Bank, Shanghai Branch
☎ 53857700

CITIC Industrial Bank, Shanghai Branch
☎ 63506350

Everbright Bank of China, Shanghai Branch
☎ 63606360

Fujian Industrial Bank, Shanghai Branch
☎ 62677777

Guangdong Development Bank, Shanghai Branch
☎ 63022233

Huaxia Bank, Shanghai Branch
☎ 62257087

People's Bank of China
☎ 58845000

Shanghai Pudong Development Bank
☎ 63296188

Shenzhen Development Bank, Shanghai Branch
☎ 58877777

BUSINESS ASSOCIATIONS

American Chamber of Commerce
☎ 62797119
🖷 62797643

Belgian Luxembourg Business Association
☎ 58791599

Benelux Business Association
☎ 32140872

British Chamber of Commerce
☎ 62185022
🖷 62185066

Canada China Business Council
☎ 63906791
🖷 63907310

Canadian Trade Commission
☎ 62798400

China-Australia Chamber of Commerce
☎ 62488301

China-Britain Business Council
☎ 62185183
🖷 62185193

China-Italy Chamber of Commerce
☎ 63511198
🖷 63511197

Danish Business Association of Shanghai
☎ 62192711

Delegation of German Industry and Commerce
☎ 50812266
🖷 50812009

Dutch Business Association
☎ 64376598

Finland Trade Center
☎ 64710388
🖷 64711338

French Chamber of Commerce
☎ 62819260, 62183618

German Chamber of Commerce
☎ 63309791
🖷 63309794

Hong Kong Chamber of Commerce
☎ 53069533
🖷 53069532

Hong Kong TDC
☎ 63528848, 63528488

Italian Trade Commission
☎ 62488600
🖷 62482169

Japanese Federation of Commerce & Industry
☎ 62752001
🖷 62701579

Liverpool Chamber of Commerce & Industry
☎ 63237703, 62185183-14
🖷 63237704

Malaysian Timber Association
☎ 62754070

Russian Federation of Industries & Commerce
☎ 62281304

Swedish Chamber of Commerce
☎ 64743533
🖷 64375654

SITA Telecom Association
☎ 62680690

Sino-Japan Economic Society
☎ 62750088

Sino-American Chamber of Commerce
☎ 64152579

Sino-American Federation
☎ 62287599

US-China Business Council
☎ 64152579
🖷 64152584

BUSINESS CENTERS

AA Business Center
☎ 53820866-639
🖷 53823218

Apollo Instant Office
☎ 62486288
🖷 62481980

Far Glory Executive Center
☎ 62292222
🖷 62295555

German Centre for Industry and Trade Shanghai
☎ 65015100
🖷 65154648

Jiahua Business Center
☎ 64868888
🖷 64864900

Maryland Business Center
☎ 62797657

Michigan Business Center
☎ 62797640

President Business Center
☎ 62113900
🖷 62119010

Regus Business Center
☎ 28909888

ServCorp Business Services
☎ 28903000

Shanghai Center
☎ 62798600
🖷 62798610

The Execuive Centre
☎ 52524618
🖷 52524616

CONSULATES

Australia
☎ 64334604
17 Fuxing West Road

Austria
☎ 64740268
1375 Huaihai Middle Road

Belgium
☎ 64376628
127 Wuyi Road

Cambodia
☎ 63619676
400 Hankou Road

Canada
☎ 62798400
1376 Nanjing West Road

Chile
☎ 62498000
65 Yan'an West Road

Cuba
☎ 62753078
55 Loushanguan Road

Czech
☎ 64712420
1375 Huaihai Middle Road

Denmark
☎ 62090500
2200 Yan'an West Road

Egypt
☎ 64331020
1375 Huaihai Middle Road

Finland
☎ 64740068
1375 Huaihai Middle Road

France
☎ 64377414
1375 Huaihai Middle Road

Germany
☎ 64336953
181 Yongfu Road

Malaysia
☎ 62481688

India
☎ 62758885
2200 Yan'an West Road

Iran
☎ 62814666
296 Xinhua Road

Israel
☎ 62098008
55 Loushanguan Road

Italy
☎ 64716980
1375 Huaihai Middle Road

Japan
☎ 62780788
8 Wanshan Road

Korea
☎ 62196420
2200 Yan'an Road

Mexico
☎ 64373451
1375 Huaihai Middle Road

New Zealand
☎ 64711108
1375 Huaihai Middle Road

Netherlands
☎ 62099076
88 Xianxia Road

Norway
☎ 63239988
12 Zhongshan East 1st Road

Poland
☎ 64334735
618 Jianguo West Road

Russia
☎ 63242682
20 Huangpu Road

Singapore
☎ 64370776
400 Urumqi Middle Road

Spain
☎ 63234265
120 Zhongshan East 1st Road

Sweden
☎ 6474 1311
1375 Huaihai Middle Road

Switzerland
☎ 62700519
88 Xianxia Road

Thailand
☎ 63234095
7 Zhongshan East 1st Road

Yugoslavia
☎ 62081388
60 Ronghua East Road

Untied Kingdom
☎ 62797650
1376 Nanjing West Road

United States of America
☎ 64336880
1469 Huaihai Middle Road

COURIER SERVICES

DHL-Sinotrans Int'l Air Courier
☎ 800-810-8000 (Toll Free)
65362900
📠 65366110

DZL
☎ 62569636

EMS
☎ 185

FedEx Shanghai
☎ 62750808
📠 62757522
Service Hotline:
☎ 5411 8333 (Puxi)
☎ 5032 0909 (Pudong)
☎ 6885 1188 (Shanghai Gateway)

Global Express Service
☎ 63551915

Shanghai Hengda Air Cargo Group
☎ 52705555

Sunsir Express Co Ltd
☎ 62405511

TNT Skypack-Sinotrans Ltd
☎ 6421 1111
📠 64216666

UPS Int'l Express
☎ 63915599
📠 63916633
Service Hotline:
☎ 21-63915555 (Shanghai)
☎ 10-65818391 (Beijing)
☎ 20-83486666 (Guangzhou)

QSE
☎ 63535327

Shanghai Express
☎ 64591777

Shanghai Aviation Express
☎ 62688657

Post Express
☎ 65400000

Quick Duck
☎ 64467728

COSCO Express
☎ 62684288

Mitex International
☎ 62948835

EVENT ORGANIZERS

Adsale Exhibition Services Ltd
☎ 62781867

CMP Media
☎ 64371178

Deutsche Messe AG (Shanghai)
☎ 68863286

Hong Kong Exhibition Services
☎ 62095209

IGEDO Int'l Modemesse Kronen GmbH & Co.
☎ 62786757

Legend Exhibition Service Co.
☎ 62890101

Oriental Expo Services Ltd.
☎ 62297336

Montgomery Network
☎ 62095209

Munich Trade Fairs Consultancy
☎ 68863366

O.E. Conference & Exhibition Co.
☎ 62274262

Pico Exhibition Services
☎ 59108330
📠 59159177
Website: www.pico.com

Royal Dutch Jaarbeurs China & Keylong Exhibitions Services
☎ 52896776, 52896770

Shanghai Conference Service Co.
☎ 64690175

Shanghai Everbright International Convention and Exhibition Center
☎ 635949888

Shanghai Exhibition Center
☎ 62790279

Shanghai Int'l Convention Center
☎ 20370000-6818

Shanghai Int'l Exhibition Center
☎ 62755800

Shanghai Int'l Exhibition Co.
☎ 63872828

Shanghai J&L Exhibition & Service
☎ 64876624

Shanghai Mart
☎ 62366888

Shanghai Modern International Exhibition Corp.
☎ 63217522

Shanghai New Int'l Expo Center
☎ 38760488

Shanghai Pudong International Exhibition Co.
☎ 62723462

Shanghai Syma-Expo Ltd.
☎ 62388811

Shanghai Union International Exhibition Co.
☎ 62997648

Shanghai World Trade Mart Co., Ltd.
☎ 62360208

Xcellent Identity Network Ltd.
☎ 62350482

EXECUTIVE SEARCH

Andersen Consulting
☎ 63915588

Asia Pacific Management Institute
☎ 38784882

Bo Le Associates Ltd.
☎ 53966686

China Human Resources Group
☎ 63179979

Dayu Job Consulting
☎ 64285063

EMDS Shanghai Office
☎ 5257 4104

Eve Business Consulting
☎ 68766568

Gainful Consulting
☎ 62700400

Hewitt Consultancy Co. Ltd.
☎ 64515230

Join-Link Consulting Ltd.
☎ 63223767

LEK Consulting LLC
☎ 62728200

Manpower Business Consulting
☎ 68752897

Nicholson International
☎ 63648895

Norman Broadbent International
☎ 62798575

Oasis Executive Searching Group
☎ 62861992

Pudong Human Resource
☎ 68541246

Russell Reynolds Services
☎ 64450955

Shanghai China Human Resources Market
☎ 58876116

Shanghai Director & Manager Resources Company
☎ 62338413

Shanghai Foreign Service Co. Ltd.
☎ 63721888, 63861898

Shanghai Fortune Consultant
☎ 62402111

Shanghai Human Resources Co. Ltd.
☎ 62774770

Shanghai Ineyes Information Co. Ltd.
☎ 52573253

Shanghai Int'l Multisearch Company
☎ 52120010

Shanghai Trade Union Overseas Employment Services Co.
☎ 62191398

Shanghai Professional Qualifications Evaluation Center
☎ 64045568
Shanghai Recruitment Service
☎ 62700400

Shanghai Witbright Science & Technology Information Consulting Company
☎ 64389536

Shanghai Zhiying Commercial Consultation Co., Ltd.
☎ 54043205

TMP Worldwide eResourcing
☎ 28903230

Wang & Li Asia Resources Online
☎ 62175626

Watson Wyatt Consultancy
☎ 52986888

FREIGHT & SHIPPING

Air Sea Transport (HK) Ltd
☎ 62561974
📠 62582419

Atlantic Forwarding (China) Ltd
☎ 64724689
📠 64728270

American President Lines Co Ltd
☎ 62476789
📠 62791602

Chiatai Enterprises Shipping Ltd
☎ 63237408
📠 63237408

China Naitonal Chartering Corp
☎ 63213103
📠 63291690

China National Materials Storage and Transportation Corp
☎ 63240593
📠 63248943

China-Japan Int'l Ferry Co Ltd
☎ 63257642
📠 63241372

Chinese-Polish Joint Stock Shipping Co.
☎ 63290818
📠 63291918

Combuilt Services Int'l (China) Ltd
☎ 63722737
📠 63291918

Compagnie Maritime D'Affretement
☎ 63233813
📠 63235935

COSCO Shanghai Int'l Freight Co Ltd
☎ 65958000
📠 65959533

COSCO Shanghai Freight and Forwarding Int'l Co
☎ 63067777
📠 63245413

Cots Enterprises Ltd / Cots Shipping Co Ltd
☎ 63561144
📠 63560404

Crown Worldwide Ltd
☎ 64720254
📠 64720255

EAS Int'l Transportation Ltd
☎ 64723060
🖷 64727718

Emery Worldwide
☎ 64722922
🖷 64721824

Eternal Way Ltd
☎ 63246260
🖷 63065147

Euro-Asia Line (HK) Ltd
☎ 63295252
🖷 63295050

Everich Shipping Ltd
☎ 65359158
🖷 65359157

Fairweather Steamship Co Ltd
☎ 63568801/4
🖷 63566637

Flynt Int'l Forwarders Ltd
☎ 64721382
🖷 64723572

Gold Star Line Ltd
☎ 63730000
🖷 63732222

Green Sail Ltd
☎ 63242210
🖷 63064331

Hanjin Shipping Co. Ltd.
☎ 62798132/3
🖷 62798154

Inchcape Shipping Service (HK) Ltd.
☎ 63269809
🖷 63269808

Intro-Well Shipping Ltd
☎ 62566008
🖷 62566008

Islamic Republic of Iran Shipping Lines
☎ 63752935/6
🖷 63182268

Jardine Shipping Agencies (HK) Ltd.
☎ 62137832/3
🖷 62129186

Kawasaki Kisen Kaisha Ltd
☎ 64728818
🖷 64728769

Kenwa Shipping Ltd
☎ 63295557
🖷 63294514

King Sharp Shipping Ltd
☎ 65355820
🖷 65357797

Kuehne & Nagel Ltd
☎ 64726251/9
🖷 64729561

LC Shipping Ltd
☎ 64711679
🖷 64715241

Land-Ocean Inchcape Int'l Container Transport Co Ltd
☎ 63214142
🖷 63215499

Maersk (China) Shipping Co. Ltd.
☎ 63201326
🖷 63203045

Mitsui O.S.K. Lines (Asia) Ltd.
☎ 63749206
🖷 63749208

Natural Ltd
☎ 64729200
🖷 64720880

P&O Nedlloyd Lines
☎ 63289886
🖷 63289616

Nippon Express Co Ltd
☎ 64726398
📠 64722261

NYK Line
☎ 63851166
📠 63280077

OOCL (China) Ltd.
☎ 62794567
📠 62794590/4610

Panalpina (China) Ltd
☎ 62103725/7
📠 62127724

Richmers-Linie
☎ 64155170
📠 64155171

Schenker Int'l (HK) Ltd.
Tel: 64723648/50
📠 64728170

Shanghai Changjiang Shipping Corp
☎ 63756375
📠 63756700

Shanghai Jinjiang Shipping Co Ltd
☎ 64723684
📠 62551995

Shanghai Marine Shipping Co Ltd
☎ 63213103
📠 63213751

Shanghai Newseas Shipping Agency
☎ 65445254
📠 65449502

Shanghai Shipping (Group) Co
☎ 63219600
📠 63291408

Shanghai Tonglian Transport Industry
☎ 63232967
📠 63234054

Sino Santa Fe Int'l Service Corp
☎ 62192551
📠 62194654

Sinotrans Shanghai Airfreight Forwarding Co
☎ 63213103
📠 63291690

Sinotrans Shanghai Storage & Transport Co
☎ 63226996
📠 63206486

Sinotrans Shanghai Co
☎ 63213103
📠 63291668

Swire Shipping (Agencies) Ltd
☎ 63751346/9
📠 63751351

Trans Wing Shipping Co Ltd
☎ 63566214
📠 63569264

Van Ommeren China B.V.
☎ 63730000
📠 63732222

Viltrans Shipping (HK) Co Ltd
☎ 62493584
📠 62488686

Wallem & Co Ltd
☎ 63201740
📠 63201636

Wellable Shipping Ltd
☎ 63565524
📠 63564405

Wide Shine Shipping Ltd
☎ 63217474/9
📠 63217572

Zim Israel Navigarion Co
☎ 63730000
📠 63732222

GOLF CLUBS

Grand Shanghai Int'l Golf & Club
☎ 62405502
🖷 62947661

Shanghai Easter Paris Golf Club
☎ 59126888
🖷 59129712

Shanghai Hongqiao Golf Club
☎ 64016666
🖷 64063502

Shanghai International Golf & Country Club
☎ 59728111
🖷 59728520

Shanghai Links Countryside Golf Club
☎ 58975899
🖷 58974607

Shanghai Qizhong Golf Club
☎ 64091256
🖷 64090526

Shanghai Seaside Golf Club
☎ 58058888
🖷 58058588

Shanghai Sun Island Resort Golf Club
☎ 59831625
🖷 59830888

Shanghai Xubao Golf Club
☎ 67481111
🖷 67480067

Shanghai Yingtao Golf Club
☎ 59767998
🖷 59769236

Tianma Country Club
☎ 57661666
🖷 57662626

Tomson Golf & Country Club
☎ 58338888
🖷 58339700

GOVERNMENT

Shanghai Administration of Culture and Radio Broadcasting
☎ 63612556

Shanghai Administration of Labor and Social Insurance
☎ 63677216

Shanghai Agriculture Administration
☎ 63212810

Shanghai Audit Administration
☎ 63787200

Shanghai Civil Defense Commission
☎ 24028888

Shanghai Construction and Administration Committee
☎ 64431576

Shanghai Customs
☎ 63232410

Shanghai Development Planning Commission (SDPC)
☎ 63212810

Shanghai Development Research Center
☎ 63212810

Shanghai Economic Commission
☎ 63586666

Shanghai Economic Cooperation Office
☎ 62463539

Shanghai Education Commission
☎ 62563010

Shanghai Ethnic and Religion Commission
☎ 52891653

Shanghai Environmental Protection Administration
☎ 62260296

Shanghai Finance Administration
☎ 62716004

Shanghai Foreign Affairs General Office
☎ 62565900

Shanghai Foreign Economic Relations & Trade Commission
☎ 62752200

Shanghai Foreign Investment Board
☎ 62368800

Shanghai Forestry Administration
☎ 64855090

Shanghai Housing Development Board
☎ 63193188

Shanghai Health Administration
☎ 62758710

Shanghai Industrial & Commercial Administration (SICA)
☎ 64220000

Shanghai Informationalization General Office
☎ 62822266

Shanghai Intellectual Property Administration
☎ 52981809

Shanghai Medical Insurance Administration
☎ 62558001

Shanghai Municipal Engineering Administration Bureau
☎ 65079898

Shanghai News and Publication Administration
☎ 64370176

Shanghai Overseas Chinese Administration
☎ 62490880

Shanghai Personnel Administration
☎ 64045566

Shanghai Port Authority
☎ 63290660

Shanghai Public Safety Administration
☎ 24023456

Shanghai Science & Technology Commission
☎ 64393089

Shanghai Sports Administration
☎ 63275330

Shanghai Statistics Bureau
☎ 35110517

Shanghai Tourism Board
☎ 64390793

Shanghai Transportation Administration
☎ 53820733

Shanghai Urban Environment Administration
☎ 62473288

Shanghai Urban Planning Administration
☎ 64276246

HOTELS

★★★★★

Four Seasons Hotel
☎ 62568888
📠 62565678

Grand Hyatt Shanghai
☎ 50491234
📠 50491111

Hilton International Hotel
☎ 62480000
📠 62483848

Hotel Inter-continental Pudong
☎ 58318888
📠 58317777

Huating Sheraton Hotel
☎ 64391000
📠 625508304

Marriott Hotel
☎ 62376000
📠 62376222

Okura Garden Hotel
☎ 64151111
📠 64158866

Peace Hotel
☎ 63216888
📠 63290300

Pudong Shangri-La Hotel
☎ 68828888
📠 68826688

Ramada Plaza Pudong
☎ 50554466

Radisson Plaza Xing Guo Hotel
☎ 62129998

Regal Int'l East Asia Hotel
☎ 64155588
📠 64458899

Shanghai JC Mandarin Hotel
☎ 62791888
☎ 800-8201225 (Toll Free)
📠 62791822
Website: www.jcmandarin.com

Shanghai Jinjiang Tower
☎ 62582582
📠 64725588

Sheraton Suzhou Hotel & Towers
☎ 512-65103388
Website: www.sheraton.com/suzhou

Sofitel Jinjiang Oriental Pudong
☎ 50504888

St. Regis Hongta
☎ 50504567

The Portman Ritz-Carlton
☎ 62798888
📠 62798800

The Westin Taipingyang (Pacific)
☎ 62758888
📠 62755420

★★★★

Baoshan Hotel
☎ 56698888
📠 56601924

Broadway Mansions
☎ 63246260
📠 63065147

Central hotel
☎ 53965000
📠 53965188

City Hotel
☎ 62551133
📠 62550211

Crowne Plaza
☎ 62808888
📠 62803353

Cybress Hotel
☎ 62688868
📠 62688007

Everbright International Hotel
☎ 48425006
📠 64820944

Galaxy Hotel
☎ 62755888
📠 62754413

Grand Youyou Hotel
☎ 58810888
📠 58810511

Holiday Inn Pudong
☎ 58306666
📠 58305555

Hotel Sofitel Hyland
☎ 63515888
📠 63514088

Hotel Nikko Longbai
☎ 62689111
📠 62689333

Hotel Telecom
☎ 58300000
📠 58354007

Jian Guo Hotel
☎ 64399299
📠 64399433

Jing'an Hotel
☎ 62481888
📠 62482657

Mayfair Hotel
☎ 62402288
📠 62105500

New Century Hotel
☎ 36084999
📠 65218728

Novotel Atlantis Shanghai
☎ 50366666
📠 50366677

Ocean Hotel
☎ 65458888
📠 65458993

Purple Mountain Hotel
☎ 68868888
📠 68868800

Rainbow Hotel
☎ 62753388
📠 62757244

Ramada Plaza
☎ 63500000

Renaissance Yangtze Hotel
☎ 62750000
📠 62750750

Shanghai Int'l Equatorial Hotel
☎ 62481688
📠 62481773

Worldfield Convention Hotel
☎ 62703388
📠 62704554

★★★

Baolong Hotel
☎ 65425425
📠 56632710

Holiday Inn Downtown Shanghai
☎ 63538008
📠 63543019

Huating Guest House
☎ 64813500
📠 64390322

New Asia Hotel
☎ 63242210
📠 63566816

New Garden Hotel
☎ 62426688
📠 62423256

Novotel Shanghai Yuan Lin Villa
☎ 64701688

Oasis Tower
☎ 62865888
📠 62862248

Pacific Hotel
☎ 63276226
📠 63723634

Qingpu Hotel
☎ 59850688
📠 59850615

Shanghai Convention Center
☎ 64716060
📠 64710089

Shanghai Hotel
☎ 62480088
📠 62481310

Shanghai Int'l Airport Hotel
☎ 62688866
📠 62688393

Windsor Evergreen Hotel
☎ 64700888
📠 64704832

Yan'an Hotel
☎ 62481111
📠 62477149

YMCA Hotel
☎ 63261040
📠 63201957

INDUSTRIAL PARKS

Baoshan Industrial Park Administration Committee
☎ 56871753

Baoshan City Industrial Park
☎ 56131344

Caohejing High-tech Park Development Corporation
☎ 64850000
📠 64850523

China-Singapore Suzhou Industrial Park Development Co. Ltd.
☎ 512-62882828
🖷 512-62881297
Website: www.cssd.com.sg

Fudan University Science Park Investment Service Center
☎ 65311017
🖷 65448060

Hongqiao ETDZ United Development Corporation
☎ 62756888
🖷 62194505

Jiading Industrial Park Administration Committee
☎ 58991818
🖷 58991812

Minhang United Development Corp
☎ 64300888
🖷 64300789

Qingpu Industrial Zone Development Corp
☎ 59735145
🖷 59735159

Nanhui Industrial Park
☎ 58003800
🖷 58004188

Ningbo Free Trade Zone Administrative Committee
☎ 574-86880139, 86881077
🖷 574-86896543, 86883518
Website: www.nftz.com

Shanghai Chemical Industrial Park
☎ 64576556

Shanghai Comprehensive Industrial Development Zone Development Corporation
☎ 59562324
🖷 59563621

Songjiang Export Processing Zone Administrative Committee
☎ 57741796
🖷 57601993

Songjiang Industrial Zone Administrative Committee
☎ 57741102
🖷 57743188

Shanghai Software Park Administrative Committee
☎ 38954510

Shanghai Int'l Automobile City Spare Parts Assembly Industrial Zone
☎ 59563324
🖷 59563621

Shanghai Pudong Kangqiao Industrial Zone Management Committee
☎ 58121488
🖷 58121188

Shanghai Spark Development United Corp
☎ 62136254
🖷 57502635

Shanghai Waigaoqiao Free Trade Zone Development Co. Ltd.
☎ 50580088
Website: www.waigaoqiao.com.cn

Shanghai Xingzhuang Industrial Zone United Development Co Ltd
☎ 64892500

Waigaoqiao Free Trade Zone Administrative Committee
☎ 50461100
🖷 50461441

Zhangjiang High-tech Park Administrative Committee
☎ 50801818
🖷 50800686

INSURANCE COMPANIES

Aetna Life Insurance
☎ 62756785

AIU Insurance Company
☎ 63508180
🖷 63508183/4

Allianz Dazhong Life Insurance Company
☎ 58798828
🖷 58798830

American International Assurance (AIA)
☎ 63216698
🖷 62474000

Pacific Aetna Life Insurance Company
☎ 68863138

Manulife-Sinochem Life Insurance
☎ 50492288

Allianz Insurance Shanghai Rep. Office
☎ 50494950
🖷 50494847

Aon Insurance Corp.
☎ 64267605

Cigna Corp. Shanghai Rep.
☎ 58826563

China Life-CMG Life Assurance
☎ 58882288

China Pacific Insurance
☎ 66779900

China Ping An Insurance
☎ 62192022
🖷 62193033

Colonial Mutual Group
☎ 63211523

Commercial Union Assurance Co. Ltd.
☎ 62491648

Continental Insurance Corp.
☎ 62497511/ 2

E. W.Blanch Ltd.
☎ 53069898

Federal Insurance
☎ 65114766

Fuji Fire Insurance
☎ 62480000

Generalcologne Reinsurance Company
☎ 58761122

Great Eastern Life
☎ 58301297

Hannover Reinsurance
☎ 53065667

Huatai Insurance
☎ 66218833

ING General Insurance Int'l
☎ 62798399
🖷 62798900

Japan Life Insurance Co.
☎ 62780441

John Hancock Tianan Life Insurance Company
☎ 68816658

Kerry Insurance Co. Ltd.
☎ 65224273

Kyoritsu Co. Ltd.
☎ 62098086

Manufactures Life Insurance
☎ 63508668

Manulife-Sinochem Life Insurance
☎ 50492288

Massmutual Insurance Asia Co. Ltd.
☎ 53965761

Mitsui Marine & Fire Insurance Co. Ltd.
☎ 68414998

Munich Reinsurance Co.
☎ 68869582

New York Life Insurance Company
☎ 62493541

OFS (Asia)
☎ 62484123

Pacific Century Insurance Co. Ltd.
☎ 58401989

Prudential
☎ 64391000-5016

Royal & Sun Alliance Insurance
☎ 68411999
🖷 68412700

Samsung Fire & Marine Insurance
☎ 62080080

Standard Life Assurance Co.
☎ 68413311

Sumitomo Marine & Fire Insurance Co. Ltd.
☎ 68410515

Swiss Reinsurance Company
☎ 63916562

Tokyo Fire & Marine Insurance
☎ 64710584
🖷 64712234

Transamerican Occidental Life
☎ 62195320

Yasuda Marine & Fire Insurance Co. Ltd.
☎ 68411199

Winterthur Insurance (Asia) Ltd., Shanghai Branch
☎ 68823351
🖷 68824600

Zurich Insurance Company
☎ 62798686

INTERNATIONAL SCHOOLS

Concordia International School Shanghai
☎ 58990380

French School of Shanghai
☎ 6405 9220

German School of Shanghai
☎ 6405 9220

KinderWorld International Kindergarten
☎ 6386 7880

L'ecole Francaise de Shanghai
☎ 59763431

Shanghai American School (SAS)

☎ 62211445, 58973097
📠 62211269, 58970011
Website: www.saschina.org

Shanghai Changning International School (SCIS)

☎ 6252 3688

Shanghai Singapore International School (SSIS)

☎ 62219288
📠 62219188
Website: www.ssischool.com

The Japanese School - Hongqiao

☎ 6401 2747

Yew Chung International School - Shanghai

☎ 62195910, 6242 3243
📠 62190675
Website: www.ycef.com

LAW FIRMS

Allens Arthur Robinson

☎ 68412828
📠 68412829

Altheimer & Gray

☎ 62890990
📠 62899911

Armstrong Teasdale LLP

☎ 62798808
📠 62798866

Blake Dawson Waldron
☎ 62798069
🖷 62798109

Boss & Yong
☎ 68869666
🖷 68869333

Boughton Peterson yang Anderson
☎ 63906790

Bull, Housser & Tupper
☎ 64400015
🖷 64400021

Clifford Chance LLP
☎ 62798461
🖷 62798462

Coppens Van Ommeslaghe & Faures
☎ 38784620
🖷 38784622

Davis Wright Tremaine LLP
☎ 62798560
🖷 62798547

Deacons Graham & James
☎ 63851605
🖷 63851603

Duan & Duan Law Firm
☎ 62191103
🖷 62752273

Haarmann Hemmelrath & Partner
☎ 50498176
🖷 50475122

Holman Fenwick & Willam
☎ 68413872
🖷 68410287

Bruckhaus Westrick Heller Lober
☎ 50491118
🖷 38780099

Bryan Cave LLP
☎ 62798166
🖷 62798165

Davis Wright Tremaine LLP
☎ 62798560
🖷 62798547

Linklaters
☎ 68415858
🖷 68415656

Johnson Stokes & Master
☎ 62880688
🖷 62880131/2

Jone Day, Reavis & Pogue
☎ 52986568
🖷 52986569

Kaye Scholer LLP & Affiliates
☎ 52984266
🖷 52984277

King & Wood
☎ 68410088
🖷 68410066

Lehman, Lee & Xu
☎ 62882698
🖷 62882699

O'Melveny & Myers LLP
☎ 62195363
🖷 52985500

Rouse & Co Int'l
☎ 63915368
🖷 63915366

Schulz Noack Baerwinkel Lawyers
☎ 62198370
🖷 62196849

Simmons & Simmons
☎ 62490700
🖷 62490706

Sinclair Roche & Temperley
☎ 68410988
🖷 68410525

Thirffry & Associes
☎ 68411388
🖷 68411266

Wessing Berenberg-Gossler
☎ 684155 25
🖷 68410066

White & Case LLP
☎ 63212200
🖷 63239252

MEDICAL SERVICES

Australian Consulate Clinic
(For Australian Passport Holders)
☎ 64334606

Baosteel Hospital
50 Mohe Road
☎ 56691101

Dr. Anderson & Partners
Rm 1001, Block D, New Century Plaza
48 Xingyi Rd, Hongqiao
☎ 62700263

Changzheng Hospital
415 Fengyang Road
☎ 63610109

Fudan Special Hospital
409 Fangxie Road
☎ 63770161

Fudan Children's Hospital
183 Fenglin Road
☎ 54524666

Huadong Hospital
221 Yan'an West Road
☎ 62483180

Huashan Hospital
12 Urumqi Middle Road
☎ 62489999

Int'l Medical & Health Care Center
585 Jiulong Road, Xuhui
☎ 63243852

Int'l Peace Medical Center
910 Hengshan Road
☎ 64070434

Int'l SOS Assistance
☎ 62484344

New Pioneer Int'l Medical Center
910 Hengshan Doad
☎ 64693898

Pacific Dental Hospital
4th Floor, 269 Wuchang Road,
Xuhui District
☎ 63062518

Pudong Shangri-La Medical Clinic
4th Floor, 33 Feycheng Road,
Pudong
☎ 68828888

Renji Hospital
145 Shandong Middle Road
☎ 63260930

Shanghai Dental Medical Center
7th Floor, Ninth People's Hospital
639 Zhizaoju Road, Xuhui
☎ 63133174

Shanghai Chinese Medicine Hospital
274 Zhijiang Road
☎ 56639828

World Link Medical Center
2nd Floor, Portman Center, West Tower
☎ 62797688

World Link Meical Clinic (Gubei)
Mandarin City, Gubei
☎ 64055788

OFFICE SPACE

Apollo Plaza
1440 Yan'an Middle Road

Jing'an District
☎ 62481980

Bank of China Tower
200 Yincheng Middle Road
Pudong New District
☎ 38824500

Bund Capital
668 Beijing East Road
Huangpu District

Central Ring Plaza
381 Huaihai Middle Road
Luwan District
☎ 62791515

Central Plaza
227 Huangpi North Road
Huangpu District
☎ 63276327

China Enterprise Tower
2 Huashan Road
Jing'an District
☎ 62729697

China Insurance Tower
99 Lujiazui Road
Pudong New District
☎ 58881433

China Merchants Tower
161 Lujiazui East Road
Pudong New District
☎ 62178899

China Petroleum Tower
969 Oriental Road
Pudong New District
☎ 68758888

China Shipping Tower
1 Pudong Avenue
Pudong New District
☎ 58795283

CITIC Pacific Plaza
1168 Nanjing West Road
Jing'an District
☎ 62676905

Conch Tower
1277 Zhongshan West Road
Changning District
☎ 62759857

East Sea Business Center
588 Yan'an East Road
Huangpu District
☎ 63523288

East Sea Plaza
1486 Nanjing West Road
Jing'an District
☎ 62471101

Eastern International Plaza
85 Loushanguan Road
Changning District
☎ 62750062

Everbright Plaza
547 Tianmu West Road
Zhabei District
☎ 63532118

Far East International Plaza
317 Xianxia Road
Changning District
☎ 62709999

Financial Plaza
333 Jiujiang Road
Huangpu District
☎ 63500153

Friendship Tower
40 Beijing East Road
Huangpu District
☎ 53080241

Ganglu Plaza
700 Yan'an East Road
Huangpu District
☎ 63723412

Global Plaza
18 Taolin Road

Pudong New District
☎ 62676905

Global World Tower
168 Yuyuan Road
Jing'an District
☎ 62490318

Goldbell Plaza
680 Zhaojiabang Road
Xuhui District
☎ 64666258

Guangdong Development Bank Tower
555 Xu'anhui Road
Luwan District
☎ 63055037

Guangming Tower
2 Jinling East Road
Huangpu District
☎ 63212812

Haixing Plaza
1 Ruijin South Road
Luwan District
☎ 64188226

Harbor Business Center
628 Daming East Road
Hongkou District
☎ 65957505

Hong Kong Plaza
283 Huaihai Middle Road
Luwan District
☎ 63863500

HSBC Tower
101 Yincheng East Road
Pudong New District
☎ 68412212

Hualian Group Tower
359 East Daming Road
Hongkou District
☎ 65466984

Huaneng United Plaza
139 Yincheng East Road
Pudong New District
☎ 68812800

Huafu Tower
585 Longhua West Road
Xuhui District
☎ 64694625

International Shipping & Finance Tower
720 Pudong Avenue
Pudong New District
☎ 50367026

Jing'an New Times Plaza
881 Nanjing West Road
Jing'an District
☎ 32170533

Jinmao Tower
88 Century Boulevard
Pudong New District

Jiushi Fuxing Tower
918 Huaihai Middle Road
Luwan District
☎ 64158818

Kerry Everbright City
218 Tianmu West Road
Zhabei District
☎ 63179568

Kunyang International Business Center
798 Zhaojiabang Road
Xuhui District
☎ 64738083

Lippo Plaza
222 Huaihai Middle Road
Luwan District
☎ 63821235

Lucky Plaza
660 Shangcheng Road
Pudong New District
☎ 68880507

Metro Tower
30 Tianyaoqiao Road
Xuhui District
☎ 64268380

Modern Plaza
218 Xiangyang South Road
Xuhui District
☎ 64667207

New Caohejing Tower
509 Caobao Road
Xuhui District
☎ 64855800

New Hualian Tower
755 Huaihai Middle Road
Luwan District
☎ 64667000

New Shanghai International Plaza
360 Pudong South Road
Pudong New District

New Town Plaza
55 Loushanguan Road
Changning District
☎ 62756888

Ocean Petroleum Plaza
583 Linling Road
Xuhui District
☎ 64395300

Overseas Chinese Tower
129 Yan'an West Road
Jing'an District
☎ 62496569

Shanghai International Trade Center
2201 Yan'an West Road
Changning District
☎ 62756712

Pan Pacific Tower
1221 Yan'an West Road
Changning District
☎ 62522218

Plaza 66
1266 Nanjing West Road
Jing'an District
☎ 32104566

POS Plaza
1600 Century Boulevard
Pudong New District

Radisson Tower
2 Huaihai Middle Road
Luwan District
☎ 63190000

Ruijin Plaza
205 Maoming South Road
Luwan District
☎ 64726202

Shanghai Commercial Plaza
1376 Nanjing West Road
Jing'an District
☎ 62798600

Shanghai Bund International Plaza
99 Huangpu Road
Hongkou District
☎ 63931116

Shanghai Industrial Tower
18 Caoxi North Road
Xuhui District
☎ 64879077

Shanghai Kerry Business Center
1515 Nanjing West Road
Jing'an District
☎ 62791515

Shanghai Landmark Tower
409 Nanjing East Road
Huangpu District
☎ 63513828

Shanghai Mart
2299 Yan'an West Road
Changning District
☎ 62360302

Shanghai Materials Trade Plaza
2550 Zhongshan North Road
Putuo District
☎ 32570000

Shanghai Medicine Towr
200 Taicang Road
Luwan District
☎ 63558088

Shanghai Merchants Tower
333 Chengdu North Road
Jing'an District
☎ 62177377

Shanghai Plaza
138 Huaihai Middle Road
Luwan District
☎ 63592138

Shanghai Securities Tower
528 Pudong South Road
Pudong New District

Shanghai Times Square
93 Huaihai Middle Road
Luwan District
☎ 63190407

Shenneng International Plaza
1 Fuxing Middle Road
Luwan District
☎ 63900800

Shui On Plaza
333 Huaihai Middle Road
Luwan District
☎ 63851600

Smick Tower
800 Shangcheng Road
Pudong New District
☎ 68755858

South Securities Tower
580 Nanjing West Road
Jing'an District
☎ 52340001

Sun Plaza
88 Xianxia Road
Changning District
☎ 62700967

Times Square
500 Zhangyang Road
Pudong New District

Tomson Center
188 Zhangyang Road
Pudong New District
☎ 58763646

Tomson Financial Center
710 Oriental Road
Pudong New District
☎ 58308888

Vanke Plaza
37 Shuicheng South Road
Changning District
☎ 62702466

Victoria Plaza
1068 Xikang Road
Putuo District
☎ 62664765

Wanbao International Business Center
660 Xinhua Road
Changning District
☎ 62803000

Wanzhong Plaza
1303 Yan'an West Road
Changning District
☎ 62106570

World Plaza
855 Pudong South Road
Pudong New District

World Trade Plaza
500 Guangdong Road
Huangpu District
☎ 63513876

Yandang Plaza
107 Yandang Road
Luwan District
☎ 63727779

Yongxin Plaza
128 Nanjing West Road
Huangpu District
☎ 63501597

Yu'an Plaza
738 Oriental Road
Pudong New District
☎ 58206268

Zhengze World Trade Tower
1590 Yan'an West Road
Changning District
☎ 62801711

Zhaofeng Global Tower
1800 Zhongshan West Road
Xuhui District
☎ 64400233

Zhaofeng World Trade Tower
369 Jiangsu Road
Changning District
☎ 62136688

Zhongcheng Plaza
818 Oriental Road
Pudong New District
☎ 58209200

Zhonghui Plaza
16 Henan South Road
Huangpu District
☎ 63748888

Zhongsheng Financial Center
2067 Yan'an West Road
Changning District
☎ 62784350

PROPERTY AGENTS & CONSULTANTS

Shanghai Home Corporation
☎ 34060973

Adrienne Farrelly Shanghai Properties
☎ 62997974
📠 62998231

Allied J & W Consulting
☎ 56957482

AllBest Property Service
☎ 63866106
📠 53510447

Autumn Leaves Housing Consultants Ltd.
☎ 34060273

CB Richard Ellis
☎ 62891200
📠 62891233

Century 21 Shanghai Wealth Realty
☎ 58518725
🖷 58604836

Chesterton Petty
☎ 64459967
🖷 64459965

Coldwell Banker
☎ 33074520

Colliers International
☎ 62370088
🖷 62372122
Website: www.colliers.com/china

Cordial Consultant
☎ 62581010
🖷 64611371

Diana Real Estate
☎ 86213415
🖷 64791148

DTZ Debenham Tie Leung
☎ 53061383
🖷 53065676

Knight Frank
☎ 62481515
🖷 62482929

FPD Savills Int'l Property Consultants
☎ 63916688
🖷 63916699

Jones Lang Lasalle
☎ 63933333
🖷 63933080

Shanghai Dairy Fine Property Consultants
☎ 62749955

Shanghai Metropolis Real Estate Consultants
☎ 62480245
📠 54049215

Shanghai Properties
☎ 62483336

Pacific Property Service
☎ 64392046

Phoenix Property Consulting
☎ 64379891
📠 64718926

Red Dragon Property Service
☎ 64483000

Shanghai Realty
☎ 62461133
📠 62461199

Sunshine Green Realty
☎ 62852507

T&D Real Estate Co
☎ 62780331
📠 62086416

The Emerald
☎ 68122222

SECURITIES FIRMS

Tai Fook Securities Group Ltd.
☎ 68419818

China Galaxy Securities Co.
☎ 62188777

Celestial Asia Securities Holdings
☎ 62881717

China Galaxy Securities Co.
☎ 64310880

China Securities Co.
☎ 63055812

Everbright Securities Co. Ltd.
☎ 64648801

Guotai-Junan Securities Co.
☎ 62580818

Haitong Securities Co. Ltd.
☎ 53594566

Shenyin-Wanguo Securities Co.
☎ 54033888

Shanghai Finance Securities Co. Ltd.
☎ 57334778

Shanghai Securitie Co. Ltd.
☎ 65223500

Shenyin & Wanguo Securities Co. Ltd.
☎ 64158888

SERVICED APARTMENTS

Aidu Apartment
☎ 62624900
📠 62624900

Ascott International
☎ 53829292
📠 53820908

Athena Garden
☎ 62782578

Belvedere Service Apartments
☎ 62132222
🖷 62510000

Changning Equatorial Serviced Apartments
☎ 62100889
🖷 62109008
Email: rsosha@public9.sta.net.cn

Chevalier Place
☎ 64338599
🖷 64339605

China Garden
☎ 62198689

Concord Serviced Apartment'
☎ 62727232
🖷 62496194

Dragon Pearl Complex
☎ 58606868

Emerald Court Serviced Villas
☎ 62621020

Evergreen Garden
☎ 62421586
🖷 62421584

Highness Garden
☎ 65049558
🖷 65620815

Hongxi Garden
☎ 62362838
🖷 64213568

Honwell Garden
☎ 62810610
🖷 62825958

Huashan Garden
☎ 58310617
🖷 58319433

Kerry Everbright City
☎ 63547778
🖷 63540142

Kingswell Gardens ServicedApartment
☎ 62621020

Kingsville
☎ 64454664
🖷 64373688

La Residence
☎ 62250047
🖷 62250056

Le Chateau
☎ 62622020
🖷 62627650

Longbai ServicedApartment
☎ 62688320
🖷 62688728

Luoxiu Apartment
☎ 58858895

Lyon Garden
☎ 62476707
🖷 62789894

Mandarin Garden
☎ 62628118
🖷 62628128

Marseilles Garden
☎ 62781731
🖷 62781730

Miramar Apartment
☎ 62706921
🖷 62702944

New Century Plaza
☎ 62780498
🖷 62702944

New Harbor Serviced Apartment
☎ 63556232
🖷 63556233

Noble Serviced Apartment
☎ 64386343
🖷 64394277

Oriental Garden
☎ 62728000
🖷 62729895

Oriental Plaza
☎ 63866677

Phoenix Mansion
☎ 58993929
🖷 50310707

Prince Mansion
☎ 62804355
🖷 62802381

Rainbow Garden Apartment
☎ 62421586
🖷 62421584

Redin Apartment
☎ 62191261
🖷 62197399

Rome Garden
☎ 62701760
🖷 62701761

Royal Orchid Villa
☎ 64165788
🖷 64045009

Royal Pavillion
☎ 62798677

Shanghai Aibo Mansion
☎ 64722600
🖷 64728850

Shanghai American Homes
☎ 62621052
🖷 62625757

Shanghai California Garden
☎ 59147777
🖷 59145663

Shanghai Canadian Garden
☎ 64722600
🖷 64728850

Shanghai Center
☎ 62798600
🖷 62798610

Shanghai Garden
☎ 64124399
🖷 64124480

Shanghai Garden City
☎ 65411855

Shanghai Golden Bridge Mansion
☎ 64722600
🖷 64728850

Shanghai Times Square
☎ 63910294

Somerset Grand Shanghai
☎ 63856888

Somerset Xuhui
☎ 64660888

Splendid Garden
☎ 62198268
🖷 62191218

Supreme Tower Serviced Apartment
☎ 58311118
🖷 58319580

Sun Plaza
☎ 62707369
🖷 62700008

Taigu Serviced Apartment
☎ 62786666
🖷 62783367

The Regalia Building
☎ 50818818
🖷 50811133

Tianci Serviced Apartment
☎ 63361199

Xiang'an Apartment
☎ 62770207

Versailles de Shanghai
☎ 62628118

Wahtai Mansion
☎ 64159915
🖷 64159916

Wantai Villas
☎ 62786666
🖷 62783367

Windsor Court & Windsor Park
☎ 62628118
🖷 62628128

Zhaofeng Garden
☎ 62108029
🖷 62109008

Zhonghui Garden
☎ 64711733
🖷 64711228

TAXI

Bashi Taxi
☎ 84000, 64312788

Dazhong Taxi
☎ 82222, 62581688

Jinjiang Taxi
☎ 62584584, 62758800

Qiangsheng Taxi
☎ 62580000

TRAVEL

Shanghai Tourism administration
☎ 64391818
🖷 64391519

China Base Travel
☎ 54562253

China Travel Service
☎ 63368800
🖷 62475878

Concordia Int'l Travel Service
☎ 62897000
🖷 62897799

Destination Travel Agency
☎ 63145505
🖷 53590632

Everbright City Travel Service
☎ 64670329
🖷 64673802

Great World Travel
☎ 63514293
🖷 63224210

Great Atlantic Travel
☎ 56919824
🖷 56888622

Guquan Travel Agency
☎ 62094372
🖷 62785889

Henerson Miramar Hotels
Reservations Center
☎ 62705539
🖷 62705489

Holy Land Travel Service
☎ 62125719
🖷 62254461

Jade Travel
☎ 62798393
🖷 62798699

Kache Professional Travel Service
☎ 62890188
🖷 62893879

Mart Tours & Travel
☎ 53823435
🖷 53826099

China Golden Bridge Travel
☎ 55054719
🖷 55085039

CITIC International Travel
☎ 52925277
🖷 52925288

China Youth Travel Service
☎ 64331826
🖷 64330507

Jinjiang Tours
☎ 64662828
🖷 64662297

New Asia Travel
☎ 63599988
🖷 63584405

Qantas Holiday
☎ 63758866
🖷 63758486

R & R China Int'l Travel Services
☎ 86216468

Shanghai China Int'l Travel
☎ 62898899
🖷 62891910

Shanghai Business Int'l Travel
☎ 53821100
🖷 62721990

Shanghai Holiday Travel
☎ 63609999
🖷 63872777

Shanghai Merchants Travel
☎ 62671121
🖷 62676163

Shanghai Far East Tourist
☎ 62891897
🖷 62891901

Shanghai Jetour Travel
☎ 62952222
🖷 62949705

Shanghai Skytour Travel
☎ 63735723
🖷 63266793

Shanghai Spring Int'l Travel Service
☎ 62520000

Smart Travel
☎ 54044042
🖷 54035133

Tibet Tourism Shanghai Representative Office
☎ 63211729
🖷 63231016

Travel Quick Services
☎ 62106740
🖷 62728248

Welcome Holiday
☎ 62725823
🖷 32100532

WildChina Inc
☎ 64039737

ADVERTISERS' INDEX

Trade Events

SEC: Shanghai Exhibition Center
INTEX Shanghai: Shanghai International Exhibition Center
SICC: Shanghai International Conference Center
SNIEC: Shanghai New International Expo Center
SECEC: Shanghai Everbright Conference and Exhibition Center

Year 2002

Date : 3-6 Dec. 2002
Event : Auto Parts & Equipment Shanghai 2002
Venue: INTEX Shanghai

Date : Dec. 2002
Event : The 2nd Shanghai Int'l Architectural Design Exhibition
Venue: Shanghai Mart

Year 2003

Date : 25-28 Feb. 2003
Event : WoodMac, FurniTek, WoodBuild China 2003
Venue: INTEX Shanghai

Date : 1 Mar. 2003
Event : PCIM China
Venue: SEC

Date : 1-7 Mar. 2003
Event : East China Fair 2003
Venue: SNIEC

Date :	3-4 Mar. 2003
Event :	The 8th International IC-China Conference & Exhibition; Embedded Systems Conferences; Electronic Design Automation & Test Expo
Venue:	Shanghai Mart
Date :	4-7 Mar. 2003
Event :	FurniWood Shanghai 2003
Venue:	INTEX Shanghai
Date :	5-7 Mar. 2003
Event :	Fi Asia – China 2003
Venue:	SECEC
Date :	14-16 Mar. 2003
Event :	AGRO EXPO China-Shanghai
Venue:	SICC
Date :	18-21 Mar. 2003
Event :	INTERKAMA China 2003
Venue:	SNIEC
Date :	21-24 Mar. 2003
Event :	Shanghai International Diamond Trade Fair 2003
Venue:	INTEX Shanghai
Date :	28-31 Mar. 2003
Event :	Woodwork Shanghai 2003, Furniture Shanghai 2003
Venue:	INTEX Shanghai
Date :	2-5 Apr. 2003
Event :	Batimat China 2003
Venue:	SEC

Date :	8-11 Apr. 2003
Event :	NEPCON Shangahi 2003
Venue:	SECEC
Date :	10-13 Apr. 2003
Event :	The 8th China Building & Construct Exposition, The 8th Int'l Building Materials & Interior Decoration Exhibition, TEXDEX 2003, Interior Decoration & Design Exhibition 2003, Shanghai Int'l House Decoration Festival, China Windoor / Hardware/ Chemical Building Metal Exhibition, China Int'l Wood China 2003, China Int'l Bath & Kitchen China 2003
Venue:	INTEX Shanghai
Date :	19-22 Apr. 2003
Event :	The 9th China Building & Decoration Expo (BATIMAT CHINA 2003); Hardware China 2003; Ceramics, Tile & Sanitary Ware China 2003; ILE China; Hotelex Shanghai 2003
Venue:	Shanghai Mart; INTEX Shanghai; SECEC
Date :	14-17 May 2003
Event :	CeBIT Consumer Electronics 2003; Satellite, Broadcast, Cable & Networks 2003
Venue:	SNIEC
Date :	27-29 May 2003
Event :	China Police & Securex China 2003
Venue:	INTEX Shanghai
Date :	27-29 May 2003
Event :	Bakery China 2003
Venue:	SECEC

Date :	31 May-2 Jun. 2003
Event :	Shanghai Int'l Water Supply, Drainage and Treatment Equipment Fair
Venue:	SECEC
Date :	3-6 Jun. 2003
Event :	Machine Parts 2003; International Bearing Industry Exhibition 2003
Venue:	Shanghai
Date :	3-7 Jun. 2003
Event :	ShanghaiTEX 2003
Venue:	SNIEC
Date :	10-13 Jun. 2003
Event :	The International Medical Equipment & Technology Exhibition
Venue:	SEC
Date :	17-19 Jun. 2003
Event :	CPhI China 2003
Venue:	SECEC
Date :	20-29 Jun. 2003
Event :	Shanghai Motor Show
Venue:	SEC
Date :	23-26 Jun. 2003
Event :	ELE/EXPO COMM SHANGHAI
Venue:	INTEX Shanghai

Date : 1-4 Jul. 2003
Event : Compressors & Systems, Control and Instrumentation, Envirotec, Pumps & Systems, Tubes & Piping; Chemtec; Fluidpower; Valves And Fittings; Watertec China 2003
Venue: INTEX Shanghai

Date : 3-6 Jul. 2003
Event : Int'l Building & Construction; Wintech - Window, Door & Roof; FloorTec; Housing Decoration Design & Service; Forestry, Timber & Wood; Traffic & Parking
Venue: SECEC

Date : 3-6 Jul. 2003
Event : The 4th Exhibition on Rotating Equipment, Fluids, Gas & Air-Handling System, Hydro Pneumatics & Motion Systems, Thermal & Mechanical Processing, Water & Waste Treatment Central System Instrumentation in China
Venue: INTEX Shanghai

Date : 8-11 Jul. 2003
Event : BevTek and BrewTek China; MeatPak China 2003
Venue: SNIEC

Date : 8-11 Jul. 2003
Event : ProPak China 2003
Venue: SECEC

Date : 17-20 Jul. 2003
Event : International Advertising/Printing/Packaging/Paper Industrial Exhibition
Venue: SNIEC

Date :	1 Sep. 2003
Event :	International Petroleum & Petrochemical Exhibition
Venue:	SECEC
Date :	2-5 Sep. 2003
Event :	Die & Mould East China 2003
Venue:	INTEX Shanghai
Date :	3-5 Sep. 2003
Event :	Asia Business Travel Market
Venue:	Grand Hyatt Shanghai
Date :	3-5 Sep. 2003
Event :	All China Leather Exhibition - Moda Shanghai
Venue:	SECEC
Date :	3-5 Sep. 2003
Event :	China International Footwear Fair
Venue:	SNIEC
Date :	4-9 Sep. 2003
Event :	China International Building & Housing Expo 2002
Venue:	INTEX Shanghai
Date :	9-11 Sep. 2003
Event :	Fashion China
Venue:	INTEX Shanghai
Date :	11-14 Sep. 2003
Event :	The 8th China International Furniture Expo; The 8th China International Furniture Manufacturing Expo
Venue:	INTEX Shanghai; SECEC

Date :	16-19 Sep. 2003
Event :	Bakery China; FHC 2003
Venue:	INTEX Shanghai
Date :	16-19 Sep. 2003
Event :	Confectionery China; Food China 2003; Hotel China 2003; Wines+Spirits China 2003
Venue:	SECEC
Date :	18-21 Sep. 2003
Event :	CeBIT Asia 2003
Venue:	SNIEC
Date :	14-16 Oct. 2003
Event :	Intertextile Shanghai Autumn
Venue:	SNIEC
Date :	15-18 Oct. 2003
Event :	Music China
Venue:	INTEX Shanghai
Date :	15-18 Oct. 2003
Event :	ProLight + Sound Shanghai
Venue:	Shanghai Mart
Date :	16-19 Oct. 2003
Event :	Building & Interior Decoration China 2002; Floor, Roof, Wall & Window China 2002
Venue:	SECEC
Date :	28-31 Oct. 2003
Event :	B+D Shanghai
Venue:	SECEC

Date :	30 Oct.-2 Nov. 2003
Event :	Boiler Shanghai 2002; Welding Shanghai 2002
Venue:	INTEX Shanghai
Date :	6-9 Nov. 2003
Event :	CTC-Construction Technology China 2002; Building Shanghai 2002; Shanghai International Exhibition on Building Materials, Building Services and Interior Decoration; International Exhibition on Public Safety, Security and Fire Control
Venue:	INTEX Shanghai
Date :	11-14 Nov. 2003
Event :	The 4th International Exhibition on Electric Power Equipment and Technology
Venue:	SICC
Date :	18-21 Nov. 2003
Event :	CeMAT Asia 2003; Energy ASIA 2003
Venue:	SNIEC
Date :	Nov. 2003
Event :	The 4th Shanghai International Industry Fair
Venue:	SNIEC
Date :	2-4 Dec. 2003
Event :	Shanghai Metal Expo 2003
Venue:	INTEX Shanghai
Date :	2-4 Dec. 2003
Event :	Marintec China
Venue:	SNIEC

Year 2004

Date : 17-20 Feb. 2004
Event : WoodMac China 2004
Venue: INTEX Shanghai

Date : 13-16 Jul. 2004
Event : ProPak China 2004
Venue: SECEC

Date : 14-17 Sep. 2004
Event : FHC 2004
Venue: SECEC

**Dates and venues are subject to changes.*